NATIVE ROADS

The Complete Motoring Guide to the Navajo and Hopi Nations

Self-guided Road Tours
featuring the History, Geology,
and Native Cultures of Northern Arizona

by
Fran Kosik

Rio Nuevo Publishers, Tucson

Rio Nuevo Publishers
P.O. Box 5250
Tucson, AZ 85703-0250
800 • 969-9558

ISBN:1-887896-16-3

Cover design: Sheldon Preston, Preston Designs and Joan Carstensen
Cover photograph: "Road to El Capitan" courtesy of the Atchison, Topeka & Santa Fe Railroad Collection, Kansas State Historical Society
Back cover photographs:
Monument Valley and migration petroglyph by Sheldon Preston, Teec Nos Pos rug photograph by Gene Balzer

Printed in Canada

ACKNOWLEDGMENTS

Many people helped me with this book over the years - especially friends I met while working at Diné College. I want to specifically thank Ursula Knoki-Wilson for what I have learned from her and for her friendship. Likewise to Mom and Dad Knoki and Jim and Caroline Bluehouse for sharing their blessings with me. To the staff in the Center for Diné Studies, Community Campus and Continuing Education, thank you for your friendship and help throughout the years. My special thanks to my good friend Lena Fowler for believing that all things are possible.

To Jim Babbitt, Ronnie Biard, Karen Berggren, Kevin Cloud Brechner, Curtis Cornelius, Brother Gerald Grantner, O.F.M., Karen Hughes, Wilson Hunter, Joe Magee, Angie Maloney, Tom McMillian, Wade Newman, Gay Nord, Ann and Pat O'Connor, Bob Rhoades, Mick Robbins, Tara Travis, Ursula Knoki-Wilson, and to my English teacher George Hardeen, thank you for your expertise and talent in making this a better book.

I would like to thank the staff at the Northern Arizona University, Cline Library Special Collections and Archives; specifically, Karen Underhill, Laine Sutherland and Diane Grua for their advice and extensive knowledge about the photographic collections at NAU and the history of the Colorado Plateau. Likewise to Carol Burke at the Museum of Northern Arizona Photo Archives.

I would also like to thank the Hopi Tribe for their review of the drive through the Hopi Nation.

A special thanks to my parents, Joe and Laura Kosik, for believing in me.

*This book is dedicated to my best friend
and husband, Duane.*

WARNING-DISCLAIMER

Extensive research and actual traveling experience have gone into the development of this book. The author has attempted to provide an accurate description of the history and lifestyle of the natives and non-natives through research and talking with people over the years. But it is not uncommon for someone from another part of the reservation to have another version of a story or to spell words differently.

The maps in this book are not drawn to scale. My primary purpose for including them is to point out what comes next. All of the motel prices were accurate when the book was printed but prices change frequently. Please call the motel directly for updated costs.

DO NOT READ THIS BOOK WHILE DRIVING. Have a passenger read this book to you. If you are alone, read when you pull over to enjoy the view.

The purpose of this book is to educate and to assist you in your travels. Neither Treasure Chest Books nor the author can accept responsibility or liability for any person or entity with respect to any loss or damage caused, or alleged to be caused, directly or indirectly by the information contained in this book.

TABLE OF CONTENTS

Native Roads

LEGEND

Camping

Photo Opportunity

RV Dump Site

Gas

Picnic Area

Showers

Groceries

Post Office

Telephone

Hospital or Clinic

Restaurant

Open range highway

Laundromat

Restrooms/or outhouse

Detour

MM Mile Marker

TUBA·CITY

The warm winter sun reflected off one of the many water towers that distinguishes the oasis of Tuba City from the rest of the tawny desert as we slowly drove up the town's wide tree-lined main street. It was exactly the kind of weather I was searching for when I left what my classmates and I referred to as "dreary Erie."

I had just graduated from nursing school and my father had given me a used, powder blue Chrysler Newport, "the tank," to make the drive across country. My sister and my best friend piled everything I owned in the world into that car, wrote the words "Tuba City or bust" all over it and started on the adventure of our lives.

I jumped at the chance to work for the Indian Health Service in Tuba City as my first job right out of nursing school. Not fully aware of what we were doing, we decided to take the scenic route over the Rocky Mountains in the dead of winter. We met many friendly people on that trip but none friendlier than the staff at the Wolf Creek Pass ski resort when "the tank" sputtered into their parking lot completely out of gas. Saved by a five gallon donation (they wouldn't take any money), we crossed over the highest mountain pass we would encounter and continued on our way.

Arriving at my new job a little wiser about elevation, winter and distances between gas stations in the West, I realized I knew nothing about the people I would care for or about the beautiful location I was lucky enough to choose for my first nursing assignment. Over the next 20 years, I have had many opportunities to learn from "The People" and to wander through this amazing landscape. I hope what I have learned will help you in your travels.

As a visitor, or someone contemplating a trip to northern Arizona, you will want to see all of the scenic wonders like the Grand Canyon, Monument Valley, Lake Powell and Canyon de Chelly. Distances from one place to another are long but the beauty remains all around you. Along the way, you may wonder about the people, land formations and history of the area. That is why I wrote this book; to give you, the road traveler, a better understanding of where you are in the context of both the Navajo and Hopi nations, the geologic formations and the history of the area. As you drive, each significant milepost is explained to give you a snapshot of the important events that helped shape this part of America.

The recommended map of the area is the ***Guide to Indian Country***, produced by the Automobile Club of Southern California and for sale at most tourist stops or bookstores for about $4. To best see many of the sites in this book, take along a pair of binoculars and a compass.

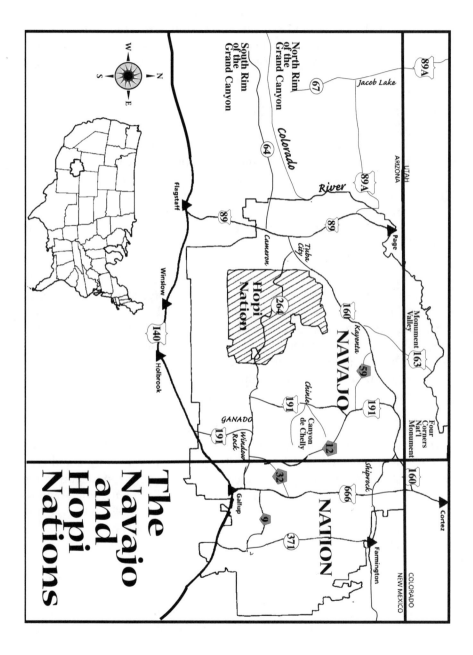

THE COLORADO PLATEAU

In traveling the Native Roads, you will traverse a spectacular piece of America called the Colorado Plateau. This region covers more than 150,000 square miles (390,000 sq km) and extends from the Mogollon Rim in central Arizona to the south, the Wasatch Range in Utah to the west, the Uinta Range to the north and the Rocky Mountains to the east.

About 4.5 billion years ago, sediments began to deposit as oceans, seas, lakes and deserts came and went, laying down one layer on top of another. All the while, forces deep within the earth were building until powerful plate tectonics began to form mountains and pushed the Colorado Plateau straight up as one unit. This happened 60-to-70 million years ago, about the same time the dinosaur era ended. The Colorado River, up to this time, meandered across a broad flat plain. As the plateau rose, the river began to run downhill with greater and greater force, eventually forming the Grand Canyon.

During this time, parts of the plateau were affected by folding and buckling of the sedimentary rock layers. Sharply-rising rock layers that appear sheared off in mid-air demarcate the edges of an uplift, known as a monocline. There are many striking monoclines to see on your travels. The Echo Cliffs along U.S. 89, 25 miles south of Page, mark the eastern boundary of the Kaibab Uplift. Comb Ridge along U.S. 163 marks the southern boundary of the Monument Uplift, which runs all the way from Kayenta, Ariz. to, Bluff, Utah.

To become familiar with the many rock formations, try to follow one rock layer as it appears and disappears over different parts of the reservation. The Chinle Formation is a good one to track because its purple and grey colors make it easy to pick out. You see it as the crumbly, round, purple and grey hills along U.S. 89 between Cameron and Tuba City, and south of Chinle near Canyon de Chelly. It makes up the bottom of the Echo Cliffs on U.S. 89, the Organ Rock Monocline on U.S. 160, and is seen again under Owl Rock on U.S. 163 heading toward Monument Valley.

In addition to sedimentary rocks, there are many igneous formations caused by underground volcanos that failed to break the surface when they erupted. Over eons, erosion wore off the top layers of sedimentary rocks exposing the harder volcanic plug. Agathla Peak and Shiprock are two primary examples of igneous formations.

GEOLOGIC TIME LINE FOR THE MOST COMMON ROCK LAYERS

	Age of Mammals **Cenozoic** 65 million years ago *Hopi Buttes*	Volcanics	
	Ganado Mesa	Bidahochi Formation	
	Chuska Mountains	Chuska Sandstone	
M E S O Z O I C — *Age of Reptiles*	*Black Mesa* — **Mesa Verde Group**	Yale Point Sandstone	
		Wepo Formation	
		Coal	
		Toreva Formation	
	Cretaceous 135 million years ago	Mancos Shale	
		Dakota Sandstone	
	Carrizo Mountains — **San Rafael Group**	Morrison Formation	
		Cowsprings Sandstone	
	Coal Mine Canyon	Entrada Sandstone	
	Jurassic 180 million years ago	Carmel Formation	
	Glen	Navajo Sandstone	
	Echo Cliffs Vermillon Cliffs — **Canyon**	Kayenta Formation	
		Moenave Formation	
	Group **Triassic** 230 million years ago	Wingate Sandstone	
	Painted Desert Petrified Forest	Chinle Formation	
		Moenkopi Formation	Shinarump
Paleozoic 600 million years ago	*Age of Fishes*	Kaibab Formation	
	Monument Valley Canyon de Chelly	Coconino Sandstone	De Chelly Sandstone
		Supai Group	
		Redwall Limestone	

Adapted from Smiley, 1984

TOURIST SEASON ON THE COLORADO PLATEAU

The high season for tourists on the Colorado Plateau is April 1 through November 1. This includes the Hopi and Navajo Nations, north and south rims of the Grand Canyon, Flagstaff and the Lake Powell/Page area. To help you plan your trip, every motel, RV park, camp site, restaurant, telephone, bathroom, police station and laundromat found on the major highway tours are listed in this book.

TIME ZONES

The Navajo Nation joins the rest of the U.S. in changing to Daylight Savings Time (DST) beginning the first week of April and ending the last week in October. The rest of Arizona and the Hopi Nation stay on Mountain Standard Time (MST) year round. The Navajo Nation switches because the reservation extends into New Mexico and Utah, states which also move to DST.

Obviously, this causes a good deal of confusion in towns that honor both time zones. In Tuba City, for example, the Tuba Trading Post and the Hopi village of Moenkopi stay on MST while Bashas' Market and the Indian Health Service Hospital switch to DST. In some homes, husbands and wives go to work in different times zones.

WEATHER

The Colorado Plateau is classified as arid. It receives less than 10 inches (25.4 cm) of rain per year. Most precipitation comes in two seasons, winter from December to March, and summer from July through August. Summer thunderstorms, known locally as monsoons, dump about 65 percent of the entire year's moisture. Amazingly, most of these summer storms have a diameter of only three miles.

The **average summer temperature** depends entirely on your elevation. A good rule of thumb is for every 1,000-foot (305 m) increase in elevation, the temperature will drop about three degrees Fahrenheit (1.7°C). On average, summer temperatures at 5,000 feet (1,524 m) are in the 90s-to-100s (32°C-38°C). At 7,000 feet (2,133 m), the daytime temperatures are usually in the 80s (27°C-32°C). Nighttime temperatures can drop considerably, especially in the mountains, so carry something warm to wear.

There are a few things you need to keep in mind when traveling in the West (like not running out of gas on a mountain pass) to avoid problems. One of these is **flash floods**. Because most of the soil is sandy, when it does rain it dumps more than the ground can absorb. Water flows downhill in washes and into slickrock funnels and spouts, collecting runoff from numerous outlets. Along the way it picks up debris and boulders. That's why it's not a good idea to cross a wash under flash flood conditions. The water may be deeper than you think and your car could easily be whisked away by the powerful water or pummeled by large rocks swept down from the higher mesas. This rule also applies to hiking in a narrow canyon during a thunderstorm.

Lightning

Navajos and Hopis have many "taboos," or words of warning, about lightning. Because this is a common danger in high country, Navajos instruct their children on appropriate behavior in a storm. If you sit down, they say, the lightning will go away. They also say not to yell when it's raining or you'll be struck by lightning. The most appropriate behavior in a thunderstorm is to avoid being in the open on a canyon rim. If you're away from shelter, squat on the ground next to a cliff or beneath an overhang. Do not touch grounded metal objects such as a railing or your camera's tripod. Lightning *will* strike the water, so if you are in a boat on Lake Powell, get off the lake and find a cliff or overhang to sit next to or under until the storm passes. In this country, storms don't usually last long.

Dust Storms

The wind is an amazingly powerful force in the desert. Bear in mind that it helped carve this land over millions of years. On a less grand scale, it would take only a few minutes for one of these sand storms to damage the paint on your car or pit your windshield. For the Navajos, the wind is the source of breath as well as the cause of illness. Winds are particularly strong in the spring, blowing generally from February through June.

You will frequently see **dust devils** cross your path. They are harmless but similar in appearance to a tiny tornado. Some Navajos think of dust devils as wind controlled by evil spirits up to no good. You, too, would be a believer if you saw a large dust devil run through a camp, throwing saddle blankets, harnesses and buckets into the air to land hundreds of feet away.

Quicksand

If you are interested in hiking, especially around the Little Colorado River, you should be aware of this mixture of sand and water that allows heavy objects, like your body, to sink. You probably learned about quicksand through western movies but never really believed there was such a thing. Yet it is a real danger and was a major obstacle to pioneers trying to cross the Little Colorado to settle in Arizona.

TRAVEL ETIQUETTE

As you motor through the Navajo, Hopi and San Juan Southern Paiute homeland, you will have the opportunity to see many of the mountains, rocks, animals, birds and plants that make up the core of the traditional belief system. Consider this: only medicine people may climb a mountain. Mountains are revered as sacred places. Traditional medicine people have been schooled in the appropriate behaviors and rituals that protect them as they travel among the Holy People to collect specific herbs, earth or rocks needed for ceremonial healing. Failure to maintain harmony through inattention to the laws of nature, they say, will result in illness.

Through one of more than 50 ceremonies, such wrong action and illness can be corrected and harmony restored. Your respect for this belief and your gentleness with all things you touch, walk on or look at is appreciated. Please do not take anything. Under the Preservation of American Antiquities Act, it is a crime to remove artifacts from federal property.

To include natives in your pictures, please ask their permission first. Many will definitely not want their pictures taken. Others, such as models working at Monument Valley or Canyon de Chelly, expect a gratuity. Hopis do not allow photography of any kind.

If you are lucky enough to see a Hopi dance, the appropriate etiquette is to stand toward the back of the crowd, leaving the front for villagers. During the dance, maintain silence and do not ask questions about the names or identities of the masked dancers, especially in front of children. Photography or sketching is prohibited in the villages or at dances. Tape recording and taking notes are also not allowed. If there is a "closed" sign at the entrance to a village, this means the ceremonial is closed to outsiders and you may not enter. Please read page 123-124 before visiting the Hopi Nation.

LAND OWNERSHIP

All Indian reservations are federal land held in trust for tribes for their exclusive use. Homesite leases within reservations were first handed out by the Indian Service, now called the Bureau of Indian Affairs, after the Navajos' release from Fort Sumner in 1868 following the infamous Long Walk. Reservation land is now under the tribe's control. Navajo tribal members are able to get their own piece of land, or homesite, by applying to their own community, a political subdivision of the Navajo Nation known as a chapter. Everyone in the community gives their opinion on the proposed homesite lease. Frequently, though, families will object to any limitation of their grazing land, making it difficult for new homesite leases to become available.

THE NAVAJO NATION

Ask a Navajo elder to tell you a story and you may be occupied for a while. Often an explanation of a current event must be put into perspective by beginning with the creation. The Navajo creation story involves three underworlds where important events happened to shape the Fourth World where we all now live.

It takes years to develop a true understanding of Navajo oral history. Diné College, formerly Navajo Community College, offers an excellent cultural orientation program for newcomers to the area. A two-day workshop called "The Winter Stories" features the legends that can only be told "after the thunder sleeps." Summer cultural orientations for health workers and educators offer an overview of the important cultural points needed to work successfully in this society. For more information about these programs, call Lena Fowler or Liana Reed at Diné College, Continuing Education, P.O. Box 731, Tuba City, AZ 86045, (520) 283-6321.

The Navajo were given the name *Ni'hookaa Diyan Diné* by their creators. It means "holy earth people." The Tewa Indians were first to call them Navahu, which means "the large area of cultivated land." Father Alonso de Benavides changed the name to Navaho in a book written in 1630. (Hewett, 1906)

According to the Diné, they emerged from three previous underworlds into this, the Fourth, or "Glittering World," through a magic reed. The first people

from the other three worlds were not like the people of today. They were animals, insects or masked spirits as depicted in Navajo ceremonies. **First Man,** or *Áłtsé Hastiin,* and **First Woman,** or *Áłsé Asdzáá,* were two of the beings from the First or Black World. First Man was made in the east from the meeting of the white and black clouds. First Woman was made in the west from the joining of the yellow and blue clouds. **Spider Woman,** or *Ná ashjé'ii Asdzáá,* who taught Navajo women how to weave, was also from the first world.

Spider Rock, Canyon de Chelly
Courtesy Museum of New Mexico, 6168

Once in the Glittering World, the first thing the people did was build a sweat house and sing the Blessing Song. Then they met in the first hogan made exactly as **Talking God,** or *Haashch'ééłti'í,* had prescribed. In this hogan, the people began to arrange their world, naming the four sacred mountains surrounding the land and designating the four sacred stones that would become the boundaries of their homeland. (The mountains do not actually contain their symbolic sacred stone.) The **San Francisco Peaks,** *Dook'o'oosłííd,* the Abalone and Coral Mountain north of Flagstaff, is the Navajos' western boundary. **Mt. Blanco,** *Sis Naajiní,* or the White Shell Mountain, in Colorado represents the eastern boundary. **Mt. Taylor,** *Tsoodził,* east of Grants, N.M., is the Navajos' Turquoise Mountain and represents the tribe's southern boundary. **Mt. Hesperus,** *Dibé Nitsaa,* in Colorado, representing the Black Jet Mountain, lies to the north.

After setting the mountains down where they should go, the Navajo deities, or "Holy People," put the sun and the moon into the sky and were in the process of carefully placing the stars in an orderly way. But the trickster, Coyote, growing impatient from the long deliberations being held, seized the corner of the blanket where they lay and flung the remaining stars into the sky.

The Holy People continued to make the necessities of life, like clouds, trees and rain. Everything was as it should be when evil monsters appeared and began to kill the new Earth People. But a miracle happened to save them, personified as **Ever Changing Woman**, or *Asdzą́ą́ Nádleehé.*

Changing Woman grew up around Huerfano Mesa, or *Dził Ná'oodiłíí,* in New Mexico. She married the Sun and bore two sons, the Hero Twins of the Navajo people. They are Monster Slayer and Child-Born-of-Water. The twins traveled to their father the Sun who gave them weapons of lightning bolts to fight the dreaded monsters. Every place the Hero Twins killed a monster it turned to stone. An example of this is the lava flows near Mt. Taylor in New Mexico, believed to be the blood from the death of *Yé' iitsoh,* or the "monster who sucked in people." All of the angular rock formations on the reservation, such as the immense Black Mesa, are seen as the turned-to-stone bodies of the monsters.

With all of the monsters dead, the Holy People turned their attention to the making of the four original clans. *Kiiyaá áánii,* or Tall House People, was the first clan. They were made of yellow and white corn. Eventually other clans traveled to the area around the San Juan River, bringing their important contributions to the tribe. Some were Paiutes who brought their beautiful baskets. Others were Pueblos who shared their farming and weaving skills. Still others were Utes and Apaches.

For her husband the Sun to visit her every evening, Changing Woman went to live in the western sea on an island made of rock crystal. Her home was made of the four sacred stones; abalone, white shell, turquoise and jet. During the day she became lonely and decided to make her own people. She made four clans from the flakes of her skin. These were known as the Near Water People, Mud People, Salt Water People and Bitter Water People. When these newly-formed clans heard that there were humans to the east who shared their heritage, they wanted to go meet them.

Changing Woman gave her permission for them to travel from the western sea to the San Francisco Peaks. They then traveled through the Hopi mesas where they left porcupine, still commonly found there today. Then they traveled toward the Chuska Mountains and on to Mt. Taylor. Finally, the people arrived at Dinetah, the Diné traditional homeland, and joined the other clans already living there. Dinetah is located in the many canyons that drain the San Juan River about 30 miles east of Farmington, N.M. (Yazzie, 1971; Underhill, 1953; Walters, 1994)

Anthropologists believe the arrival of the Navajo at Dinetah happened between 1300 and 1680 A.D. Life there was not easy. Constant attacks from Ute raiders, as well as the threat of Spanish invasion during the 17th and 18th centuries, made life very dangerous. Because of the combination of outside threats, as well as a severe drought in 1740, the Navajos began to move out of their center place in Dinetah. (Walters, 1994)

When settlers and prospectors started to travel across Navajo hunting areas in the late 1800s, they were frequently killed, or, at the very least, harassed to scare them away. The U.S. Cavalry came to the rescue of the settlers and tried to negotiate peace treaties with people they designated as "chiefs." In actuality, they were talking to *naat'áanii,* people with great speaking abilities who were respected for their leadership skills. Some were medicine-men, or *hataałii,* like Manuelito, who was born in 1820 in Utah and was a great warrior known as *Nabaah Jiltaa,* or "Warrior Grabbed Enemy."

When one clan's *naat'áanii* signed a treaty, the military thought peace would reign with all of the Navajo people. This was not the case. Information about a treaty signed by one band of Navajos was not necessarily shared with other bands. Finally, the military would not tolerate any more "broken" treaties. Because of its 1840 promise to Mexico under the Treaty of Guadelupe de Hidalgo, and the country's interest in settling the West, Gen. James Carlton commissioned one-time friend of the Navajos, Kit Carson, and his volunteer soldiers to pave the way for miners and settlers. The plan was to kill or capture Navajos and march the survivors to Fort Sumner in New Mexico, more than 400 miles away. This became known as **The Long Walk**.

By 1864, Carson's troops captured some 8,000 Navajo men, women and children after slashing and burning their way across the reservation. This destroyed all of the Navajos' food and water supplies. Completely subjugated, the Navajos surrendered and lived at a place called Bosque Redondo on the Pecos River near Fort Sumner for four years. When they arrived, there was no housing for them. Most lived in hogans made out of anything they could find or holes dug in the earth.

Group of Navajo Captives, Fort Sumner, New Mexico, 1866
Courtesy Museum of New Mexico, #38191

Gen. Carlton's grand idea was to turn the Navajos, and about 500 Apaches, into farmers on a tiny piece of land only 40 miles square (104 sq km). But the land was so barren, finding firewood required searching for miles. Water was so alkaline, it was undrinkable. The soil was so poor, crops wouldn't grow.

At last, in 1868 when news of the starvation conditions reached the ears of sympathetic Americans, and because of the prohibitive cost of feeding thousands of people in a concentration camp, the War Department agreed to let the Navajos go. They were given the option of relocating to Oklahoma or going back to their traditional homeland. To the military, the home of the Diné was nothing more than useless wasteland. But to the Navajo, it was the place of their emergence and where their ceremonies have the most power.

General William T. Sherman met with a council of 12 Navajo men, including Barboncito and Manuelito, to negotiate their release. He explained that the treaty would allow for each person to receive rations. To this one of the Navajo leaders said, "No. All we want you to give us is an old buck goat. We will tie him by his horns to a pinyon tree and let him butt it with his head until he is dead. That will show our young men what it is like to fight against the government." Actually, they got $5 worth of clothing and $10 each year if they were farming. Families could select 160 acres to farm and got $100 in farming equipment and seeds. The tribe was to divide 15,000 sheep and 500 cattle evenly between families. For each group of 30 students between the ages of six and 16, a school house was to be built and a teacher provided. (Shinkle, 1965)

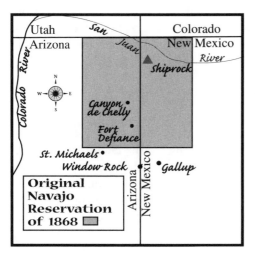

The first signer of the Treaty of 1868 was Barboncito, known as "Peace Chief." The treaty granted the Navajos a reservation of a little more than 6,120 square miles (15,912 sq km) on land that straddled the boundary between the New Mexico and Arizona territories. But this limited acreage would not support the growth of sheep herds so families began crossing reservation boundaries, living in sheep camps far from other clans. (Shinkle, 1965)

Because of the huge distances between camps, the BIA devised the boarding school system to meet their obligation to educate all Navajo children. Navajo parents had no idea that the education their children would receive would be so alien to their way of life and, in effect, be another prison sentence. (More about boarding schools in the chapter on Tuba City, pages 115-117.)

NAVAJO LEGAL SYSTEM

The American judicial system was imposed on the Navajo people in 1882 by the secretary of the Interior. Called the Courts of Indian Offenses, these forums were based on a punishment system of justice and ignored ancient Navajo customs and beliefs about concepts of right and wrong.

One hundred years later, Navajo judges began to look for more culturally appropriate ways to deal with disputes. In 1982, the **Navajo Peacemaker Court** was formed. This court operates on three fundamental Navajo beliefs. First, all people are equal and no one may make a decision for, or coerce, another person into a decision. Second, the social system revolves around the belief in *ke'*, or respect for one's relatives and responsibility to them; and last, a deep respect for tradition and the belief that problems are solved through ancient prayers and ceremonies handed down from one generation to the next.

With these basic principles to guide them, the peacemaker judge brings the disputing parties together to talk out the problem and come to a consensus. The goal is for both parties to walk away with their heads held high. The peacemaker judge is not an authority on the legal system and may not have a college education. But he or she is someone able to speak well and lead the negotiations to a peaceful conclusion.

Navajo courts have jurisdiction over all civil matters on the Navajo Nation. In criminal matters, the tribal courts have limited jurisdiction. Navajo and Hopi police are cross-deputized with the Arizona Department of Public Safety and have authority to arrest lawbreakers. In criminal matters, a non-native is transported off the reservation to the closest county jail and court-house.

NAVAJO CLAN SYSTEM

When a Navajo baby is born, he or she belongs to the clan of the mother. The clan name passes on through her to her children. When a young man marries, it must be to someone completely outside of his clan. Even though people in his clan are not all blood-related, it is considered inappropriate to marry within one's own clan. The children are "born to" a woman's clan and take her clan name, and are "born for" a man's clan. Navajos precisely know who they are through identification by their mother's, father's, maternal grandfather's and paternal grandfather's clans.

Whenever one Navajo meets another, the appropriate etiquette is to introduce one's maternal and paternal clans on both sides of the family. In this way, it is possible to find a "mother" or "uncle" in a clan relative living hundreds of miles away and, therefore, a benefactor who will help you on your travels.

NAVAJO HOMES

Most of the newer houses and small subdivisions you will pass on the highway are there to make it easier for Navajo children to catch the school bus. These families probably have another camp in a more remote location where they graze their sheep and cattle. Today, just about every camp has a hogan with a frame or cinder block house or a trailer close by. The modern homes are for the extended family to live in with the hogan used by the grandma or reserved for ceremonies.

Hogan construction follows a very specific blueprint handed down by the Holy People to maintain the spiritual meaning of the dwelling and its use for curing ceremonies. The male hogan, rarely seen today, was three logs placed in the ground at the northern, southern and western cardinal positions. Two poles form the entry and the entire hogan is covered with dirt. Tso Bonito Zoo in Window Rock has a good example of a male hogan.

Forked Hogan ca. 1918-1920
Marie Olson Collection, Cline Library, Special Collections and Archives, NAU 516-30

The more common dwelling is the female hogan built in a round shape with six or eight sides of logs laid one on top of the other to form a wall. The entire hogan was covered with earth except for the smoke hole in the top. All hogans must have their entrance facing the rising sun to greet the Holy People in the morning. Traditional hogans have dirt floors to maintain a connection to the earth (Mother Earth) and an opening to the sky (Father Sky).

If you find that you must stop at a Navajo camp, drive up slowly to the front of the hogan and stop. Do not get out of the car. Sit and wait a few minutes. If someone is home, they will come out to greet you and invite you in.

Female Hogan in Canyon de Chelly, ca. 1930-1940
Philip Johnston Collection, Cline Library, Special Collections and Archives, NAU PH 413-194

NAVAJO FOOD

Traditional foods consists of corn, beans, squash, pumpkins, pinyon pine nuts, peaches, apples, prairie dog, rabbit and other game as it was found. When Navajos took up sheepherding from the Spanish in the 17th Century, mutton became the primary food source. Every part of the sheep is used in some sort of dish. Sheep intestines are completely cleaned and filled with a mixture of sheep blood, potatoes, corn meal mush and fat to make blood sausage called *dił*. The real delicacy is sheep head, or '*atsiί,* which is slowly baked in the ground for many hours before being eaten. The most common meal found at most social gatherings is mutton stew and fry bread. The stew is made from every part of the sheep except the intestines and head. The meat is boiled with potatoes, onions, celery and salt. It is served with fry bread (see Tuba City for recipe) or a tortilla. Coffee has practically replaced Navajo tea as the national drink.

COMMON VEGETATION

Throughout your visit to the Colorado Plateau, you will travel into and out of numerous **pinyon-juniper woodlands,** known as pygmy forests and found at 4,000-to-7,500 feet (1,219 m-2,286 m).

These trees are an important element in the Native American lifestyle. For thousands of years, the native peoples have relied heavily on the nuts for their survival. The seed of the Colorado Pinyon (*Pinus edulis*), which dominates this area, is extremely rich in fat. It is about 66 percent fat, 14 percent protein and 18 percent carbohydrate. For starving people in between a successful hunt, the storage of pinyon nuts often meant the difference between life and death. (Lanner, 1981)

The pinyon nut saved the Domínquez-Escalante expedition of 1776 from starvation, (see pages 77-79 for an explanation of this historic party). But the famous Donner party in Nevada was not so lucky. Ignorant of the secrets of the pinyon, they passed right through a forest at the peak of its harvest and were forced to commit cannibalism to survive the Sierra winter. (Lanner, 1981)

Pinyons are gathered from the end of August through November. A bumper crop comes about every seven years. You can buy small bags of roasted pinyon nuts, salted and in their shell, for $1 at most roadside beadstands. But beware: like a bag of peanuts, they can be very addicting. (Be sure to take the shell off before eating them.)

Sagebrush, or *Ts' ah,* grows at about 6,500 feet (1,981 m). This is a wonderful plant and has many medicinal properties. It is considered to be one of the "Navajo life medicines" and is said to cure headaches just from smell-ing it. (Mayes, 1989) Perhaps the most classic smell in the West is the wonderful scent of wet sage after a rainstorm.

Other common plants are **yucca** and **Mormon Tea.** Soap is made from yucca roots. It's used to wash the hair of the Hopi bride and groom, as well as those involved in various Navajo ceremonies. Mormon Tea, used by the Mormons and by traditional healers, brews into a tea for various remedies to restore health. If you decide to try some, be aware that the tea does contain ephedrine which can accelerate your heart rate.

Sheep Shearing, not dated.
Ganado Mission Collection, Courtesy Sage Memorial Hospital

ANIMALS COMMON TO THE AREA

Dibé **(Sheep)**: Many families continue to raise sheep as their sole means of support. All of the Navajo reservation is open range. This means that *you* are responsible if a sheep, horse or cow runs in front of your vehicle, caus-ing an accident. The water runoff from the road surface acts as a irrigation system, encouraging grasses to grow alongside of the road when the rest of the pasture land is barren. Watch your speed and the roadsides for grazing animals. Open range highways are marked throughout the book with this horse herd graphic:

Tłízí **(Goat):** Most of the goats you see grazing beside the road are Angora. The mohair is spun to make Navajo rugs. Drums made of goat skin are used during healing ceremonies.

Gálgii **(Raven):** Larger than the common crow, ravens can be confused with a hawk because they alternate soaring with flapping their wings. Their feathers are used by medicinemen in certain ceremonies and were used on the shafts of arrows by warriors and hunters.

Gahtsoh **(Jack Rabbit):** Much larger than a rabbit, the jackrabbitt has very powerful, large hind legs. The fibula bone is carefully prepared by medicinemen and used as a whistle, a necessary piece of equipment in some ceremonies. At one time, the fur was braided with yucca to make blankets. Rabbit skin blankets over 3,000 years old have been excavated at Basketmaker sites in Tsegi Canyon. (Guernsey, 1921)

Máii **(Coyote):** The average coyote is 24 inches tall (61 cm) and weighs about 40 pounds (18 kg). It eats smaller rodents, especially prairie dogs. The coyote, also referred to as "the trickster," is the major character in many Navajo stories about right and wrong, with the coyote always on the wrong side. According to Navajo healer Ursula Knoki-Wilson, the coyote itself is not evil. He is just a daring character easily persuaded by evil forces to take impulsive risks that usually have a bad outcome. To some, a coyote crossing your path is warning of impending danger. He is therefore doing you a favor. To avoid the danger, the traveler must stop and think good thoughts before continuing. The Hopis believe coyote is more gullible than he is evil. The word in Hopi to describe a person who believes everything he is told is *ihu,* meaning sucker. (Malotki, 1993)

Dlǫǫ **(Prairie Dog):** Once a common food to the Navajo, the prairie dog lives in "prairie dog towns" throughout the reservation. They build sophisticated underground tunnels which may stretch for miles with many entrances and exits.

HEALTH PRECAUTIONS

The prairie dog sometimes carry fleas infected with the bacteria that causes the **bubonic plague**. This was once a highly-contagious and deadly disease, but is now completely treatable with antibiotics. It's seasonal and generally affects only a small number of people. U.S. Public Health Service officials watch prairie dog colonies for "die-offs" which indicate infection with the disease. When this happens, warnings are announced to keep domestic animals from roaming and to avoid contact with dead animals.

Hantavirus: Traditional healers and elders soon deduced what it was when two young people mysteriously died from a respiratory ailment within days of each other in 1992. They remembered that in 1918, and again in 1933, there were also many unexplained deaths. The similarity was a lot of rain followed by a bumper crop of pinyon nuts. These conditions led to an explosion in the population of deer mice. This time around, the U.S. Centers for Disease Control and the U.S. Public Health Service were able to pinpoint the virus responsible for causing this potentially fatal pulmonary syndrome. Deer mice and other rodents carry the virus in their saliva, feces and urine. It's believed the people affected somehow came into contact with the virus by cleaning up mice droppings or by sweeping, raising airborne dust which contained the virus. The best way to protect yourself from exposure is to avoid sleeping near rodent burrows or touching sick or injured animals. If you find mice droppings in your hotel or cabin, do not disturb them. Instead, report them to the caretaker who will remove them wearing a mask and gloves and spraying them with disinfectant.

 **NAVAJO RUG WEAVING**

Spider Woman, one of the Holy People, taught Navajo women how to weave. Spider Man taught her how to build the loom in a very specific way. The loom that was created is much like the Pueblos' vertical loom. Pueblo refugees came to live with the Navajos after the Pueblo Rebellion of 1680 and were known to weave cotton long before the Spanish arrived in 1540 with 3,000 sheep from Spain. The Navajos started to collect their sheep herds around 1640 in raids against the Spanish. (Wheat, 1984)

What to look for if you want to buy a Navajo rug

The best place to buy a rug is from the weaver. This often takes time so the next best place is from a roadside vendor or a trading post. Examine the rug closely and use all of your senses to determine if you have an authentic Navajo handmade rug.

Look at the rug.

Lay it flat and look at both sides to see if the weaving is straight and the sides are even. Then fold the rug in half to see if the edges match up. Do this both for the length and width of the rug. Next, fold the rug in half and peel it back to see if the two halves mirror each other. Look at the colors. They should be the same throughout the rug.

Many weavers leave a "spirit line," or a single line exiting the rug across one of the borders, to prevent their spirit from being trapped in this living entity they have just created. Today, some weavers do not put in the line. It's left to the weaver's discretion and may mean that this particular weaver did not feel a need for a spirit line.

Rug weaver at her loom, ca. 1930s
Fred Harvey Collection, Museum of Northern Arizona Photo Archives, MS 301-3-18

Smell the rug.

If it smells like goat or sheep, this is a good indication the rug is Navajo. However, many exceptional Navajo rugs are made from commercial yarn and won't have this smell.

Touch the rug.

Feel how tight the weave is. Imitation Navajo rugs made in Mexico will have a loose weave and feel soft to the touch. A good Navajo rug will have a consistent weave throughout. Two characteristics found in almost all Navajo rugs are: 1) there are no exposed warp threads (the strong thread running the length of the rug) as found in Mexican or East Indian rugs and 2) a Navajo rug will have double cotton warp threads on the selvage edges (top and bottom edges of the rug). Mexican rugs will have only one, but you will have to gently separate the colored threads on the edge to see the selvage warp. (Brechner, 1995)

Talk to the weaver.

If at all possible, meet the weaver and ask her what type of wool she used and whether the colors are natural or commercial dyes. If this is not possible, most reputable trading posts will know quite a bit about each weaver and her rug. Her name and what part of the reservation she's from should be on the rug.

If you know what you are doing, one of the best places to get a good price on a rug is the **Navajo Rug Auction** at the Crownpoint Elementary School in Crownpoint, N.M. Throughout the year on the third Friday of the month, the auction offers more than 200 rugs from all regions of the Navajo Nation. Viewing is from 3 - 6 p.m. with the auction starting at 7 p.m. For more information, call (505) 786-5302.

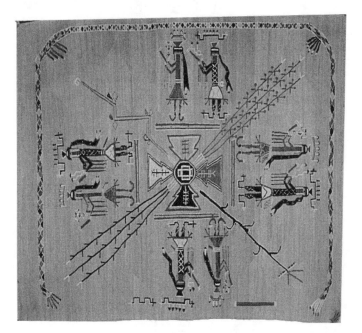

Navajo Sandpainting Rug
Weaver: Hosteen Klah
1930-1936

Photograph by Gene Balzer
Museum of Northern Arizona

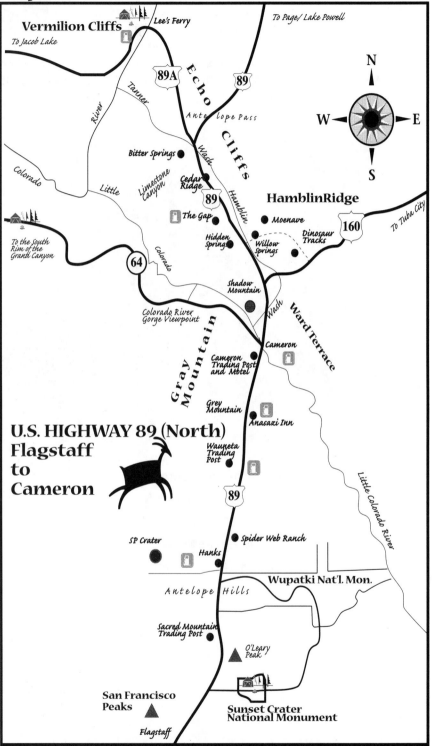

Chapter 2

Vermilion Cliffs

To Jacob Lake

Lee's Ferry

To Page/ Lake Powell

89A

89

Echo Cliffs

Tanner

River

Antelope Pass

Bitter Springs

Wash

Colorado

Little

Limestone Canyon

Cedar Ridge

89

Hamblin

HamblinRidge

160

To Tuba City

The Gap

Moenave

Hidden Springs

Willow Springs

Dinosaur Tracks

Colorado

Shadow Mountain

64

Colorado River Gorge Viewpoint

To the South Rim of the Grand Canyon

Wash

Ward Terrace

Cameron

Cameron Trading Post and Motel

Gray Mountain

Grey Mountain

Anasazi Inn

Little Colorado River

U.S. HIGHWAY 89 (North)
Flagstaff
to
Cameron

Wauneta Trading Post

89

SP Crater

Spider Web Ranch

Hanks

Wupatki Nat'l. Mon.

Antelope Hills

Sacred Mountain Trading Post

O'Leary Peak

San Francisco Peaks

Sunset Crater National Monument

Flagstaff

N
W E
S

48 miles (77 km) from Flagstaff to Cameron

U.S. HIGHWAY 89

Highway 89 was called Lees Ferry Road before 1931. It was a wagon road that connected Flagstaff with Tanner's Crossing over the Little Colorado at Cameron and continued north along the Echo Cliffs to Lees Ferry. (Indermill, 1990)

San Francisco Peaks from the north, 1905
Detroit Publishing Co. Collection, Cline Library, Special Collections and Archives, NAU PH 90.10.1

MM 425 SAN FRANCISCO PEAKS (West)

Rising to a height of 12,643 feet (3,831 m), the San Francisco Peaks are Arizona's highest mountains. Franciscan missionaries living in the Hopi village of Oraibi in 1629 named these mountains to honor their founder, St. Francis of Assisi.

The peaks, or *Dook'o'oosłííd,* represent one of the four sacred mountains of the Navajo and the winter home of the Hopis' kachinas, *Nuvatu kya' ovi.* They are also the western boundary of traditional Hopi lands, or Hopi *tutskwa.* These mountains hold meaning for everyone living in northern Arizona. You will see them dominating the southern horizon throughout your travels on the Hopi mesas.

The group of peaks that make up the center of this extinct volcanic range are **Agassiz, Fremont**, and, the tallest, **Humphreys Peak**. Despite having blown its top a millennium ago, the peaks today rise from the high plain at about 6,000 feet (1,818 m) in elevation to more than twice that. Mt. Humphreys was named for Andrew Atkinson Humphreys, a surveyor for the railroad. Mt. Agassiz honors the memory of Jean Louise Rodolphe Agassiz, a famous geologist and zoologist who developed the theory of the ice age, and Mt. Fremont commemorates John Charles Fremont, governor of Arizona from 1878 to 1882. Fremont was also a well-known botanist who started his plant collection in the 1840s. The Fremont Cottonwood, named for Gov. Fremont, is one of the most common trees you will see along streams and washes in the Southwest. (Mayes, 1989)

Basques shepherds are an interesting yet little-known group of people who lived and worked on the San Francisco Peaks from the late 1800s to the 1980s. Originally from an area between France and Spain in the Pyrenees Mountains, the Basques emigrated to the west to seek their fortunes when life in their own country became too difficult. Some sailed to the New World with Christopher Columbus in 1492 and with Coronado's expedition in 1540.

Some people think the word Arizona is actually the Basque word, "arriz ona," meaning the good or valuable mineral ore. Another variation may be "arrtiza ona," meaning the good or valuable rocky place. Either definition is appropriate.

Life in America was not easy for the "Amerikanuak," a Basque living in America. This was especially true during the Gold Rush of 1848 when thousands of Basques emigrated to California. Most would not find their fortune in precious metals but instead offered their services to land owners interested in developing large sheep herds.

Basques were soon in demand, renowned throughout the West for their successful and productive management of sheep. They accepted four-year contracts with landowners, taking their salary in sheep. At the end of his contract, the shepherd would venture off on his own as a private sheep rancher.

It was not an easy life to care for animals that must constantly graze on less than ideal grassland. To get the most nutrition from available grasses, shepherds moved their sheep to the San Francisco Peaks from summer through early fall. Before winter, the flock moved to low country where the ewes dropped their lambs in the spring. Navajo shepherds also follow this pattern of cyclical migration, known as transhumance. (Stein, 1991)

One of the more beautiful times of the year to visit northern Arizona is when the band of aspen that encompass the middle of the San Francisco Peaks change colors, usually at the end of September or beginning of October. It is also when many of the wildflowers are in bloom.

Surrounding the peaks are more than 2,200 square miles (5,720 sq km) of volcanic remnants and more than 400 extinct volcanos. The most prominent and most recent volcanic cone is **Sunset Crater.**

MM 425 SUNSET CRATER Northeast, the volcanic cone with the red rim

Known to Navajos as Yellow Top Mountain and to Hopis as Red Hill, this cinder cone was given its name because of its sunset colors by John Wesley Powell, the famed explorer of the Colorado River and Grand Canyon. The Hopis believe their Wind God, *Yaponcha*, lives in a crack in the black rock near the crater.

Sunset Crater is the last of numerous volcanos that developed in this area and is thought to have erupted around 1064. Two lava flows created this volcanic cone: **Kana-a Flow,** which headed northeast toward the Little Colorado, and **Bonito Flow**, which traveled northwest. (Anderson, 1958)

SCENIC DETOUR

MM 430.5 Sunset Crater Volcano/ Wupatki National Monument

The entrance fee to Sunset Crater Volcano and Wupatki National Monument is $4 per car. The National Park Service accepts Golden Eagle, Golden Age, and Golden Access Passports. This is a 35-mile (57 km) winding road with no gas stations or food available other than snack machines located in the visitors centers at Sunset Crater Volcano and Wupatki. To see everything in both parks, plan at least four hours and bring a lunch. Both visitors centers open at 8 a.m. and close at 5 p.m. (MST). All of the trails and ruins close at dusk.

The volcano became a national monument in 1930 due in part to a movie company's interest in dynamiting Sunset Crater to simulate a volcanic explosion. Here you can explore and learn about vulcanism, cinder cones, and lava flows. The visitors center has exhibits on these topics and a self-guided tour through Bonito lava flow is available. Even though Sunset Crater is off-limits to hiking, you can climb **Lenox Crater**, 1/4 mile (.40 km) south of the visitors center. Impressive lava flows and scenery can be seen from the many overlooks.

Mile 33.5 BONITO PARK (SOUTH)

Beautiful views of the San Francisco Peaks to the west and Sunset Crater Volcano to the east.

Mile 32.7 BONITO CAMPGROUND (North)

Located directly across from the Sunset Crater Volcano visitors center, this 43-site campground operates on a first-come, first-served basis. Maximum vehicle length, 35 feet, no RV hook-ups. $8/night. Closed in winter. For more information call (520) 526-0866.

Mile 32.6 SUNSET CRATER VOLCANO VISITORS CENTER (South)

The center has interpretive displays about vulcanism and the Sunset Crater area. It also has an earthquake monitoring system that records earth movements all over the world. Open from 8 a.m. to 5 p.m. (MST).

Mile 31.3 BONITO LAVA FLOW (North)

Flowing from the base of Sunset Crater, the molten lava cooled very quickly to form the hard outer covering seen here. Inside, the lava continued to flow as a liquid, spreading over a wide area. Because the lava flows look much like the surface of the moon, NASA sent Neil Armstrong, the first man to walk on the moon, and other astronauts to train at Sunset Crater. They practiced how to walk on the jagged rocks in space suits to collect moon specimens. Outside the park, craters were blasted into a volcanic cinder field to duplicate the Sea of Tranquility, where Apollo 11 would land.

Bonito Lava Flow with the San Francisco Peaks
Photograph by Christine Stephenson

Ice caves are found throughout this flow. In the 1880s, Flagstaff saloon owners harvested the ice for their restaurants.

Mile 31 Self-guided walking tour through a lava flow.

Mile 29 CINDER HILLS OVERLOOK (South)

You can see the beginning of the Kana-a Flow that follows the road all the way to Wupatki. *Kaná a* is the name for the Hopis' friendly kachina that lives here. The Hopis lived on the southern edge of Black Mesa when Sunset volcano erupted in 1065. There is a story in their oral history about a Hopi community destroyed by a cloud of ash. People saw a strange light in the mountain moving toward them and warned the villagers to get out of its way. Some who were pursuing pleasures and did not follow the Hopi teachings were destroyed but the good people who carried out their responsibilities and duties were saved. (Thybony, 1987)

Mile 25.3 PAINTED DESERT VISTA AND PICNIC AREA (West)

Mile 24 STRAWBERRY CRATER WILDERNESS (West)

The jagged, sharp-looking lava found here is a good example of *aa* lava. A Hawaiian word, it is pronounced ah-ah. *Pahoehoe* (pronounced pa-hoy-hoy), also Hawaiian, is smooth lava.

Mile 14 WUKOKI PUEBLO (East)

Meaning "big house" in Hopi, the Sinagua people lived in this three-story dwelling from the early 1100s to 1210 A.D. For more information about the Sinagua see pages 265-266.

Mile 13.6 WUPATKI PUEBLO AND VISITORS CENTER (West)

Wheelchair accessible to the upper pueblo.

The ruins were named *Wapatkikuh*, or "Tall House Pueblo," by anthropologist Dr. Jesse W. Fewkes who completely mapped the area in 1896.

Wupatki plays an important part in the Hopi Snake Clan legend. The Zuni Parrot Clan was said to have traditionally stopped here. The Havasupai claim knowledge of these ruins through their ancestors. And like so many ruins of the Southwest, this one also bears a Navajo name, *Anaasazi Bikin*, or "House of the Ancient Ones." (Van Valkenburg, 1941)

The ball court is the most unusual feature at the ruins. It's thought to be similar to ball courts built by the Aztecs and Mayans. Next to the ball court is a blow hole that acts like a barometer. When the atmospheric pressure is low, air is forcefully blown out of the hole, when it is high, air is sucked into the hole.

Mile 12.4 CLYDE PESHLAKAI'S HOME(East)

In a rock house north of the monument headquarters. Closed to visitors.
Clyde Peshlakai was a custodian of Wupatki National Monument in 1936. His father, Peshlakai Etsidi, traveled in 1902 and again in 1904 to Washington to advocate for an increased land base for the Navajo. Protestant Minister William Johnston from Tuba City accompanied him to meet with President Theodore Roosevelt. Roosevelt was sympathetic to the needs of the Navajo and added the Leupp area, about 20 miles (32 km) south of Wupatki, to the Navajo reservation.

Mile 10.5 PAINTED DESERT VIEWPOINT

As you come down off Woodhouse Mesa, the vegetation changes to Desert Scrub dominated by sagebrush and salt bush. The names and characteristics of these plants are identified at the Wupatki visitors center.

Mile 9.4 DONEY PICNIC AREA (South)

Ben Doney was a fortune hunter who lived here from 1883 to 1930 and spent most of his time looking for the **Lost Padre Mine**. He believed this area was the site of a lost Spanish mine from the 17th Century. The story described the mine's location as being in a red hill 40 miles (64.5 km) west of the Hopi villages. Doney sunk many shafts looking for the mine but never found anything. (Thybony, 1987)

The large and small volcanic cinder cones here bear his name. **Doney Trail** leads to the top of the cinder cone and takes about one-half hour to climb. It offers a great view of the Painted Desert, Sunset Crater and the San Francisco Peaks Volcanic Field. Keep your eyes open for golden eagles which nest on Doney Mountain. Not wheelchair accessible.

Mile 4.1 CITADEL PUEBLO (West)

Built in the late 1100s, this pueblo offers a 360-degree view. It's called the Citadel because its design suggests the builders wanted protection from attack; although there is very little evidence that warfare was a serious threat. Behind the ruin is a large limestone sink originally thought to have provided the community with a water source but it is too porous to hold water. Cisterns and drainage systems were built to collect rainwater during the wet years, and when it didn't rain the Little Colorado River, about 10 miles (16 km) away, was the closest source of fresh water.

Sitting below the Citadel is **Nalakihu Ruin** which means "house standing alone" in Hopi. The Museum of Northern Arizona excavated the ruin in 1933 and found many owls buried here as well as pottery shards that came from as far away as Prescott, Ariz., about 150 miles (242 km). The scientists do not know if the rather large pots were carried all the way from Prescott or if a group of people had migrated to this area, bringing the pots with them. (Thybony, 1987)

Mile 3.8 TURN OFF TO LOMAKI PUEBLO (North)

The name of this pueblo, built in the 1100s, means "beautiful house" in Hopi. The 1/4 mile (400 m) trail that leads to it passes by **Box Canyon Ruin.** Both ruins sit on the edge of earth cracks that are found throughout Wupatki-Sunset Crater National Monument. **Earth cracks** are thin vertical openings in the Kaibab Limestone caused from the movement of the earth.

END SCENIC DETOUR

Or begin scenic detour if you are traveling south. This is a 35-mile (57 km) loop through Wupatki/Sunset Crater National Monument that connects back with U.S. Highway 89. Mile markers 433-443 can be seen only if you do not take the scenic tour of Wupatki/Sunset Crater Volcano National Monument.

🐐 MM 433 O'LEARY PEAK (East)

Named for Dan O'Leary, a guide for the military during the Indian Wars of the 1800s. This volcanic dome is more than 200,000 years old and is part of the San Francisco volcanic field.

🐐 MM 436.5 SACRED MOUNTAIN TRADING POST (West)

Built in 1915, this trading post was once known as Deep Wells. Bill Beaver bought the post in 1960 and renamed it Sacred Mountain Trading Post. Today it is an operating post, supplying native crafts people with materials for bead work and jewelry in exchange for finished jewelry, rugs and art work. Beaver speaks Navajo and was influential in assisting local Navajo artists develop their roadside businesses which you will see along U.S. 89. He also is credited with encouraging the San Juan Paiute basketmakers to rejuvenate their skills. (Indermill, 1990).

ROADSIDE VENDORS

The first automobile to travel from Flagstaff to the Grand Canyon made the trip in 1902. Traveling over a rutted wagon road, it took the tourists three days to make the 70-mile journey from Flagstaff to Grandview Point on the South Rim of the canyon. Encouraged by the increase in tourism, the first Navajo vendor stand was probably put up by Navajos living close to the wagon trail. Today, vendors typically congregate in large groups of beadstands. Many sellers are related and from the same area. Outside vendors are not welcomed into this lucrative method of direct selling to tourists. For many vendors, roadside selling is the only means of support and the entire family, including children old enough to make change, will participate in running the roadside beadstand.

The typical roadside stand is a variation of the traditional Navajo shade house, or *chaha'oh*. The shadehouse has four forked wood posts with a cross beam on each side. Long boughs of juniper or pinyon, dried reeds or a blanket cover the top of the cross beams for shade.

Navajo Shade House, not dated.
Brown, Bahl and Watson Collection, Cline Library, Special Collections and Archives, NAU PH 92.14.114

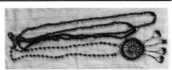

One of the more common items sold at the stands are necklaces called "ghost beads" made of juniper seeds. To the Navajo, these beads bring protection in unfamiliar places and protect children from nightmares.

Photograph by Christine Stephenson

MM 442.5 ANTELOPE HILLS (Both sides of the road)

You will see herds of wild antelope on both sides of the road around this

area. A truly American animal, the antelope has roamed the prairies of this country for more than 12 million years. Hunted almost to extinction like the plains buffalo, sharp shooters killed antelope from coach windows of passing trains and slaughtered them in mass to supply meat for hungry gold and silver miners. Standing only three feet high (1 m) and weighing about 125 pounds (57 kg), the antelope's only defense is their keen eyesight. Watch for them in the early morning.

Antelope at Indian Gardens, Grand Canyon, Arizona, ca. 1930s
Fred Harvey Collection, Museum of Northern Arizona Photo Archives, #301-3-118

Sinagua Trading Post (East)

AAA 24 hour Towing Service (520) 679-2331

MM 443.2 PAINTED FACES (East)

Don't miss this...if you can find it. Three faces painted in the style of Hopi kachinas decorate these fence posts. According to Cecil and Eva Fisher, owners of the Sinagua Trading Post for the past 16 years, they do not know who the artist is but every once in awhile someone comes back and re-paints the faces.

MM 445 JUNCTION FOREST SERVICE ROAD 545

Entrance to Wupatki National Monument. See pages 31-35 for information about the National Monument.

Three Faces
Photograph by Fran Kosik, 1994

MM 446 HANKS TRADING POST

Directly behind Hanks to the west is **SP Crater**. Like Sunset Crater, SP is a cinder cone and has an extensive *aa* lava flow that traveled northward. *This is the closest gas station before you enter Wupatki National Monument if you are traveling south.*

MM 450.5 SPIDER WEB RANCH (East)

This is the headquarters for the CO Bar ranch, owned by the Babbitt family of Flagstaff. The five Babbitt brothers moved to Arizona from Cincinnati, Ohio, (hence "CO" Bar cattle brand) in 1886. The first thing the brothers did when they arrived in Flagstaff was purchase 864 head of cattle. To buy their first herd, they used most of the $20,000 from the sale of their home and business in Cincinnati. Over the next 40 years, they built a cattle empire of more than 100 brands with a grazing area covering most of northern Arizona from the Mogollon Rim south of Flagstaff, north to Tuba City, west to the Grand Canyon and east almost to the New Mexico border.

The Babbitt family still owns most of the grazing land on both sides of U.S. 89 to Gray Mountain. If you are lucky, you will see real cowboys rounding up the herd to take them to market or to transfer them to another grazing area.

MM 452.5 WAUNETA TRADING POST (West)

MM 458 GRAY MOUNTAIN (West)

This looming gray expanse to the west rises to an elevation of 7,500 feet (2,286 m) and extends all the way to the Grand Canyon, about 70 miles away. The Navajo shared this plateau with the Havasupai for almost 150 years. (Van Valkenburgh, 1941)

Former Navajo Tribal Chairman Peter MacDonald, in his autobiography *The Last Warrior*, tells a story about Apollo 15 astronauts, Jim Irwin and David Scott, who were training on the moon-like landscape of Gray Mountain in 1971. Wearing space suits, the two astronauts practiced driving the moon buggy over the rocky terrain gathering specimens and traveling to and from a mock-up of the lunar landing module.

Seeing these strange creatures, a medicine man who was grazing sheep in the area came over to MacDonald for an explanation. When MacDonald told him the astronauts were practicing to travel to the moon the elder asked if he could send a message with them. MacDonald explained to the astronauts that Navajo legend describes the Diné stopping on the moon on their way to visit their father, the Sun. The message was for any Navajos still living on the moon. Too happy to oblige, the astronauts gave the medicineman a tape recorder for his message. When the medicineman was finished MacDonald interpreted the tape for the astronauts. In essence, the medicineman had warned the moon-dwelling Navajos to beware of these two men because they will want to make a treaty with you. (MacDonald, 1993)

SERVICES AT GRAY MOUNTAIN

LODGING
Anasazi Inn at Gray Mountain
High Season: $79.95 (2 beds or 1 single king size bed)
Low Season: $69.95 (2 beds or 1 single king size bed)
Tax: 6.1 percent Reservations:(520) 679-2214

RESTAURANT
Gray Mountain Trading Post
Serves breakfast, lunch and dinner. Summer hours: 6 a.m-10 p.m.
In summer, the trading post offers a steak cookout behind the motel for a minimum of 10 people. The motel will take you on a mule-driven wagon to

the cook-out. Because the town is off the reservation, it is legal to purchase alcohol here. Possession of alcohol on the reservation, however, is illegal.

The Navajo Nation changes to Daylight Savings Time (DST) with the rest of the country from April to October. The Hopi Nation and the rest of Arizona stay on Mountain Standard Time (MST) year round.

 MM 460 - ENTERING THE NAVAJO NATION

Dine' Bikeyah -- Navajoland -- has had many boundaries decided for it by the federal government. But to the Navajos, four sacred mountains enveloping the land mark their territory. The San Francisco Peaks, the *Abalone and Coral Mountain,* north of Flagstaff is the Navajos' western boundary. Mt. Blanco, or *White Shell Mountain,* in Colorado represents the eastern boundary. Mt. Taylor, east of Grants, N.M., is the Navajos' *Turquoise Mountain* and represents the tribe's southern boundary. Mt. Hesperus in Colorado represents the *Black Jet Mountain* and lies to the north.

MM 466 NAVAJO ARTS AND CRAFTS ENTERPRISE (West)

This business in the hogan-shaped building is owned and operated by the Navajo Nation. It offers quality handmade authentic Navajo jewelry, rugs, pottery, as well as unusual T-shirts and sweat shirts. Open from 8 a.m.-6 p.m. DST.

MM 466 NAVAJO TRIBAL TOURIST OFFICE (West)

If you are planning to camp or hike on the Navajo Nation you must obtain a permit. Camping permits are $2 per person per night. A back-country permit for hiking is $5 per person; $10 for 2-10 people and $20 for more than 10 people. The permit is good for 14 days. For more information, contact: Navajo Nation Parks and Recreation, P.O. Box 308, Window Rock, AZ 86515. (520) 871-6645.

◁ Junction U.S. 89 with Arizona State Highway 64 to the Grand Canyon

For information about services available in Cameron, see page 60.

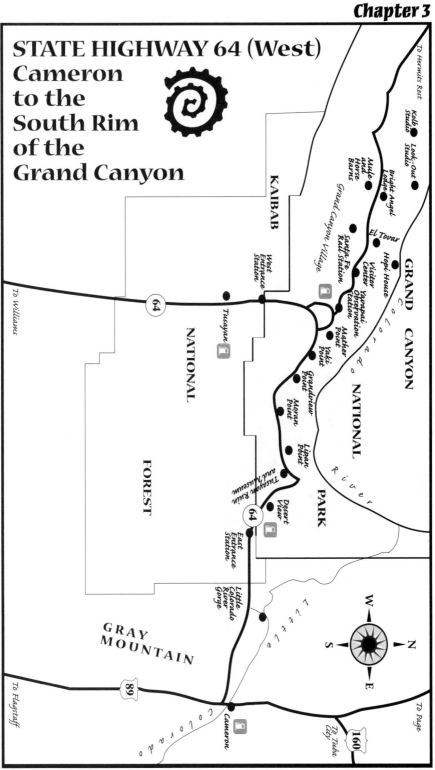

Chapter 3

STATE HIGHWAY 64 (West)
Cameron to the South Rim of the Grand Canyon

KAIBAB

GRAND CANYON

NATIONAL

NATIONAL

FOREST

PARK

To Hermits Rest

Kolb Studio

Look-Out Studio

Mule and Horse Barns

Bright Angel Lodge

El Tovar

Hopi House

Santa Fe Rail Station

Grand Canyon Village

West Entrance Station

Visitor Center

Yavapai Observation Station

Mather Point

Yaki Point

Grandview Point

Moran Point

Lipan Point

To Williams

64

Tusayan

Colorado River

Tusayan Ruin and Museum

Desert View

64

East Entrance Station

Little Colorado River Gorge

GRAY MOUNTAIN

Little Colorado

W N S E

89

To Flagstaff

To Page

To Tuba City

160

Cameron

Colorado

NATIVE ROADS

57 miles (92 km) from Cameron to the South Rim

⊙ MM 290 GRAY MOUNTAIN (South)

Gray Mountain is part of the Kaibab Monocline formed when the earth uplifted about 250 million years ago. This gradual uplift caused the meandering Colorado River to run at a steeper gradient, giving it more power to cut through the less resistant rock layers. It eventually led to the creation of the Grand Canyon. The elevation at the South Rim is 7,000-to-7,500 feet (2,135-2,287 m) with the average gradient on the Colorado River of 7.8 feet per mile (2.38 m per km).

Because of the elevation, temperatures are moderate in summer, averaging in the 70s and 80s (21°C-27°C). Winter can be very cold and snow storms are frequent. The average temperature during the day will be in the 30s to 40s (0°C-5°C). Average rainfall annually is about 11 inches (28 cm).

⊙ MM 286 LITTLE COLORADO RIVER GORGE (North)

Rimmed with Kaibab Limestone, this 1,200-foot (366 m) gorge is a Navajo tribal park with tremendous scenic views. Many local artists sell jewelry, pottery and rugs here. There are port-a-potties but no water.

Little Colorado River Gorge, ca. 1930s
Fred Harvey Collection,
Museum of Northern Arizona Photo Archives, MS 301-5-78

⊙ **MM 275 KAIBAB NATIONAL FOREST:** At this point you enter a pygmy Utah juniper-pinyon pine forest, found at elevations of 4,000-to-7,000 feet (1,200 m-2,135 m). You can camp anywhere in the forest without a permit.

EAST ENTRANCE TO THE GRAND CANYON: $20 per vehicle for a permit valid for seven days at both the South and North Rims. Visitors on foot or bicycle pay $10. Golden Eagle passes cost $50 per year and are good at all National Park Service sites. Golden Age Passports for people over 62 cost a one-time, life-time fee of $10. But don't lose your card or you'll have to pay again. Golden Access Passports for handicapped individuals are free. Buying the Golden Eagle Pass is a bargain if you want to visit any of the other national parks in the area like Wupatki-Sunset Crater Volcano National Monument or the Petrified National Forest.
http://www.thecanyon.com/NPS/index.htm

Fred Harvey Bus at Desert View, ca. 1930s
Fred Harvey Collection, Museum of Northern Arizona Photo Archives, MS 301-4-480N

DESERT VIEW POINT: From this vista you can see the Painted Desert and where the Colorado River has cut through the Kaibab Plateau. To the east is Cedar Mountain.

You can see the **Desert View Watchtower** all the way from Highway 160 just outside of Tuba City — if you know what to look for. You will, after you see it up close on the edge of the South Rim for the first time. Mary Colter designed and built the watchtower in 1932. An architect for the Fred Harvey Co., she designed and supervised the construction of many of the buildings at Grand Canyon.

Despite the obstacles women faced in the late 1800s, Mary Colter was not a woman to let life pass her by. Her parents immigrated from Ireland to Pittsburgh, Penn., where Colter was born in 1869. She graduated from the California School of Design as an architect and in 1902, was hired by the Fred Harvey Co. to decorate the Alvarado Hotel in Albuquerque. Three years later she designed the Hopi House next to the El Tovar. (Evans, 1985)

Desert View Watchtower, aerial view ca. 1930s
Fred Harvey Collection, Museum of Northern Arizona Photo Archives, 301-4-480

Colter was in her sixties when she developed the concept of the watchtower for the Fred Harvey Co. who wanted a rest station for passengers traveling from Cameron to the Grand Canyon. Colter used the watchtowers of Mesa Verde and Canyon de Chelly as her prototypes. To accomplish the effect she wanted, stones for the exterior of the building had to be naturally shaped. This required picking each stone by hand from a local quarry. (Grattan, 1992)

Colter commissioned famous Hopi artist **Fred Kabotie** from the village of Shungopavi to paint murals in the Hopi Room in the watchtower. He used the theme of the **Snake Dance** as his subject. The Snake Dance is an important Hopi ceremonial held in August to bring rain for the maturing of the crops. Other Kabotie murals are in the **Painted Desert Inn** at the Petrified Forest National Park.

Standing on top of the 1932 watchtower, you are at the highest point on the South Rim, 7,522 feet (2,279 m) above sea level. From the 360 degree view you can see the Colorado River, the Painted Desert to the east and the San Francisco Peaks in the south.

One of Mary Colter's famous buildings you can't see from the rim is the beautiful and remote **Phantom Ranch** built by the Fred Harvey Co. in 1921. Colter named the ranch for the nearby Phantom Creek and designed the main building and cabins to blend in with the rustic environment. Later buildings added by the U.S. Geological Survey followed her design.

When the ranch was completed in 1922, it attracted wealthy politicians, movie stars and artists because of its remote and quiet location. Now the ranch caters to anyone who can get a reservation. The waiting list is sometimes as long as two or three years but it is worth the wait. A little known fact about the ranch is that at one time it had a beautiful swimming pool, hand dug by the Civilian Conservation Corps of the Roosevelt New Deal era. Cool, clean water was piped into the pool from the Bright Angel Creek and flowed over a man-made waterfall. It was truly a wonderful way to end what can be a long, hot hike or mule ride. The National Park Service filled in the pool in 1972 because of maintenance and sanitary problems.

Dining hall at Phantom Ranch with pool, not dated.
Emery Kolb Collection, Cline Library, Special Collections and Archives, NAU 568-4690

Phantom Ranch can be reached only by foot or horseback. To make a reservation, or for any other accommodations within the boundaries of the canyon, contact: Amfac, Parks & Resorts (303) 29P-ARKS between 7:00 a.m.-6:00 p.m. (MST), seven days a week. Plan in advance; reservations within the park, especially at Phantom Ranch, are very hard to get on short notice. http://www.heard.org/EDU.HARVEY/gc/gc6.htm

 **DESERT VIEW CAMPGROUND:**

First come-first served, no hook-ups and it is closed during the winter. Fee: $10 per night. In summer, most canyon campgrounds are full by noon.

LIPAN POINT: From this view point you can see a great expanse of the canyon, including the inner gorge, Vishnu's Temple, Cape Royal and the Colorado River, as well as Echo Cliffs, the Painted Desert and Navajo Mountain off in the distance.

TUSAYAN RUINS AND MUSEUM: About 800 years ago, 30 Anasazi Indians lived at this small site near the canyon's edge. The museum offers interpretative displays of prehistoric life in the canyon. Buy a brochure for 25 cents and take a self guided tour through the ruins. Guided tours are also offered. The museum is open daily from 9:00 a.m.- 6:00 p.m. (MST).

MORAN POINT: From 1867 to 1879, the United States conducted the

great surveys of the American West. John Wesley Powell's 1871-1872 trip through the Grand Canyon on the Colorado River was one of these surveys. The government hired Thomas Moran to document the landscape encountered on this trip. He did this by making hand drawings from photographs taken by E.O. Beaman and Jack Hillers who traveled down the river with Powell. To some experts, Moran's work at both Yellowstone and the Grand Canyon are considered to be some of the most important and definitive drawings of the newly explored land. (Kinsey, 1992)

Thomas Moran, Grand Cañon of the Colorado, ca. 1874
John Wesley Powell Collection, Cline Library,Special Collections and Archives, NAU PH 268-35

GRANDVIEW POINT: Directly below this viewpoint, in the Redwall Limestone on Horseshoe Mesa, is the long-defunct **Last Chance Copper Mine.** Peter Berry and Ralph and Niles Cameron developed the mine during the 1890s. Burros carried the ore out of the canyon on the Grandview Trail that Berry hand-built for about $12,000. The mine never broke even because of the high cost of transporting the ore. By 1895, Berry realized that the motherlode he sought was in the pockets of tourists so he built the Grandview Hotel at the head of his trail, the first hotel at the Grand Canyon. Grandview became the most popular trail for tourists to get an unobstructed view of the canyon. (Anderson, 1958, Good, 1985)

Grandview Trail: While beautiful, this is considered a strenuous, six-mile round trip trail. It drops 2,600 feet (793 m) quickly to Horseshoe Mesa where you can see the remains of Berry's and the Camerons' copper mine. Hopis use the flecks of green copper from here to paint their kachina masks and dolls. There is no water on this trail. Each hiker needs at least two quarts of water but during the summer a gallon (4 liters) per hiker is a necessity.

DUCK ON ROCK VIEW POINT: There is a plaque here showing the topographic features of the canyon. This viewpoint got its name because the formation looked like a duck until its bill fell off. (Berggren,1995)

YAKI POINT: Here you will find the head of the **South Kaibab Trail** that leads to Phantom Ranch. The ranch can also be reached via the Bright Angel Trail.

Junction of State Highway 64 with East Rim Drive. Turn right.

MATHER POINT: Stephen Mather was named the first director of the National Park Service in 1916. From Mather Point the north rim is 10 miles (16 km) away and is 1,000 feet (305 m) higher in elevation than this point on the South rim.

YAVAPAI OBSERVATION STATION: Here you'll find viewing tubes with sites that point out geologic features. An interesting exhibit is the geologic clock. Based on a three minute geologic cycle to create one rock layer, each tick on the clock represents 11 million years. Open daily from 8 a.m.

NATIVE ROADS

to 8 p.m. (MST). The **Rim Trail** starts here and follows the canyon edge through Grand Canyon Village, ending at Hermits Rest. The trail is paved from Yavapai Point to Maricopa Point, 3.5 miles (5.6 km). Shuttle buses run from 6:30 a.m. to 10:30 p.m. (MST) during the summer at approximately 15 minute intervals so you can walk as far as you want and then catch a shuttle bus back to where you started.

SOUTH RIM VISITORS CENTER: Open from 8:00 a.m. to 6:00 p.m. (MST) every day, the center offers information about the services and educational programs offered within the park.

MATHER CAMPGROUND:

Located one mile (1.6 km) south of the visitors center. Requires reservations from March 1 through Nov. 30. But you can make reservations up to five months in advance on a first-come, first-served basis. Toilets, showers and phone, open year round, 320 campsites, seven-day limit, $12 per site, no hookups. Handicap accessible. Contact: DESTINET, P.O. Box 85705, San Diego, CA 92186-5705, (800) 365-2267.

Turn right to El Tovar and Hopi House

EL TOVAR

This national historic landmark takes its name from Don Pedro de Tovar, an officer in Coronado's expedition of 1540. He never actually saw the Grand Canyon. His charge was to explore the Hopi villages and report back to Coronado waiting in Zuni. When he returned, he told Coronado of a great river farther west that the Hopis had described to him. Coronado dispatched Captain Don Garcia de Cardeñas to find the river.

No expense was spared in 1904 to build El Tovar. Designed by an architect from Chicago, the famous hotel cost $250,000 to build. Native Arizona stone makes up the foundation of the building but Oregon logs were used for the walls. Water, always a problem on the South Rim, came every day by train from more than 120 miles (193 km) away. In 1932, a pumping station brought fresh water up from Indian Gardens. Today, water is pumped from Roaring Springs on the North Rim. (Evans, 1985)

Guests staying at El Tovar had only the best food prepared for them by an Italian chef. Dinner was served on antique plates and silverware and the hotel had its own garden, dairy cows and chickens to assure the freshest food for its patrons. It even had its own greenhouse to grow fresh flowers for the tables. (Evans, 1985)

Fred Harvey was an entrepreneur with an uncanny ability to see the future and the services that people would be willing to pay for. Born in England in 1836, he came to this country as a teenager and earned money washing dishes in a New York restaurant. By the time he was 21, he was a successful restaurateur in St. Louis but lost his business during the Civil War.

He moved to Kansas and landed a job working for the Chicago, Baltimore & Quincey Railroad, traveling extensively on the train. It didn't take him long to see the potential in providing eating and sleeping accommodations to the increasing number of rail travelers. Around 1886, he presented a proposal to the Atchison, Topeka & Santa Fe Railroad to manage restaurants and hotels at each of the company's major stations. At the time of Fred Harvey's death in 1901, his company managed 45 hotels and restaurants from Cleveland to Los Angeles.

Probably his most famous "restaurant concept" was the "**Harvey Girl**." The topic of many movies, these wholesome young ladies from the East received free chaperoned travel to the wild West plus room and board. In return, they had to promise not to marry for one year–often referred to as the most frequently broken promise in history.

A Harvey House, 1926
The Kansas Historical Society, Topeka, Kansas

The Harvey Girls, in their starched white aprons, learned how to make tourists feel welcome and comfortable. El Tovar was one of the hotels that used Harvey Girls to wait on their exclusive clientele. *Price $111-$271. Same day reservations call (520) 638-2631 or for advanced reservations call (303)-297-2757. Amfac Parks & Resorts, Suite 600, 14001 E. Llif, Denver, CO 80014.*

HOPI HOUSE: Across the parking lot from El Tovar stands the Hopi House designed by Mary Colter. The Fred Harvey Co. wanted a building to sell Indian arts and crafts that represented the local history and fit in with the canyon environment. Built primarily by Hopi labor, it was patterned after authentic dwellings in Old Oraibi. Mennonite missionary H.R. Voth, who lived in the Hopi village of Oraibi, played an important part in obtaining Hopi ceremonial objects displayed here when the House opened in 1905. (See page 134 for more about Voth.) (Grattan, 1992; Whiteley,1992)

MULE AND HORSE BARNS: Lending the western scent of manure to the character and charm of the South Rim are the historic barns, built in 1907, on the south side of the railroad tracks. The mules, used to transport visitors to the bottom of the canyon and back, are cared for here.

If you want to take a **mule ride** into the canyon, you need to plan ahead. Trips are booked one year in advance but you can place your name on a waiting list for cancellations at the Bright Angel Transportation Desk, located in the Bright Angel Lodge, when you arrive at the canyon. *To make reservations, write or call: Amfac Parks & Resorts (303) 297-2757.*

YAVAPAI LODGE (LEFT): *Price: $79-$89. Same day reservations (520) 638-2631 or for advanced reservations call (303) 297-2757 or write Amfac Parks & Resorts, Suite 600, 14001 E. Llif, Denver, CO 80014.*

BRIGHT ANGEL LODGE: The lodge sits on the site of the old Bright Angel Camp that included two historic cabins. **Buckey O'Neill** built his cabin sometime in the 1890s while part-owner in the Anita Copper Mine located 15 miles south of here. He talked the Santa Fe Railroad into building a line from Williams to his mine to transport the ore. When the copper ran out, the Santa Fe extended the rail to the rim to take advantage of the growing tourist trade. (Manns, N.D.)

The second cabin was **Red Horse Station** built here in 1896 by J. Wilbur Thurbern, a stage coach operator who brought visitors from Flagstaff to Grandview Lookout. The station sits about 100 yards (91 m) from the mule corral at the head of the Bright Angel Trail. In 1902, Ralph Cameron bought the camp and added a second story to the Red Horse Station calling it the **Cameron Hotel**.

Colter built Bright Angel Lodge in 1935 and wanted to keep the designs of the older Red Horse Station and Cameron Hotel so she used native stone and timber. Truly the first historic preservationist, she understood the irreplaceable value of handmade cabins, saving and incorporating them into the plans for the Bright Angel Lodge. (Grattan, 1992)

One of the more interesting features as you walk into the lodge is the **geologic fireplace** in the lobby. Each rock layer of the canyon is represented in the fireplace, with Kaibab Limestone at the very top. Every stone in the fireplace came out of the canyon by mule train. There is also a Fred Harvey Museum in the lodge. *Rates: $35-$111, reservation number and address same as Yavapai Lodge.*

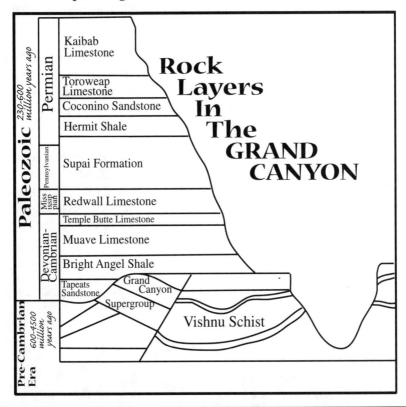

To see the Look Out, Kolb Studio and the Bright Angel Trail, you will have to park your car and walk on the Rim Trail behind the Bright Angel Lodge. Take the shuttle bus to see the Orphan Mine, Powell Memorial and Hermit's Rest.

THE LOOK OUT: Mary Colter designed the lookout for the Fred Harvey Co. in 1914 to completely blend into the rim environment. The chimney is almost indistinguishable from a distance, looking like a pile of rocks. Weeds grow on top of the roof so that when looking at the Bright Angel trailhead from a distance, it is almost impossible to see the camouflaged lookout. (Grattan, 1992)

⚙ **KOLB BROTHERS STUDIO:** Emery and Ellsworth Kolb were photographers from Pennsylvania who made their way to the Grand Canyon in 1901 and set up a studio on the rim of the canyon. Their idea was to take pictures of tourists hiking down the Bright Angel Trail. But in 1902, the United States forester, who controlled the canyon, refused to allow the brothers to build on the rim. The Kolbs made a deal with Ralph Cameron to set up a temporary studio in a tent beside the Cameron Hotel.

As more and more tourists came to the canyon, attracted by the Fred Harvey enterprise and the newly constructed El Tovar Hotel, the photographers' makeshift studio couldn't handle all of the business. Somehow they were able to talk Cameron into giving them a piece of his mining claim at the head of the Bright Angel Trail to build their elaborate studio.

In the early 1900s, photography was a cumbersome and delicate operation. It required clean water not available on the South Rim. After taking the visitors picture at the head of the trail the brothers hiked to their darkroom at Indian Gardens, 4.6 miles (7.4 km) one-way. Emery processed the film with water from the spring and then ran back up the trail to meet the group as they arrived back from their muleride.

Kolb Studio, 1915
Emery Kolb Collection, Cline Library, Special Collections and Archives, NAU PH 568-772

To supplement their meager earnings from taking tourist photographs, the brothers explored the canyon and sold pictures of areas never seen before. Their most daring and famous adventure was the first filming of a boat trip through the Grand Canyon. Starting out on the Green River in 1911, the two brothers using specially designed wooden boats, began their historic journey and arrived at Bright Angel Trail six weeks later. Taking a few days to develop footage and restock, the brothers continued down the river and after 101 days arrived in Needles, Calif.

To capture this amazing journey, that included running more than 365 rapids, one brother steered the boat while the other dealt with the bulky motion picture equipment, shooting from the bow. A dangerous rapid was recorded from the shore by one brother while the other ran the rapid. If you have a chance, see the Imax™ movie, *Grand Canyon: The Hidden Secrets,* to get an idea of just how dangerous and complex capturing the river on film must have been in 1911.

Imax™ Theatre *is located in the town of Tusayan at the south entrance to the park. The movie is shown in the summer from 8:30 a.m. to 8:30 p.m. and in the winter from 10:30 a.m. to 6:30 p.m. every hour on the half hour daily. Adults: $7.50; children under 12, $4.50; children under three are free. (520) 638-2203.*

In the basement of their studio on the South Rim, the Kolbs built an auditorium to show canyon visitors their amazing film. Because of an on-going battle with the Fred Harvey Co. and the forest service, the brothers couldn't show their film at the canyon. Undaunted, they took their show on the road, traveling to Washington, D.C., to lecture to sold-out crowds at the National Geographic Society. Ohio was to be the brothers downfall. Emery did not want to go to Ohio, thinking they would lose money on the appearance. Ellsworth insisted and when the show did not break even, the brothers decided to split permanently. A coin was tossed and Emery won the studio and photography business. Ellsworth moved to Los Angeles to pursue his interest in flying. The brothers never reconciled, only visiting each other on occasion.

An interesting story that involves the Kolbs is the mystery of the fate of Glen and Bessie Hyde. Newlyweds from Idaho, the Hydes traveled to the Kolb studio in 1928 to have their picture taken after traveling 26 days from the Green River to the Bright Angel Trail in their homemade wooden boat. When the Kolbs found out the Hydes did not have life jackets on board their boat, they offered them inner tubes just in case. The Hydes refused, saying they were both very good swimmers. Unfortunately, the Kolbs were the last people to see the honeymooners alive.

Glen and Bessie Hyde, 1928
Photographed by the Kolbs before their disappearance.
Emery Kolb Collection, Cline Library,
Special Collections and Archives, NAU PH 568-5386A

Bessie's father started a hunt for his daughter soon after she failed to show up on schedule in Needles, Calif. One of the first airplanes to fly below the rim was dispatched from March Air Force Base in California to look for the couple. They found Bessie and Glen's boat below Diamond Creek with their gun, camera, notebook and a copy of *Through the Grand Canyon*, written by Ellsworth Kolb, lying inside. The search party discovered the couple's footprints seven miles (11 km) above Diamond Creek and Glen's footprints were found down river by a rapid.

Emery Kolb's theory of what happened to the couple is probably the most likely scenario. Typically, the couple would work as a team, with Bessie leading the boat down river by rope while Glen scouted the next rapid. It is possible that Bessie fell into the water, her 90 pound (41 kg) frame pushed by high winds, and Glen may have jumped in to save her, both drowning in the process. (Evans, 1985) No one really knows what happened to the couple and no human remains were ever found. An interesting twist to this story occurred 48 years later. After Emery and Ellsworth were dead and buried, someone found a skeleton in Emery's garage. Many people speculated that this was somehow the body of Glen Hyde, and that Emery and Bessie had conspired to kill Glen so that she would not have to continue on this extremely hard journey.

Luckily, Emery kept a diary that explained why he stored this skeleton for so many years. He had found it while exploring an old mine and on occasion would pull it out to entertain his grandson. (Suran, 1991)

Emery is buried in the Grand Canyon Pioneers' Cemetery. In 1974, two years before his death at the age of 95, he took his last trip down the river to experience the thrill of Crystal Rapids. A flood in 1966 altered this rapid, making it one of the more dangerous sections of water on the Colorado River.

🌀 **BRIGHT ANGEL TRAIL:** The Kolb Studio marks the head of the Bright Angel Trail, part of the Cross Canyon Corridor Historic District. This man-made trail follows a fault in the sandstone cliffs. Prehistoric Indians used this pathway and the Havasupai, who now live down river from this point in the canyon, lived at Indian Gardens in the early 1900s.

Although the trail is 7.8 miles (12.6 km) long and not recommended for someone without sufficient water and appropriate foot wear, a short jaunt to **Mallory's Grotto** is worth the effort. As you pass through the first tunnel, note the Havasupai pictographs on the left above a ledge.

Ralph Cameron, a miner who owned the Last Chance Copper Mine with his brother and three other prospectors, spent two months making the ancient path passable from the rim to Indian Gardens for pack mules and horses. Peter Berry, one of the trail builders, recorded the Bright Angel Trail as a toll road in the Yavapai County Courthouse in 1891. At that time, it was legal for private citizens to build roads on public land and charge a toll for 10 years. If the owner did not break even within that time, he could get an extension for five more years.

When Berry got his extension in 1901, Ralph Cameron bought his rights and charged each tourist or miner $1 every time they used the trail. Realizing that this was the way he would make his fortune, Cameron established ownership of the trail by staking mining claims at every important point on the trail. He filed a claim on the rim, Indian Gardens, the Devil's Corkscrew and Pipe Creek.

Detail of toll sign next to the Kolb Studio, 1915
Emery Kolb Collection, Cline Library, Special Collections and Archives, NAU PH 568-772

NATIVE ROADS

When the Grand Canyon was made a national monument in 1908, the problem of Cameron's toll road was a thorn in the side of the park service. The local people sided with Cameron but the Santa Fe Railroad, which wanted to develop the tourist business at the canyon, viewed Cameron's toll road as an unnecessary barrier to visitation of a national treasure. To get around the problem, the National Park Service built the South Kaibab Trail which was a shorter and slightly easier route to the river.

In 1920, Cameron, by then a U.S. senator, tried to eliminate funding for the Grand Canyon from the Interior Department's budget but his colleagues outvoted him. After losing reelection to the senate, Cameron left Arizona permanently. In 1928, Coconino County took control of the Bright Angel Trail and promptly deeded it to the National Park Service. (Cleeland, 1986)

The **Bright Angel Trail** is 19 miles (31 km) round-trip. Like all canyon trails, it's a strenuous hike, descending 4,400 feet (1,342 m) over well-maintained switchbacks to Indian Gardens and on to the Colorado River. The Silver Suspension Bridge crosses the river to Phantom Ranch. The trip takes most hikers two days and requires a reservation at either Indian Gardens Campground (15 campsites), Bright Angel Campground (31 campsites) or at Phantom Ranch. Because of the limited number of camp sites, it is necessary to make reservations well in advance of your hike. *Contact Backcountry Reservation Office, P.O. Box 129, Grand Canyon, AZ 86023, (520) 638-7888. To generate more revenue to maintain and improve services in the Canyon, the National Park Service instituted a new fee structure. Backcountry Permit fee $20; Backcountry Camping fee $4 per person per night.*

ORPHAN MINE: Daniel Hogan, a prospector and former Rough Rider under Theodore Roosevelt, discovered this mine when he noticed copper on the wall of the canyon about 1,000 feet (305 m) below the rim. He got a patent for the mine in 1906, but it wasn't until 1956 that the U.S. Geological Survey discovered the true wealth of the mine — uranium. The Western Gold and Uranium Co. began mining more than 45 tons (40,909 kg) of ore daily from the Orphan Mine, sending it to the Rare Metals Processing Mill outside of Tuba City. (See page 162-163 for more about Rare Metals.) There is no mining going on within the Grand Canyon today. (Anderson, 1958)

POWELL MEMORIAL: This memorial lists the names of all of the men who completed the two trips with John Wesley Powell in 1869 and 1871-72. Three men who deserted Powell's first expedition at Separation Canyon are not on the memorial. Seneca and O.G. Howland and William Dunn, not knowing how much farther the river would run and thinking they would surely die of dehydration and starvation, quit the party and attempted to hike out of the canyon, only to be killed by Shivwits Paiute Indians. The Powell party safely completed the journey just a few days later.

⊙ HERMIT'S REST: Trying to get Ralph Cameron to relinquish his control of the Bright Angel Trail was a slow and tedious process requiring seven trips to the Arizona Supreme Court. Finally, the park service and the Fred Harvey Co. developed the attitude that if you can't beat him, go around him. At a cost of $185,000, the Harvey Co. built an eight-mile road to the west end of the canyon where sightseers could hike down Hermit's Trail to get to the Colorado River and Phantom Ranch. Mary Colter designed Hermit's Rest in 1914 for the Harvey Co. to look like a haphazardly-constructed miner's cabin made out of native stones and timbers. Even the entrance arch was crudely constructed with a broken bell from a Spanish Mission hanging from the center. Seeing the massive fireplace as you enter Hermit's Rest will help you to understand the genius in Colter's ability to bring out the primitive charm and power of a structure through her rustic architectural style.

Hermit's Trail is a very strenuous, unmaintained trail that leads to the Colorado River, dropping 4,240 feet (1,293 m). On this 17-mile (27 km) round-trip hike there is no safe water to drink. The trip takes at least two days to hike, and is recommended for experienced desert hikers only.

WHO WAS THE HERMIT? Prospector Louis Boucher mined this corner of the canyon in the late 1800s. Because this area was so remote from the more popular section of the canyon, people thought of him as a hermit.

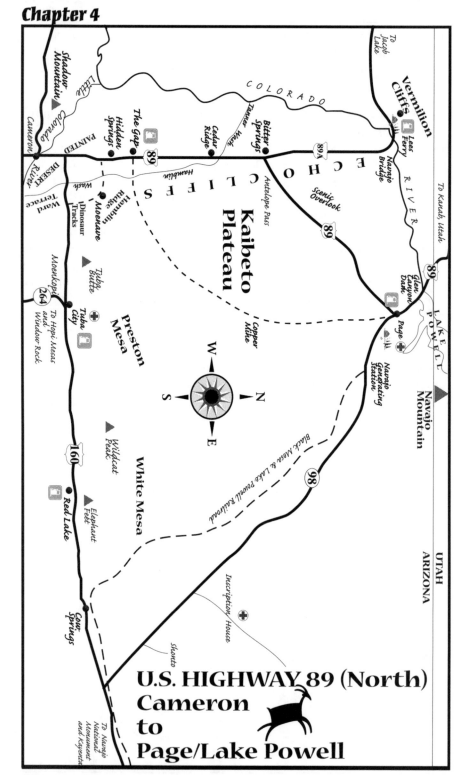

Chapter 4

Shadow Mountain

To Jacob Lake

COLORADO

Vermilion Cliffs

Lees Ferry

89A

Navajo Bridge

ECHO CLIFFS

RIVER

To Kanab, Utah

Little Colorado

Cameron

PAINTED

DESERT

Hidden Springs

The Gap

Cedar Ridge

Tanner Wash

Bitter Springs

89

Hamblin Wash

Antelope Pass

Scenic Overlook

89

Ward Terrace

Dinosaur Tracks

Moenave

Hamblin Ridge

Kaibeto Plateau

Moenkopi

264

To Hopi Mesas and Window Rock

Tuba Butte

Tuba City

Preston Mesa

Copper Mine

Glen Canyon Dam

Page

LAKE POWELL

Navajo Generating Station

Navajo Mountain

W N S E

160

Red Lake

Wildcat Peak

Elephant Feet

White Mesa

Black Mesa & Lake Powell Railroad

98

UTAH

ARIZONA

Cow Springs

Inscription House

Moenkopi

Shonto

To Navajo National Monument and Kayenta

U.S. HIGHWAY 89 (North)
Cameron
to
Page/Lake Powell

MM 467 CAMERON TRADING POST (West)

To adventurers or homesteaders traveling through here in the early 1900s, Mabel's Oasis was a welcomed sight. Owned by Mabel and Hubert Richardson, the couple took great pains to make this a green mecca for travelers to enjoy. In 1911, Mabel planted Chinese elms, apple trees, ivy and rose bushes behind the trading post and in front of what is now the gallery. Today's remodeled trading post, with its beautiful dark wood floors, display cases and antique furnishings is truly an exquisite place to visit. For sale are unusual items like a Spanish silver horse halter, silver jewelry and concho belts dating back to the 1860s. Every October, the trading post holds an auction of old bead work, pottery, rugs, baskets, dead pawn and modern Navajo rugs and jewelry. For more information, call (520) 679-2231.

The Cameron Trading Post, once known as the Little Colorado Trading Post, is now owned and operated by Joe Atkinson, the grand nephew of the Richardsons. He bought the place from trader Gilbert Ortega in 1977 and began remodeling the old sandstone buildings, adding a 65-bed motel.

It is worth a stop just to hear the trading post's wonderful wood floor creak underfoot, get a feel for what old trading days were like, and to enjoy a meal looking out onto the Chiquito Colorado, the name for the Little Colorado River in 1854.

Cameron is named for Ralph Cameron, a former U.S. senator and friend of the Richardsons. Before becoming a senator, Ralph and his brother Niles supervised the 1899 construction of the Bright Angel Trail in the Grand Canyon. Originally developed to serve Cameron's mines and others in the Grand Canyon, the trail was first taken over by Coconino County and, finally, by the National Park Service. The trail is now *the* most popular hiking trail leading to the Colorado River on the south rim of the Grand Canyon. See Chapter Three for more on the Camerons and the Bright Angel Trail.

Cameron and other miners used burros to pack equipment and supplies into the Grand Canyon. Many of the burros, or *télii,* you may see on your travels along U.S. 89 north and U.S. 64 are direct descendants of burros set free by miners who gave up on their poorly producing mines in the Grand Canyon.

Burros in Cataract Canyon, ca. 1899
Cataract Canyon Collection, Cline Library, Special Collections and Archives, NAU PH 90.15.15

SERVICES IN CAMERON

Cameron Trading Post and Motel: A room with two queen beds runs around $90 per night, including taxes. Winter rates are much lower. All rooms in the summer are booked by 4 p.m. (MST). Wheelchair accessible rooms are available with access to the gardens and the Little Colorado River viewpoint. For reservations call: (800) 338-7385, (520) 679-2231

RV Park: Full hookup includes water, electricity and sewage but there are no public restrooms or showers. $14 nightly including tax.

Cameron Trading Post Dining Room: Open for breakfast, lunch and dinner from 6 a.m.-10 p.m (MST) year round.

MM 467 LITTLE COLORADO RIVER

The Little Colorado originates at Mt. Baldy in Arizona's White Mountains and travels northward to Joseph City, Winslow and Wupatki National Monument before reaching the Colorado River in the Grand Canyon.

At Cameron, the river, known by river guides alternately as the "LCR" or "Little C," can no longer meander as it has on most of its journey. It must stay confined within this solid rock canyon. Here it begins to make a very rapid 2,000-foot (610 m) descent in elevation in just 30 miles (48 km) to the Colorado River. See pages 254-255 for more information about this unusual river.

Little Colorado River Bridge at Cameron, 1912
Arizona Historical Society-Pioneer Museum

MM 467 TANNER'S CROSSING

Until 1912, the only way across the dangerous Little Colorado River in this area was Tanner's Crossing six miles (9.7 km) up river from Cameron. The name for the crossing comes from Seth Tanner, one of the original Mormon settlers of Tuba City and an incessant explorer. Used mostly by Mormon pioneers traveling from Utah to settle in Arizona, Tanner's Crossing was dangerous because of hidden pockets of quicksand and the river's seasonal flash floods. In 1911, the Bureau of Indian Affairs hired the Midland Bridge Co. to build a one-lane, iron suspension bridge over the Little Colorado's gorge.

The original bridge still stands directly west of the modern highway bridge along U.S. 89 at Cameron. Today it carries only the Four Corners Pipeline owned by the Atlantic Richfield Co. which used it in the 1960s to transport oil from the fields near Farmington, N.M., to Los Angeles. Now the direction of the oil is reversed. Since most of the oil is now brought down from Alaska, it is sent through this pipeline from Los Angeles to Farmington.

MM 468 HAMBLIN WASH GORGE (West)

This gorge enters the Little Colorado just north of the bridge.

MM 474 WARD TERRACE (East)

You have followed this ridge since Cameron. It is named for Lester Ward, a paleobotanist who found an extensive fossil field in this area in 1899. One of the skeletons he found was the water-dwelling *Phytosaur*. This reptile was about 18-feet long and closely resembled the present day crocodile but with a much longer snout filled with long, sharp teeth. The *Phytosaur* lived in or near lake beds and streams that covered this area during the Triassic era so its fossils are predominantly found in the Chinle Formation. Behind Ward Terrace are the Red Rock Cliffs that form the western edge of the Moenkopi Plateau. (Houk, 1990; Breed, 1968)

MM 474 SHADOW MOUNTAIN (West)

This dark, mysterious-looking mound is a volcanic cinder cone that was called A 1 Mountain in the 1890s. The Arizona Cattle Co. used the A 1 brand on cattle it raised in this area. (Babbitt, 1967)

MM 480.5 Junction of U.S. 89 and U.S. 160 east to Tuba City

MM 486 MOENAVE (East)

Set against the backdrop of Moenave Sandstone cliffs, this is a green oasis with springs fed from the Kaibito Plateau. These springs have supported

Havasupai and Hopi farms since before the Domínquez-Escalante Expedition passed through this area in 1776. The Navajo Tribe now owns this land. (Indermill, 1990) Mormon trail blazer Jacob Hamblin began farming here after making friends with Hopi farmer Tuuvi at Moenkopi. He sold his farm in 1874 to John D. Lee who used it as a hiding place from authorities wanting to arrest him for his part in the Mountain Meadow Massacre. Lee's stay at Moenave lasted only five months. He was found by lawmen, taken back to Panquitch, Utah, and executed standing in his own coffin. See pages 85-87 for a complete explanation of the Mountain Meadow Massacre. (Brooks, 1950)

MM 486 HAMBLIN RIDGE(East)

Composed of Moenave Sandstone, these red rocks serve as a backdrop for Moenave. Hamblin Ridge ends at The Gap where the Echo Cliffs begin.

MM 486.5 BADLANDS OF THE PAINTED DESERT (East)

The Painted Desert is a swatch of color that runs northwest all the way from the Petrified National Forest near Holbrook, passes to the north of Winslow at the Little Painted Desert County Park, skirts around the edges

of Sunset Crater and Wupatki National Monument and extends to the Echo Cliffs on U.S. 89. The same colorful Chinle Formation that makes up most of the Painted Desert, is again exposed around Ganado on State Highway 264 and on U.S. Highway 191 around Round Rock.

Badlands of the Painted Desert, ca. 1930s
Fred Harvey Collection, Museum of Northern Arizona, 301-3-145

MM 487 WILLOW SPRINGS (East)

A constant source of water from the Kaibito Plateau made this a lush farming area for the Havasupai and a popular water stop for Mormon pioneers and prospectors. One rock near the spring bears the names of many Mormon pioneers who passed through here. The first Mormon name written in 1873 was that of H.K. Perkins. He was a member of the Haight Expedition responsible for developing the Mormon wagon trail. More than 100 Mormons were "called" by Mormon Church President Brigham Young to settle along the Little Colorado River. Perkins helped build a road from Utah to Winslow, Ariz. to carry supplies and families. Another prayer Perkins inscribed on the same rock says, "Oh that men would praise the Lord for his goodness and his wonderful works." (Wicoff, 1990, Hooper, 1977)

Home at Willow Springs, ca. 1900
Warren Family Collection, Cline Library, Special Collections and Archives, NAU, PH 412.1.44

Trading Post Ruins: *A rutted road leads to the trading post and a Navajo family lives close to the ruin. The best way to see the ruins is through binoculars from Highway 89. Looking behind the silver water tank, the ruins blend in with Hamblin Ridge. Keep looking and you'll see it.*

George McAdams built this post around 1889 after he sold his Red Lake Trading Post to the unfortunate Sam Dittenhoffer. (See pages 164-165 for more on Red Lake.) McAdams was a famous gambler who believed the Willow Springs location would give him more opportunities to play poker with the constant flow of pioneers traveling the Mormon Trail. (Richardson, 1974)

Billy Williams and his brother Ben built a small post here around 1885 before McAdams . But it is really their father John who makes an interesting story. John belonged to the fraternity of desperate characters who arrived in this part of the West in the late 1800s. He spent most of his life pursuing lost gold and silver mines. The incident that really increased his addiction was when Jack Carson, a teamster for the military at Fort Defiance, noticed an unusual color in a dry wash bed. He started to dig, easily unearthing about three pounds of gold. Realizing his strike was too big to work alone, he secreted the location of his mine leaving a lone pole with a marker pointing in the direction of his claim.

At Fort Defiance, he enlisted the help of John Williams, then a clerk at the trading post, to start working the mine for a third of its profits while he went to California to get his brother. Williams was too happy to oblige. He closed the trading post and moved his family to the mining site with only a hastily drawn map to show him the location of the gold. When he arrived, the pole marker was gone. Even though Williams eventually found the fallen pole, he could not find the gold. The only person who could, Carson, died on his way to California.

Williams became obsessed with dreams of lost gold mines. After exhausting the possibility of finding the rich deposit Carson promised, Williams moved his family to Blue Canyon near Tuba City where he opened the first trading post in the canyon. His real reason for choosing this location was to be closer to the lost mines rumored to be somewhere on Navajo Mountain.

Too restless to run a trading post, Williams left Blue Canyon in 1890 to start a company to mine "flour gold" from the San Juan River. He used an ingenious method of staking cow hides to the bottom of the river to catch the gold flakes against the grain on the fur side of the hide. He did manage to collect more than a pound of gold this way but it eventually proved to be too costly and Williams gave up his hope of ever finding gold in the Southwest. (Yost, 1958)

MM 488.5 HIDDEN SPRINGS (West)

This area is the home of the 240-member San Juan Southern Paiute Tribe, which did not obtain federal recognition as a tribe until 1990, despite having occupied Hidden Springs since before Navajos arrived in this region. The Paiutes' ancestral home included southern California, southern Nevada, southern Utah and northern Arizona. Traditionally hunters and gatherers, they foraged over a wide area in groups of 10-15 people, keeping their material belongings to a minimum. They developed elaborate basketmaking skills to carry the things they needed. (Holt, 1992)

Because of the distance between bands and their relatively small numbers, the Paiutes did not get a reservation of their own. Instead, they became part of the Navajo Tribe for federal administrative purposes. The government figured they had become part of the Navajo clan system through intermarriage. However, the Paiutes held onto their own language, culture and traditions despite their small numbers. Finally, tired of being the stepchild of the larger tribe, the Paiutes launched their long quest for federal acknowledgment. Evelyn James, who led the recognition fight, is now the president of the tribe.

The making of baskets, or *yingups,* is one of the San Juan Paiutes' greatest arts. They have supplied the Navajo people with traditional wedding baskets for years.

WHAT IS A NAVAJO WEDDING BASKET?

A Navajo wedding is rich in symbolism and every action of the bride and groom is steeped in traditional meaning. The basket represents the fundamental beliefs of Navajos. The center is the point of emergence or birth, with the four sacred mountains, sky and earth all included in the design. As part of the wedding ceremony, sacred blue corn mush is eaten from each of the four directions of the basket by the bride and groom. After they have finished, family and guests share the remaining mush with the couple. When the mush is consumed, the couple is married. The basket then becomes a gift from the bride to the groom's family.

Sumac twigs are used to make Navajo wedding baskets. They are stripped, dyed and soaked so they will bend easily for weaving. A good basket can cost from $125 to $250. However, a fine used one can sometimes be found for about $60 at the Tuba City flea market held each Friday. See the map on page 104 for directions to the flea market.

Photograph by Christine Stephenson, 1994

MM 498 THE GAP TRADING POST (West)

"The Gap" refers to the huge break in the Echo Cliffs. In 1957, before completion of Highway 89 through Antelope Pass, the dirt road across from the trading post was the only route to the Glen Canyon dam site.

The road is unimproved, has no directional signs and so is not recommended. For the intrepid, it travels to the top of the Echo Cliffs onto the Kaibito Plateau and leads to Coppermine near Page. Trader Thomas Keam of Keams Canyon was also a prospector who found copper here around 1880. In 1915, the Pittsburgh Copper Co. began working the area but because of the poor quality of the copper, the mine is no longer open. (Anderson, 1958)

NATIVE ROADS

The first trading post at The Gap was housed in buildings left by copper miners who failed to find anything of value in the Echo Cliffs. From 1924 to 1943, the post along the frontage of Highway 89 was owned by Joe Lee, great-grandson of John D. Lee of Lees Ferry fame. Lee was well-known for his talent as a storyteller, horseman and friend to the Navajos whose language he spoke fluently. Film producers in Hollywood heard about his knowledge of the area and hired him to recruit 300 "warriors" for the movie *The Last Frontier*, shot on location at The Gap in 1924. (Brown, 1940) The Lansky Players, now Paramount Pictures, filmed Zane Grey's *Heritage of the Desert* at The Gap, Willow Springs and Tuba City. (Richardson, 1974)

The trading post is now owned by the Thriftway Corp. Open from 7.a.m. - 9 p.m. (DST). (520) 283-8932.

MM 502.5 MOENKOPI FORMATION(East)

The chocolate-colored mudstone seen here is a good example of one of the oldest rock layers, formed more than 230 million years ago during the Triassic Era. Iron oxide makes the rocks red and its particles have an affinity for magnetic north. They aligned facing north when the rock was formed which helped scientists determine the ancient location of the North Pole in relation to the movement of the continents. The pole of 200 million years ago was over the northern Pacific Ocean and Arizona was very close to the equator. This helps explain why northern Arizona experienced subtropical climates during the dinosaur age. (Breed, 1968)

MM 504 CEDAR RIDGE (West)

The elevated plateau here marks the beginning of Hamblin Wash cutting through the soft Chinle Formation, draining water south to the Little Colorado River. Heading north is the beginning of Tanner Wash draining water north to the Colorado River.

MM 504 ECHO CLIFFS (East)

Named for the echo created when Frederick Dellenbaugh, a member of Powell's 1871 trip down the Colorado, shot his Remington 44 from the top of the highest peak at Lees Ferry. This ancient monocline, running north-south along U.S. Highway 89, is the result of a major rock uplift rising more than 1,300 feet (396 m) through a vertical fault. The cliffs expose most of the geologic members of the Glen Canyon Group except the Wingate Sandstone. At the bottom of the cliff is the Moenave Formation, then the Kayenta Formation. At the top is Navajo Sandstone. (Nations, 1981)

The Mormons' famous **Honeymoon Trail,** also called the Mormon Trail, ran along the base of these cliffs. Pioneer settlers used this trail from 1877 through 1890 to travel to St. George, Utah, to be married in the Mormon temple. Most of the honeymooners lived in one of the many Mormon communities settled on or near the Little Colorado River.

Because of the great distances of the time, most couples were first married locally in a legal, civil ceremony. When time or business permitted, they would travel the 300 miles (483 km) to seal their vows before God. The trail actually starts at Winslow, over Tanner's Crossing in Cameron, runs through the Painted Desert, along the Echo Cliffs, below the Vermilion Cliffs by Lees Ferry, through House Rock Valley and around the Buckskin Mountains into what is now Pipe Springs National Monument, and then into St. George.

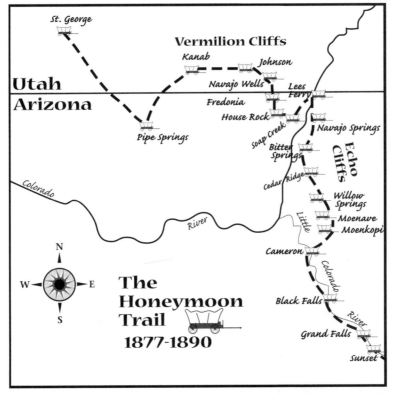

To mark the trail for others, Mormons planted tall **Lombardy Poplars,** easily seen for miles on the barren red landscape. For the hardy soul interested in knowing what it was like to have lived the pioneer life, you can take a wagon train ride from Pipe Springs National Monument to St. George, Utah. These trips are run by Mel Heaton from Moccasin, Ariz., 18 miles east of Fredonia, Ariz. (520) 643-7292 (evenings).

MM 507 NAVAJO CORN FIELDS (East)

See page 172 for an explanation of Navajo dry farming.

MM 507.5 LOMBARDY POPLARS (East)

MM 511 LIMESTONE CANYON (West)

Six miles (10 km) north of Cedar Ridge, Mormon pioneer Jacob Hamblin used this as a watering place. (Barnes, 1960)

MM 515 VERMILION CLIFFS (Straight ahead)

MM 521.5 TANNER'S WASH

Named for Seth Tanner, a Mormon explorer like Hamblin who lived in Tuba City.

MM 522 LIMESTONE RIDGE (East)

 Junction U.S. 89 with U.S. 89A: Bear to right to go to Page/Lake Powell

ANTELOPE PASS

To build Highway 89 to Page, a 300-foot (91 m) cut was made through the Echo Cliffs at an elevation of 6,533 feet (1,992 m).

MM 527 SCENIC OVERLOOK (West)

This is one of several fine panoramic vistas along this route. Looking due west, you can see the Colorado River Gorge etched into the Marble Plateau of House Rock Valley. The cliffs to the north, are the Vermilion Cliffs named by John Wesley Powell for their bright red color. For more than a century, ranchers have struggled to raise their stock on the flat table land of the Paria Plateau. Lack of water has always been their nemesis until the advent of trucks, which now haul water to the stock.

Just 15 miles (24 km) north where the valley narrows is historic **Lees Ferry**, once the only crossing of the Colorado River for hundreds of miles. On the horizon 10 miles (16 km) across to the west is the Kaibab Plateau, the land mass that forms the North Rim of the Grand Canyon. While part of Arizona, this huge stretch of territory — known as the **Arizona Strip** — has all but been cut off from the social and political life of the state because of the Grand Canyon. For the past century, Arizona residents have identified culturally with Utah more than Arizona for all but elections and taxes. Even today, only Utah newspapers and television reach into this isolated area.

The Kaibab Plateau has always been rich in timber and wildlife, making it a popular hunting region in the state.

MM 531 NAVAJO MOUNTAIN (East)

Navajo Mountain, South Side, 1937
Aerial photograph by E. Beckwith,
Museum of Northern Arizona Photo Archives, MV 2238

This mountain, just north of the Arizona-Utah border, has strong spiritual significance to all Indian tribes living on the Colorado Plateau. The Hopi migration stories tell of their travels to Navajo Mountain and the Hopi Snake Clan has shrines here. Navajo Mountain also plays an important part in the Navajo creation story.

Rising to an elevation of 10,416 feet (3,177 m), you can see Navajo Mountain throughout the Four Corners area. The Navajo call it *Naatsis'áán* or "enemy mountain cave." To them it was the place to hide from their enemies, the refuge for Hoskinnini's band of Navajos who were able to escape Kit Carson's soldiers. (See pages 180-181 for more on Hoskinnini.) To help Carson in his effort to find and subjugate the Navajo people, the soldiers built a heliograph station on top of Navajo Mountain. Directions were flashed using mirrors to troops looking for Navajos in other parts of the reservation.

On his second trip down the Colorado River in 1872, John Wesley Powell climbed out of Glen Canyon, and seeing Navajo Mountain for the first time, named it Mount Seneca Howland. Most people in the area already knew it as Navajo Mountain so his name did not stick like so many of his other descriptive names. (Barnes, 1960) Seneca Howland, his brother O.G. and William Dunn abandoned Powell's company on the first exploration of the river three years earlier. The three hiked out of the Grand Canyon fearing they would die of starvation, only to be killed by Shivwits Indians.

Rainbow Bridge: One of the Colorado Plateau's more famous natural Navajo sandstone bridges is found at the northern base of Navajo Mountain. Rainbow Bridge is the largest natural bridge in the world, with a 278-foot (85 m) span and rising 309 feet (94 m) above the canyon floor. The bridge is 33 feet (10 m) wide at the top and 42 feet (13 m) thick. See page 80 for information on boat tours to Rainbow Bridge.

The Paiutes call Rainbow Bridge *Barohoini*, meaning "the rainbow upon which one could travel to the sun." The Navajos know it as *Tsé'naanání'áhí* and have a similar story about the bridge.

The most common modern story about the race to officially discover Rainbow Bridge tells of Wetherill's expedition with Dr. Byron Cummings, dean of arts and sciences at the University of Utah, meeting W.B. Douglass, a federal surveyor who was in the region on a competing expedition looking for rumored natural bridges.

Rainbow Bridge, not dated.
Warren Family Collection, Cline Library, Special Collections and Archives, NAU P.H. 412.2.18
Keith Warren and his wife operated the Cedar Ridge trading post in 1900. This photograph was taken sometime between 1910 and 1945.

Rivals, but being good sports about their race, the two groups teamed up. On Aug. 14, 1909, Dr. Cummings rounded the bend to become the first non-native to spot their goal. One year later, President Taft signed a proclamation to make Rainbow Bridge a national monument.

After many protests, the family of the Paiute guide "Mike's Boy," who led the Douglass group, succeeded in having the National Park Service recognize Mike, at the age of 102, as the rightful discoverer of this natural wonder. But according to testimony in a 1972 federal lawsuit brought by the Shonto Chapter of the Navajo Tribe, it is clear that he was not the first man to see the bridge. The Chapter brought the lawsuit to oppose the flooding of Forbidding Canyon by the rising water of Lake Powell, fearing it would inundate this sacred site.

Testimony in the suit showed that in 1909, John Wetherill and Paiute guide Na'ashja' Beghay reported finding a Pueblo shrine dating to 1270 A.D. near the northeastern corner of the bridge. Wetherill also reported that the informant who first told him about the bridge, "Salt People His Eye Alone Man," told him a Navajo altar below the bridge was frequently visited by Navajo medicine men.

1909 Wetherill Expedition to Rainbow Bridge

Stuart Malcolm Young Collection, Cline Library, Special Collections and Archives, NAU PH 643.1.130. *Stuart Malcolm Young was the grandson of Brigham Young and photographed the 1909 expedition to Rainbow Bridge with Wetherill and Cummings. From left to right, back row: Ned English, Dan Perkins, Jack Kienan, Vern Rogerson, Neil Judd, Dan Beauregard. From left to right, front row: Jim Mike-San Juan Pauite guide, John Wetherill, Professor Cummings, W.B. Douglass and Malcolm Cummings.*

WHAT MAKES A NATURAL BRIDGE?

Natural bridges appear when an ancient river cuts its way through sandstone. In some places, like the Goosenecks of the San Juan River (just north of Mexican Hat, Utah), the river rolls in a U-shape. Over thousands of years, as the gorge deepens and the water meets softer sandstone the river carves a tunnel straight through the side of the U. Water cuts the tunnel deeper and deeper until the overlying rock layer appears to be a bridge standing high above the current level of the water. (Vokes, 1942)

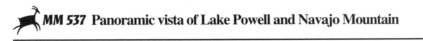

MM 537 Panoramic vista of Lake Powell and Navajo Mountain

Leaving the Navajo Nation, change to Mountain Standard Time.

MM 546 NAVAJO GENERATING STATION (East)

Sulfur dioxide emissions from this generating station have long been suspected of causing haze over the Grand Canyon. Environmental groups, led by the Grand Canyon Trust, initiated a lawsuit against the power plant to improve the visibility in the canyon. An agreement reached in 1991 requires the Navajo Generating Station to install $430 million of scrubbing devices on all three smokestacks and to reduce the sulfur dioxide emissions by 90 percent by the year 1999.

The power plant is owned jointly by the U.S. Bureau of Reclamation, the Salt River Project, the Los Angeles Department of Water and Power the Arizona Public Service Co, Nevada Power and Tucson Electric Power.

U.S. 89 Loop through Page

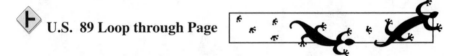

Town of Page: Situated atop Manson Mesa at 4,300 feet, this was the staging site for the construction of the Glen Canyon Dam in 1957. The land was part of the Navajo Reservation but the Navajos traded the Page site for oil-rich land in Utah. The first homes built in Page were for Bureau of Reclamation employees. It wasn't until 1975 that Page incorporated as a city on 16.7 acres (0.7 sq km) donated by the Bureau of Reclamation. The town is named for John Page, commissioner of the bureau under the Franklin Roosevelt administration from 1937 to 1943.

JOHN WESLEY POWELL MEMORIAL MUSEUM: Located at the corner of Lake Powell Blvd. and N. Navajo Drive, open from 10 a.m.- 6 p.m. (MST) on Sunday and 8 a.m.-6 p.m. (MST) Monday through Saturday from June to September. The museum offers educational displays about Powell's two trips down the uncharted Colorado River. Memorabilia about the founding of Page and the ethnohistory of native cultures are on display. River trips, jeep tours and boat tours can be arranged here. (520) 645-9496.

INTERESTING SIDE TOUR

One of the rare geologic features of this region is the **Slot Canyon**. Sculptured salmon-colored canyons the width of a hallway are the result of a crack in the sandstone that allowed water to flow into and enlarge the crack

Photograph by Christine Stephenson

over thousands of years. As water passed through the irregular crack, racing water placed force unevenly, leading to a hollowing effect. This is a wonderful challenge with great rewards for photographers. The slot allows diffuse sunlight to filter throughout the canyon, filling it with pastel hues of incredible beauty. To tour slot canyons on the Navajo Nation, contact the LeChee Chapter House, P.O. Box 1257, Page, AZ 86040, (520) 698-3272. Commercial tours are also available of **Antelope-Corkscrew Canyon** by Overland Adventures, P.O. Box 1144, Page, AZ 86040, (520) 645-5501 or Duck Tours, P.O. Box 2253, Page, AZ 86040, (520) 645-2955.

SERVICES IN PAGE

LODGING

Best Western at Lake Powell	208 N. Lake Powell Blvd.	(800) 528-1234
		(520) 645-5988
Best Western Weston Inn	207 N. Lake Powell Blvd.	(800) 637-9183
		(520) 645-2451
Courtyard by Marriott	600 Country Club Dr.	(520) 645 -5000
Empire House	100 S. Lake Powell Blvd.	(520) 645-2406
Holiday Inn Page	287 N. Lake Powell Blvd.	(520) 645-8851
Inn at Lake Powell	716 Rim View Dr.	(800) 826-2718
		(520) 645-2466
Navajo Trail Motel	800 Hemlock St.	(520) 645-9509
Page Boy Motel	150 N. Lake Powell Blvd.	(520) 645-2416
Page Super 8 Motel	75 S. 7 Ave.	(520) 645-2858
Amie Ann's Bed & Breakfast	349 S. Navajo Blvd.	(520) 645-2323
Lake Powell Int'l. Hostel	141 8th Avenue	(520) 645-3898

 *CAMPING*

Page-Lake Powell Campground: Located on Arizona Highway 98, less than one mile (1.6 km) south of town. Tents and RVs. Showers available. With hook-ups, about $20; no hook-ups, about $17.

RESTAURANTS

Beans Gourmet Coffee House	644 N. Navajo	(520) 645-6858
Bella Napoli	810 N. Navajo	(520) 645-2706
Burger King	807 N. Hwy. 89A	(520) 645-3365
Butterfield Stage Co. Steak House	704 Rim View Dr.	(520) 645-2467
Canyon Bowl and Bistro	24 Lake Powell Blvd.	(520) 645-2682
Dos Amigos	608 D. Elm St.	(520) 645-3036
Glen Canyon Steak House	201 N. Lake Powell Blvd	(520) 645-3363
Kentucky Fried Chicken of Page	25 Lake Powell Blvd.	(520) 645-2172
M Bar H Cafe	819 N. Navajo	(520) 645-1420
McDonald's of Page	300 Lake Powell Blvd.	(520) 645-2271
Pizza Hut	6 S. Lake Powell Blvd.	(520) 645-2455
	for delivery	(520) 645-9707
Porters Sunset Grille	125 S. Lake Powell Blvd.	(520) 645-3039
RD's Drive-In	146 Lake Powell Blvd.	(520) 645-2791
The Sandwich Place	662 Elm St.	(520) 645-5267
Sonic Drive In	707 N. Navajo Dr.	(520) 645-9636
Strombolli's Restaurant and Pizza	711 N. Navajo	(520) 645-2605
Subway Sandwiches	813 N Hwy. 89	(520) 645-3301
Taco Bell	33 N. Lake Powell Blvd.	(520) 645-5352
Zapata's Mexican Restaurant	614 N. Navajo Dr.	(520) 645-9006

HEALTH SERVICES

✚ Page Hospital and Samaritan Health Services

24 hour emergency care, north Navajo and Vista Avenue (520) 645-2424

AUTOMOBILE SERVICE

AAA Authorized Road Service	(520) 645-8117
B & L Automotive & Tire	(520) 645-3276
R & S Towing	(520) 645- 9416
Sand Land Auto Wreckers	(520) 645-5465

 **Resume U.S. Highway 89 north, turn right.**

🦌 GLEN CANYON BRIDGE

This dramatic bridge stands 700 feet (213 m) above the Colorado River, making it one of the highest steel arch bridges in the world. Completed in 1959, it was an engineering marvel because of the complexities of building in such a remote and dangerous site. The bridge has a span of 1200 feet (366 m) across the majestic Glen Canyon, named by John Wesley Powell, and links U.S. Highway 89 in Arizona with the Utah.

The Navajos refer to the Colorado River as "life without end." It's a female being who marries the male waters of the Little Colorado and the San Juan River.

GLEN CANYON DAM

This is the last dam built on the Colorado River and is considered a major engineering triumph. Started in 1956, the dam rises 710 feet (216 m) above the Colorado River and produces more than 1,288,000 kilowatts of hydro-electric power per day.

Norman Rockwell overlooking Glen Canyon Dam, 1969
U.S. Bureau of Reclamation, Upper Colorado Region Collection,
Cline Library, Special Collections and Archives, NAU PH 90.13.20
Norman Rockwell was a participant in the Bureau of Reclamation Art Program in 1969.

For decades, the dam has been the center of controversy between environmentalists and energy interests. At issue has been the rising and falling water fluctuations of the river resulting from the release of water from the dam to produce electricity. Those fluctuations have washed away sandy beaches and interfered with aquatic and plant life along the Colorado River. At its peak during summer months, the river would rise and fall 13 vertical feet (4 m) in a day, often stranding the huge rafts of river runners on beaches until water levels rose again. But those fluctuations were eliminated by the Grand Canyon Protection Act of 1993. *Self-guided tours of the dam are available from 8 a.m. to 4 p.m. (MST) every day.*

CARL HAYDEN VISITOR CENTER

Just over the Glen Canyon Bridge is the visitor center for the Glen Canyon Recreation Area. Perched on the very edge of the cliff, the center's massive windows let you peer down into the canyon for a good view of the lake, Glen Canyon Dam and the chasm of Glen Canyon. The National Park Service operates the information desk and will answer your questions about boating, camping, hiking and fishing in the Glen Canyon Recreation Area. Open 7 a.m.-7 p.m. (MST) in the summer and 8 a.m.- 5 p.m. (MST) during the rest of the year.

SCENIC DETOUR

Lake Shore Drive

Take a right out of the visitor center onto Hwy. 89. Follow the signs to Wahweap Marina. No mile markers; set your odometer to zero. You will be required to pay an entrance fee. The National Park Service has initiated a "fee demonstration program" to provide additional funds for use in the park. Vehicle entrance fee: 1-7 days $5; annual $15; individual entrance $3; annual $15; boating $10; annual $20.

.3 MILES (.48 km) CASTLE ROCK VIEWPOINT

Before the Glen Canyon Dam flooded the land, Cecil B. DeMille filmed the 1923 silent version of the epic drama *The Ten Commandments* below Castle Rock. This famous landmark consists of sandstone, limestone and mudstone from the Morrison Formation. Ancient rivers deposited the building materials for this formation during the Jurassic era over 180 million years ago.

2 MILES (3 km) NAVAJO MOUNTAIN VIEWPOINT

There is an interesting plaque explaining the significance of this mountain to the Navajo people and the topography of the area.

3 MILES (5 km) EL VADO DE LOS PADRES (Crossing of the Fathers)

The Dominguez and Escalante Expedition of 1776

At six places on your tour around northern Arizona, you will find markers commemorating the Domínguez-Escalante Expedition of 1776. This groundbreaking mission provided the first maps of the topography west of Santa Fe, New Mexico. Based on this information, fortune seekers in 1816 opened the Spanish Trail to the gold mines in California.

Father Atanasio Domínguez was in charge of the Spanish missions in New Mexico in 1775. He was sent here from Spain by his superiors to do three things. First, he was to assess the spiritual and economic conditions of all of the missions in New Mexico and make a detailed report. Second, he was to determine the damage to the historic archives in Santa Fe caused by the Pueblo Revolt of 1680. (See page 123 for more on this revolt.) Third, he was to develop a land route from Santa Fe to the Spanish capital at Monterey, Calif.

Assisting him in his third task was Father Silvestre Vélez de Escalante, the priest for the Spanish mission in Zuni. Domínquez needed his knowledge about the Hopis and what might lay beyond their villages. Escalante spent a week with the Hopis in 1775 and had learned that there was a gorge to the west so deep and long that it was impassable. Based on this information, Escalante decided that the best route to Monterey would be north over an already well-known Spanish route past Mesa Verde in Colorado. Their plans were to cross the Dolores and Colorado Rivers and then to turn west to cross the Sierra Mountains at a pass used by earlier expeditions.

Dominguez-Escalante Trail
of 1776-1777 ·····················

Ten men accompanied the two priests on their exploration but none more important than Captain Don Bernardo Miera Y Pacheco, a cartographer. Using an astrolabe, an ancient instrument to determine the position of the sun, moon and stars, he made detailed maps of their journey. Leaving Santa Fe on July 29, 1776, which was actually very late in the season for crossing the Sierras, they encountered many problems. Thirst, dehydration and illness plagued the group until finally, on Oct. 11, 1776, just north of present-day Cedar City, Utah, lots were cast to decide if they should continue on to Monterey, and face the possibility of being snowbound in the Sierras, or return home. A return to Santa Fe was chosen but the route was to be over territory never before charted and without a local guide to help them. One attempt to cross the Colorado River was made at the mouth of the Paria River, close to where Lees Ferry is today, but it was found to be too difficult and dangerous. Trapped, the padres' only hope was to climb out of

Native Roads

Glen Canyon and find another crossing. On Nov. 6, 1776, after many failed attempts and nearly starving, they crossed the Colorado River at this site. They continued on through the Hopi villages to Zuni and arrived in Santa Fe on Jan. 2, 1777. They had covered more than 2,000 unknown miles (3,226 km) over America's most difficult terrain.

In 1976, the Domínquez-Escalante Bicentennial Expedition retraced the fathers' route by horseback to commemorate the spirit of the 1776 expedition. (Cerqone, 1976)

The Crossing of the Fathers was well-known by Navajo and Paiute traders. Called Ute Ford, Jacob Hamblin crossed here on his first journey to the Hopi villages in 1858. It is believed that sometime between 1870 and 1880, the Mormons dynamited this ford to keep the Paiutes and Navajo from raiding Mormon communities in Utah. (Van Valkenburgh, 1941)

LAKE POWELL

The result of building the dam was, of course, the birth of the lake, named after John Wesley Powell. He was a one-armed Civil War hero who, in 1869, became the first to navigate the entire length of the uncharted Colorado River. He repeated the feat again in 1871. Ten years later he became the simultaneous director of the U.S. Geological Survey and the Bureau of Ethnology. Even though Powell was responsible for naming the Grand Canyon (almost named "Big Canyon" by another surveyor) and other landmarks on the Colorado Plateau, he did not place his own name on anything.

It is with irony that the Bureau of Reclamation gave Lake Powell his name. Powell did not agree with the proposed remaking of the West into a mirror image of the green farming communities of the East. But the popular notion in the late 1800s was that water follows human settlements. Knowing this faulty thinking was not going to work in the arid West, Powell fought expansionist politicians who were hell-bent to open this land to farmers. He was only one voice against many and today the huge cities of Phoenix and Los Angeles testify to his failure to convince policy makers to take a slow cautious approach to settling the West.

Lake Powell is more than 180 miles (290 km) long and has more miles of coastline than California. The flooding of Glen Canyon led to the inundation of many ruins, natural coves, bridges, caves, petroglyphs and historic sites, as well as the natural beauty of a magnificent canyon. Archeological projects completed between 1950 to 1970 saved many of the known historic artifacts.

An interesting story about a rare petroglyph found in Navajo Canyon involves the super nova of July 4, 1054, A.D. According to Mt. Palomar Observatory researcher William Miller, a petroglyph of a crescent moon with a round circle below it is one of only four recordings of the supernova found in the world. Other recordings were found in the archives of Japanese and Chinese astronomers.

Super Nova Petroglyph, not dated.
Photograph by Robert Euler
Museum of Northern Arizona Photo Archives, NA 5653.9a

The super nova was so bright in the eastern sky, lying just below the crescent moon, that the rising sun did not block its light. For ancient people known for their understanding and reverence of the night sky, it is surprising that there are not more recordings of this major astronomical event. Miller describes the exploding star of 1054 as the "brightest object, other than the sun and moon, ever to appear in the sky during the recorded history of man." (Miller, 1963)

Today the lake dazzles the eye with its combination of blue water, white clouds and red rocks. Fishing for striped bass is popular. Rainbow trout do not survive in the warm lake water. They live below the dam in the Colorado River. It is still possible to enjoy many of the back canyons of Glen Canyon via the lake. Some ruins and petroglyphs can be seen if you rent a boat or take the Wahweap tour boat.

Hole-In-The-Rock: *The fastest and safest way to see this historic site, located 65 miles (104 km) up lake, is by boat. Alternatively, you can drive to Escalante, Utah, and take the unpaved Hole-In-The-Rock road to the edge of the Kaiparowits Plateau, but it is a very long trip.* Just below the junction of the Colorado and the Escalante rivers is testament in the rock of the industrious and tenacious nature of the early Mormon pioneers. Sent by Brigham Young to settle the San Juan Valley, a group of Mormon settlers thought they could take a more direct route from Cedar City, Utah, to their destination than the crossing at Lees Ferry. Once they arrived at the edge of the Kaiparowits Plateau, they could find no descent to the river suitable for wagons. Instead of turning back, the pioneers blasted a road three quarters of a mile long with a vertical descent of 1,000 feet (305 meters). Even more amazing, they hitched up their teams and drove their wagons down the incline without any loss of human or animal life.

Charles Hall drove the first wagon down the precarious route. He later found a better crossing about 20 miles (32 km) upriver where Halls Crossing Marina is located today. See page 197 for a map of the Hole-In-The-Rock route.

Hole-In-The-Rock, 1969
U.S. Department of the Interior,
Bureau of Reclamation, Upper Colorado Region
Cline Library, Special Collections and Archives, NAU PH 90.13.18

At the intersection of Shoreline Drive turn right to Wahweap Marina, Lodge and Restaurant

BOAT TOURS *Make arrangements at Wahweap Lodge*

For reservations contact: Lake Powell Resorts and Marinas, 2916 N. 35 Avenue, Suite 8, Phoenix, AZ 85017-5261, (800) 528-6154.

Paddle Wheel Cruise around Wahweap Bay: $9 adult, $6.45 child plus tax at 11 a.m., 12:30 p.m. and 2 p.m. during the summer.

Dinner Cruise on Canyon King Paddle Wheel: $41.20 plus tax per person

All day tour to Rainbow Bridge and two canyons: $64.65 adult, children under 11 $34.50 plus tax, includes box lunch.

Half-day trip to Rainbow Bridge and back: $51.30 adult, children $27.30 plus tax

Navajo Tapestry Tour of Navajo and Antelope Canyons: 9:30 a.m. and 1:30 p.m., $19.65 adult, $13.10 child plus tax

LODGING

Wahweap Lodge: Luxurious accommodations with views of Wahweap Bay and Castle Rock from your room. Room rates range from $90-$100 in summer and $60-$70 in winter. Reservations: Lake Powell Resorts and Marinas, 2916 N. 35th Ave., Suite 8, Phoenix, AZ 85017-526, (800) 528-6154 or in Page, (520) 645-2433.

The Lodge has an excellent restaurant called **The Rainbow Room** that overlooks the lake. Open from 6 a.m. to 11 a.m. for breakfast, 11 a.m. to 3 p.m. for lunch and 5 p.m. to 10 p.m. for dinner. Reservations are not accepted. (520) 645-2433.

Lake Powell Motel: *Past the Glen Canyon Dam on U.S. 89 north, four miles (6.5 km).* Moderately priced, $60-$70 in summer and $30-$40 during low season. Reservations: (520) 645-2477 or Lake Powell Resorts and Marinas in Phoenix.

BOAT RENTALS AT STATELINE MARINA

5 miles (8 km) heading north on Stateline Drive. Ski boats 16-to-20 feet (5-6 m) long and wave runners can be rented at Stateline. It is a good idea to make reservations at least one or two days before you arrive at Lake Powell during the high season from May 15 through Oct. 14. Houseboats 36 and 44 feet (11-14 m) long are available to rent for two, three or five days. Prices vary depending on size and time of year. Reservations for houseboats are recommended at least six months in advance. Call Lake Powell Resorts and Marinas, 2916 N. 35 Ave., Suite 8, Phoenix, AZ 85017-5261, (800) 528-6154.

FISHING: The best fishing is for large mouth, small mouth and striped bass but you can also find northern and walleye pike, catfish, crappie and carp. Depending on where you want to fish, you may need a license for both Arizona and Utah. The southern-most part of the lake is in Arizona and the rest is in Utah. If you rent a boat at Stateline Marina, you are in Utah. Fishing licenses are sold at Wahweap or Stateline Marina or any sporting goods store in Page.

CAMPING

WAHWEAP CAMPGROUND AND RV PARK

Campground: First-come, first-served, drinking water, no showers or hook-ups. $7.

RV Park: Coin showers and laundry with hook-ups, $20.69; $13.46 in winter. Reservations: (800) 528-6154.

Lone Rock: *(Located on U.S. Hwy 89 N at MM 556.5)* Considered a party area by most locals, this primitive camping area is loud and crowded on weekends during the summer. No running water, out–houses only. Near-by hills make this an attractive place for all-terrain vehicles, which sometimes run all night.

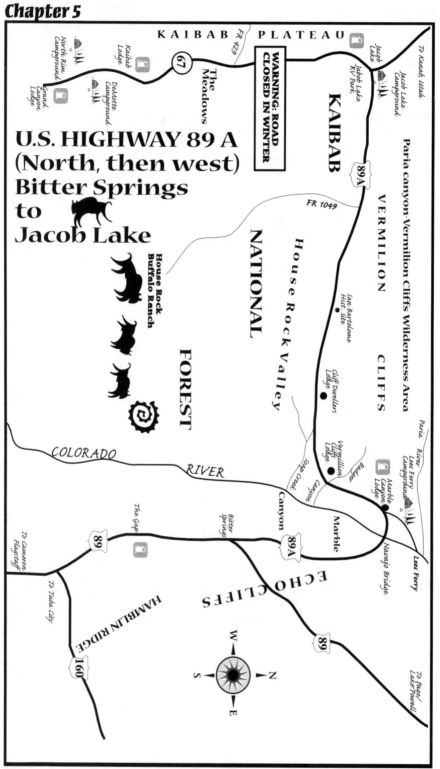

Chapter 5

U.S. HIGHWAY 89 A (North, then west) Bitter Springs to Jacob Lake

WARNING: ROAD CLOSED IN WINTER

KAIBAB PLATEAU

The Meadows

67

FR 429

North Rim Campground

Kaibab Lodge

DeMotte Campground

Grand Canyon Lodge

Jacob Lake

Jacob Lake Campground

Jacob Lake RV Park

To Kanab Utah

KAIBAB

89A

VERMILION CLIFFS

Paria canyon-Vermilion Cliffs Wilderness Area

FR 1049

NATIONAL

House Rock Valley

House Rock Buffalo Ranch

FOREST

San Bartolome Hist. Site

Cliff Dwellers Lodge

Vermilion Cliffs Lodge

Soap Creek Canyon

Badger Canyon

COLORADO RIVER

Paria River

Lees Ferry Campground

Marble Canyon Lodge

Marble Canyon

Lees Ferry

Navajo Bridge

89A

The Gap

89

Bitter Springs

To Cameron Flagstaff

To Tuba City

ECHO CLIFFS

HAMBLIN RIDGE

160

89

To Page/Lake Powell

N
W   E
S

56 miles (90 km) from Bitter Springs to Jacob Lake

MM 525 BITTER SPRINGS (West)

A Navajo tribal housing project whose water, despite its name, really does not taste that bad.

MM 525 ANTELOPE PASS (East) From here you can see where High-

way 89 cuts through a pass blasted out of the Echo Cliffs.

MM 527 VERMILION CLIFFS (West)

Capped by Navajo Sandstone, these sheer and imposing cliffs were named by John Wesley Powell because they appear vermilion, or bright reddish orange, particularly at sunrise and sunset.

MM 539 NAVAJO BRIDGE AND THE COLORADO RIVER

The older of these two bridges was the first bridge to span the Colorado River. It was constructed in 1929 by the Kansas City Structural Steel Corp. financed by a cooperative effort between Arizona and Utah. All of the steel was made in Kansas City and shipped to Flagstaff by rail then carried by truck, over 145 miles of primitive roads, to the bridge site. Steel was driven down Lees Dugway and carried across the Colorado River on the ferry to build the

Navajo Bridge with the Vermilion Cliffs in the background, 1929
Cline Library, Special Collections and Archives, NAU PH 114.2

western side of the bridge. When it was completed it was the highest bridge of its type in the world standing 467 feet (142 m) above the Colorado River with a span across of 834 feet (254 m). The historic bridge is now a pedestrian walk-way with a view of the imposing canyon and river below.

NAVAJO BRIDGE INTERPRETATIVE CENTER

On the west side of the new bridge is a native stone visitor center that provides information about the area. The gift shop sells books and maps specific to the area. The building is open from 9 a.m. to 5p.m. daily (DST) from mid-May to mid-October. The restrooms are open year round. On the east side of the bridge are Navajo arts and craft vendors.

Leaving the Navajo Nation, change to Mountain Standard Time.

The Colorado River, not dated.
Philip Johnston Collection, Cline Library, Special Collections and Archives, NAU PH 413-605

LEES FERRY

(You may wonder why Lees Ferry is without an apostrophe. According to the <u>*Sixth Report of the United States Geographic Board: 1890 to 1932*</u> *the name was officially changed from Lee's Ferry to Lees Ferry.)*

Turn north, past the bridge just before Marble Canyon Lodge. Along the 5-mile (8 km) winding road to the Colorado River are interpretive sites where you can read about the geology of the area. One of the interesting features are the "balancing rocks," – examples of the forces of erosion wearing away the soft underlying sandstone faster than the harder rock on top.

At the bottom of the hill just before you cross the Paria River, turn west onto a dirt road to the **Lonely Dell Ranch Historic District.** You can purchase a walking tour guide for 25 cents at the ranch. To the east is a **river drive**; or you can continue straight down the entrance road to the launch ramp, or "Mile Zero" of the Colorado, where commercial river rafting trips begin. Just past the launch ramp is the **Lees Ferry Historic District** where a primitive Mormon fort still stands.

The most important point for colonization of the Southwest was this very remote section of the Colorado River. Because of the near impossibility of crossing the river for 300 miles (480 km), the ferry allowed for the rapid Mormon settlement in Arizona.

In 1860, Jacob Hamblin was the first Mormon to see the possibilities for a ferry site at this location. Turned back by failed attempts to cross the fast-moving Colorado, he was finally able to cross in a raft in 1864. As more and more settlers needed to use the ferry, the Mormons built a fort to protect them from attacks by Navajos living in the area. It wasn't used very much for fighting and eventually turned into a trading post.

John D. Lee and his wife Emma came here in 1872 as punishment by Mormon leaders for Lee's involvement in the Mountain Meadows Massacre. Mountain Meadows, located in Utah on the pioneer trail to California, is the site where approximately 23 men, 10 women and 34 children of the Fancher wagon train were slain by Paiutes and Mormons.

The Mormon involvement in something so out of character with their religious convictions is a complex topic to discuss. In a nutshell, the massacre stemmed from a background of persecution that forced the Mormons to leave Missouri in 1838. When hostilities between townspeople and the Mormons turned violent, the governor forced them to leave saying, "The

Mormons must be treated as enemies and must be exterminated or driven from the state if necessary for the public peace." (Brooks, 1950)

From there they moved to Nauvoo, Ill., where they prospered. Their leader, Joseph Smith, managed to secure a charter for the town, making it almost independent from the state with its own army for protection. At the same time, Smith was running for president of the United States. This led to dissension among members of his own faith, and Smith excommunicated many of his critics. To voice their opposition to their former leader, the banished group started a newspaper called the *Nauvoo Expositor*. An enraged Joseph Smith ordered the paper's headquarters destroyed. This violence, and growing anti-Mormon sentiment in the area, led to the arrest of Smith and his brother in 1844. Gov. Thomas Ford was called to mediate between the "Gentiles" and Mormons but he arrived too late. An angry mob had pulled Joseph and Hyrum from their jail cells and murdered them.

This was the final straw for Brigham Young, Joseph Smith's successor. Knowing that the Mormon people needed a place where they could worship in their own way, he sent a Mormon scouting party west. In 1847, Brigham Young declared the Great Salt Lake Valley to be their new home.

Non-Mormon settlers, on their way to the gold fields in California, were soon on the heels of the Mormons, some hurling taunts and insults as they passed through Mormon communities. One group named their team of oxen "Joseph Smith" and "Brigham Young" and shouted that they hoped someone would kill Brigham Young as they had Smith. The Mormons began to resent outsiders. With each passing day there were fresh rumors of 2,500 federal troops traveling west to destroy the Mormon people.

A kind of frenzy began to possess the Mormon communities. Often fueled by inaccurate reports and rumors, this resentment and fear finally surfaced in the attack on the Fancher wagon train in 1857. Why the Mormons picked this particular train to attack is not clear. One explanation was that it was an attempt to maintain good relations with the Paiutes who outnumbered the Mormons four-to-one. By cooperating in an attack on the wagon train, it would show solidarity with the Indians trying to rid themselves of the unending flow of white settlers through their traditional hunting area. The supplies and alleged gold carried by the Fancher party were also speculated by some as being an attractive incentive for attacking the train.

The Fancher party was able to hold off the first wave of Indian attackers for about a week. Then John D. Lee got the job of persuading the besieged survivors into laying down their weapons and coming out from the protection of their wagon train. Not realizing it was the Mormons who were their enemy, the company did as requested. The men led the way and the women and older children followed behind. When Lee gave the command to halt, the Mormons began shooting and killed anyone old enough to talk.

Because of his insidious role in tricking the settlers out of their relatively secure place, Lee became the scapegoat for the entire affair. To hide from federal authorities, and as punishment from the church for his involvement in this crime, he fled to this Colorado River crossing with his wife Emma in 1872. (Brooks, 1950)

One of the colorful stories about Lee while he was living at the ferry was that he had many opportunities to explore the canyon for gold. Around 1885, a prospector found a large deposit of gold in the canyon near "Vulcan's Throne" (a volcanic cinder cone located in the western section of the Grand Canyon). Lee prospected in this area many times and locals think he had his own mine or gold dust buried somewhere in the Grand Canyon. If he did, he never told anyone, not even his wife Emma.

After Lee's execution for his part in the massacre in 1877, Emma married miner Franklin French, known for his building of the Tanner-French Trail in the Grand Canyon. Emma believed Lee had found gold and told French all that she knew about where Lee might have hidden it. French searched for the gold many times but without success. (Kelly, 1946)

Lees Ferry, ca. 1900
Warren Family Collection, Cline Library, Special Collections and Archives, NAU PH 412.1.2

Warren Johnson and his two wives, Permelia Jane Smith and Samantha Nelson, ran the ferry after Lee's death from 1875 to 1895. Three of Johnson's children died of diphtheria within three months of each other. They are buried in the cemetery located in the Lonely Dell Ranch up the Paria River very close to the ferry. (Barnes, 1960) *(Across the street from Marble Canyon Lodge is a memorial to the efforts of the Johnson family.)*

To many Mormon settlers, the thought of crossing the Colorado River caused more fear than the thought of all of the other dangers that lie ahead as they traveled through Navajo territory. Mormon President Daniel Wells and Bishop Lorenzo Roundy fell off the ferry when the bow dipped under high waves in 1879. The bishop's body was never recovered. Once across the river it was then necessary to climb "Lee's backbone," a two-mile (3 km) ascent out of the canyon followed by a sharp descent once on top.

Lees Ferry Dugway, not dated.
Emery Kolb Collection Special Collections and Archives, NAU #568-6473

The dugway was built in 1898 so travelers wouldn't have to climb the arduous Lee's Backbone. (Rusho, 1992) The Grand Canyon Cattle Company bought Lees Ferry in 1909 and in 1916 Coconino County purchased the ferry and ran it until 1929 when the Navajo Bridge opened. (Rusho, 1992, Barnes, 1960)

Lees Ferry Campground

A U.S. Fee Area operated on a first-come, first-served basis. $10/night; Golden Age/Access $5 night. Camp sites have shade provided by a metal awning. No trees. Community bathrooms, running water. Public showers and laundry are located at Marble Canyon Lodge on U.S. 89A by the post *office. Telephone, RV dump site. Information: Glen Canyon National Recreation Area's Lees Ferry Ranger Station (520) 355-2234.*

Fishing at Lees Ferry: Lees Ferry is well–known for excellent fishing for rainbow trout year-round. Artificial flies and lures only. No live bait of any kind is allowed and no trout between 16 and 22 inches (40-56 cm) may be kept. The limit is two fish in your possession. You may take a boat 16-feet (5 m) or larger with at least a 25 h.p. engine on the river upstream 14.5 miles (23 km) to the Glen Canyon Dam. No boating is allowed down river from Lees Ferry without a permit.

RIVER TRIPS ON THE COLORADO RIVER

Please contact each company for complete details on the type of trip offered. Some companies offer motorized or oar-powered trips. Others offer dory or paddle trips. Each company will also have different schedules and prices.

Arizona Raft Adventures, Inc. 4050-X E. Huntington Drive, Flagstaff, AZ 86004
 (800) 786-RAFT, (520) 526-8200

Arizona River Runners, Inc. P.O. Box 47788, Phoenix, AZ 85068-7788,
(520) 867-4866

Canyon Explorations, Inc. P.O. Box 310, Flagstaff, AZ 86002
(800) 654-0723, (520) 774-4559

Canyoneers, Inc. P.O. Box 2997, Flagstaff, AZ 86003
(800) 525-0924 outside Arizona, (520) 526-0924 in Arizona

Colorado River & Trail Expeditions, Inc. P.O. Box 57575, Salt Lake City, UT 84157
(800) 253-7328, (801) 261-1789

Diamond River Adventures, Inc. P.O. Box 1316, Page, AZ 86040
(800) 343-3121 (520) 645-8866

Expeditions, Inc. Route 4, Box 755, Flagstaff, AZ 86001
(520) 774-8176, (520) 779-3769

Grand Canyon Dories P.O. Box 216, Altaville, CA 95221
(209) 736-0805

Grand Canyon Expeditions Company P.O. Box O, Kanab, UT 84741
(800) 544-2691, (801) 644-2691

Hatch River Expeditions, Inc. P.O. Box 1200, Vernal, UT 84078
(800) 433-8966, (801) 789-3813

Hualapai River Runners P.O. Box 246, Peach Springs, AZ 86434
(800) 622-4409 outside Arizona; in Arizona (520) 769-2210 or (520) 769-2219

Mark Sleight Expeditions, Inc. P.O. Box 40, St. George, UT 84771-0040,
(801) 673-1200

Moki Mac Expeditions, Inc. P.O. Box 21242, Salt Lake, UT 84121
 (800) 284-7280, (801) 268-6667

OARS, Inc. P.O. Box 67, Angels Camp, CA 95222
(209) 736-4677, (209) 736-2924

NATIVE ROADS

Outdoors Unlimited 6900 Townsend Winona Road, Flagstaff, AZ 86004
 (800) 637-7238, (520) 526-4546
Tour West, Inc. P.O. Box 333, Orem, UT 84059
(800) 453-9107, (801) 225-0755
Western River Expeditions, Inc. 7258 Racquet Club Drive, Salt Lake City, UT 84121
(800) 453-7450, (801) 942-6669
Wilderness River Adventures P.O. Box 717, Page, AZ 86040
(800) 992-8022 or (520) 645-3296

MARBLE CANYON LODGE AND TRADING COMPANY

Just past Navajo Bridge after the turnoff to Lees Ferry. Built in 1926 by "Buck" Lowry in anticipation of the completion of Navajo Bridge this lodge offers a restaurant open from 6 a.m. - 9:00 p.m. (MST). Room Rates: 2 people/2 double beds $60; 2 people/1 bed $55;1 person $45 (Winter rates: reduce prices by $5) Marble Canyon Lodge, Marble Canyon, AZ 86036, (520) 355-2225. The gas station is open from 6 a.m.-9 p.m.

DOMINQUEZ-ESCALANTE TRAIL MARKER (North)

Right next to the post office at Marble Canyon Lodge. The famous Spanish expedition passed this point on Oct. 26, 1776. It spent five days near the present-day Lees Ferry where its members attempted to swim across the river. When this failed, they built a log raft, but this, too, failed. Near starvation, they ate the last horse in their expedition and decided to climb out of Marble Canyon through an "impassable" notch in Echo Cliffs. Once on top of Glen Canyon they were able to work their way down to the river again and find the "Crossing of the Fathers" near what is now Wahweap Marina. (See pages 76-78 for more on this expedition.)

MM 542 LEES FERRY LODGE AND VERMILION CLIFFS BAR AND GRILL (North)

Constructed in 1929 of native stone, it served the needs of uranium miners

working in the area. Each room opens onto a garden patio. About one-tenth of a mile (160 m) from the lodge, heading west on 89A and on the south side of the road are two markers for the **Honeymoon Trail**. You will see these markers as you drive to the North Rim. There are two more on the way to Cliff Dwellers Lodge.

The **Vermilion Cliffs Bar and Grill** offers 150 different kinds of cold bottled beer. Even though the food is good in the summer, in the winter it gets even better to satisfy the gourmet demands of the world–class fisher-men visiting Lees Ferry. Open 6:30 a.m. - 10 p.m. (MST) every day. Lodge Rates: $50 for two, year round. No TV or telephone in rooms. Reserva-tions: Vermilion Cliffs, HC67-Box 1, Marble Canyon, AZ 86036, (520) 355-2231. Next door the **Lee's Ferry Anglers Guides & Flyshop** is open from 6:30 a.m. to 11:30 a.m. and 4:30 p.m. to 7:30 p.m., seven days a week. http://www.leesferry.com/~anglers/area.html

MM 542 BADGER CANYON AND SOAP CREEK

Directly across from Vermilion Cliffs Lodge. According to an old story, Badger Canyon and Soap Creek got their names because a couple of sheep herders wanted a change in their diet. Left to watch the sheep with limited food, it was going to be a long time before the next supply wagon came through. Even though they could eat mutton anytime, the shepherds longed for something different. One day one of them was lucky enough to trap and kill a badger. To make it edible, they boiled it all day and all night. In the morning when it was time to move camp, the badger was still too tough to eat so they took it with them. Arriving at their next camp site, they took water from the new stream and continued to boil the badger. To their sur-prise, the fatty badger mixed with the plentiful gypsum in the water, turn-ing it to soap. Thus the names Soap Creek and Badger Canyon.

MM 547 CLIFF DWELLERS LODGE

The lodge was built in 1949 by Glen Canyon guide and entrepreneur Art Greene. The restaurant at Cliff Dwellers is open from 6 a.m. - 11 a.m. and 5 p.m. - 9 p.m. (MST). No lunch is served. Lodge Rates: 1-2 people/double beds $57;1-2 people/one queen $67. (After Oct. 1, the rates drop to $39.95 for all rooms.) No TV or telephones in the rooms. Reservations: Cliff Dwell-ers Lodge, HC 67-30, Marble Canyon, AZ 86036, (520) 355-2228 or (800) 433-2543 (reservations only).

VERMILION CLIFFS SCENIC HIGHWAY: Watch for **California Condors**

as you drive along this newly designated scenic road. Ten condors weigh-ing about 25 pounds with a wingspan of 9.8 ft. (3 m) have been released into the Vermilion Cliffs Wilderness Area from the San Diego Wild Animal Park and the Los Angeles Zoo. The birds live on large carcasses of deer and other game and can travel up to 150 miles (240 km) a day in search of food. There are only 88 California Condors in existence.

MM 557.8 SAN BARTOLOME HISTORIC SITE (North)

An interpretive site that explains the natural history and geology of the Arizona Strip. It also explains the near starvation condition the Domínquez-Escalante Expedition was in when they reached this spot.

WHAT IS THE ARIZONA STRIP? It is the most remote and isolated area of Arizona, separated from the rest of the state by the 279-mile-long (449 km) Grand Canyon. Back in the early 1900s, Utah wanted to acquire the strip because most of its residents identified more closely with Utah than with Arizona. To investigate if the annexation of the strip was in the best interest of Arizona, well-known poetess and travel writer Sharlot Hall took a historic two-month journey to visit the region. Named state historian in 1909, she believed it was her duty to visit every part of Arizona and accurately record its history. For 75 days, she and her wagon driver, Allen Doyle, visited most of the strip country and recorded much of its history, natural resources and the people who lived there. When she returned, she wrote articles about the importance of keeping the Arizona Strip a part of Arizona. In 1912, she retired as state historian and in 1928 moved to Prescott where she started the **Sharlot Hall Museum.** The museum is housed in the renovated "Old Governor's Mansion" that was the first territorial capital of Arizona. (Crampton, 1975)

MM 548-MM 566 HOUSE ROCK VALLEY

Runs from Cliff Dwellers to House Rock Junction where highway 89A starts to climb up the Kaibab Plateau. Mormon settlers gave the valley this name after finding shelter under two large boulders that had fallen together. Jacob Hamblin had a home here. Between 1870 and 1880, he traveled the Mormon trail, taking settlers across the Colorado at Lees Ferry to their new homes on the Little Colorado River in Arizona.

WHY ARE THERE HUGE BOULDERS LYING BESIDE THE ROAD?

These boulders once rested at the top of the Vermilion Cliffs. They are from the much harder Shinarump layer. They fell to the valley floor when the softer Moenkopi Sandstone underlying the Shinarump eroded away.

SCENIC DETOUR FOR THE WELL PREPARED

MM 560 HOUSE ROCK BUFFALO RANCH

It is twenty-one miles (34 km) to the ranger's home on a graded dirt road. Poor ground clearance can be dangerous for passenger cars. Use caution: washes fill when it rains on the nearby Kaibab Plateau. Without help from the ranger, your chance of actually seeing one of the 90 buffalo living here is minimal because of the size of the preserve. This 60,000-acre (244 sq km) ranch is home to Arizona's largest buffalo herd managed by the Arizona Game and Fish Dept.

Buffalo are not indigenous to Arizona but 87 were brought here from Texas in the early 1920s by "Buffalo Jones." Charles Jesse Jones was hired by the National Park Service to determine whether the area around the North Rim of the Grand Canyon could accommodate a buffalo herd. To do this, he contacted Edwin Wooley who ran a stage coach from Kanab, Utah, to Bright Angel Point on the North Rim. Wooley was also the owner of one of the largest cattle ranches in the Kanab-Fredonia area.

After Jones was assured that the buffalo would thrive in this area, he tried to convince Wooley of the economic value of cross breeding buffalo with Galloway cattle to develop "cattalo." Wooley agreed to the experiment and delivered 100 head of Galloway heifers for breeding. But when the resulting offspring were too large for the heifers to give birth without assistance, the idea was scrapped. In 1926, 100 buffalo were sold to the Arizona Game and Fish Dept. for $10,000 and moved from the North Rim to this preserve where 90 buffalo live today.

Buffalo in House Rock Valley, not dated.
Grand Canyon Pioneer Society, Metzger Collection, Special Collections and Archives, NAU PH 90.9.57
Art Metzger lived at the Grand Canyon in 1913, ranching with his brother. In 1928 he became Post-master at the Grand Canyon.

Struggling Ohio writer Zane Grey became a western writer because of his meeting with Buffalo Jones in New York in 1906. Jones was a famous hunter who led the slaughter of many wild animals almost to extinction. Realizing the error of his ways in his later life, he became a champion of endangered species. Grey came to the Southwest to write about Jones transformation from hunter to protectionist. He spent weeks with Jones and learned how to be a cowboy. This experience became the material for his first successful western novel, *The Last of the Plainsmen,* written in 1908. (Scott, 1979)

Buffalo hunts are held once a year by lottery. One buffalo is allowed per hunter's lifetime and permits cost around $700. If you want to see the herd, call the Arizona Game and Fish at (520) 774-5045 and make an appointment with the wildlife manager.

MM 566 SNOW CHAIN-UP AREA

Here is a subtle reminder that the Kaibab Plateau is more than 9,000 feet (2,745 m) in elevation and receives an average of 12 feet (3.6 m) of snow each year. A record 25 feet (7.7 m) of snow covered the plateau in 1985. In this high country the snow can start as early as September. The National Park Service closes the North Rim on Oct. 21 but the park remains open for day use until Dec. 1. There is no lodging, food or gasoline in the national park from then until its final closing on Dec. 1. The park may close earlier depending on the weather.

KAIBAB PLATEAU

Kaibab means "mountain lying down" in the Paiute language. It is a good name for this extensive plateau that rises high to an elevation of 9,100 feet (2,775 m). Mormons called it Buckskin Mountain because it has the largest population of mule deer in the world. The plateau also contains the country's largest virgin forest, and it is the only place on earth you will find the **Kaibab squirrel**.

The Kaibab squirrel became separated from its cousin, the South Rim's Abert squirrel, when the Kaibab Plateau was rising and the Colorado River cut its way through the plateau to make the Grand Canyon. Over millions of years, this squirrel got caught on the northern side, adapting to the colder environment. These tassel-eared squirrels adjusted very well to the climate by developing a thick coat that blends well with the surrounding trees to hide it from predators. Stop at the Kaibab National Forest visitor center next to Jacob Lake Lodge to feel a luxurious Kaibab squirrel pelt.

✠ MM 568 SCENIC VIEW (West)

From here you can see House Rock Valley, Vermilion Cliffs, Echo Cliffs and the Colorado River. There is also a **Domínquez-Escalante Marker** here.

MM 572 Leaving Pinyon-Juniper Forest- entering Ponderosa Pine Forest

Ponderosa Pine forests are found between 7,000–to–8,000 feet (2,135-2,440 m).

JACOB LAKE Junction U.S. 89 A and Arizona Highway 67

SERVICES AT JACOB LAKE

Jacob Lake Inn:

Two people/two double beds $82. Cabins: one room with one queen bed $71. Jacob Lake Inn has a very long and complicated pricing list. Your best bet is to call (520) 643-7232. This and the Kaibab Lodge (25 miles) are the only motels in the North Kaibab National Forest so be sure to make your reservations well in advance because they fill up quickly. Jacob Lake Inn is open year round. **Restaurant:** open 6:30 a.m.-8:00 p.m. (MST) http://www.jacoblake.com/

National Forest Service Jacob Lake Campground

Open May 15 to Nov. 1 (depending on snow fall). Fifty-three camp sites with picnic tables and fire grills, paved roads, running water, toilets, handicap access. $10 per vehicle/night. Tents, trailers and motor homes less than 26 feet (8 m) are welcome. No hook-ups. Reservations: (800) 283-CAMP. You may reserve a campsite up to five months in advance of your trip.

KAIBAB NATIONAL FOREST SERVICE VISITOR CENTER:

Hours 8 a.m. - 5:30 p.m. everyday. Closed in winter. The center offers information and interpretive displays about the Kaibab Plateau and the North Rim. (520) 643-7298. http://www.fs.fed.us

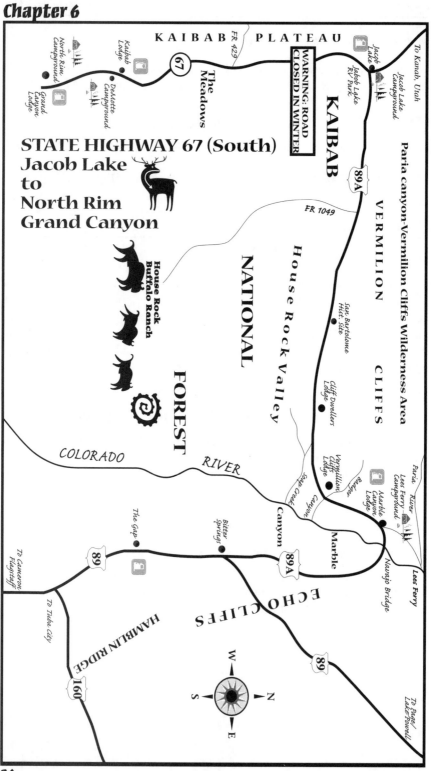

Chapter 6

KAIBAB PLATEAU

FR 429

North Rim Campground

Kaibab Lodge

67

The Meadows

WARNING: ROAD CLOSED IN WINTER

DeMotte Campground

Grand Canyon Lodge

STATE HIGHWAY 67 (South)
Jacob Lake
to
North Rim
Grand Canyon

Jacob Lake

Jacob Lake RV Park

To Kanab, Utah

Jacob Lake Campground

KAIBAB

Paria canyon-Vermillion Cliffs Wilderness Area

89A

FR 1049

VERMILION

House Rock Buffalo Ranch

NATIONAL

House Rock Valley

CLIFFS

San Bartolome Hist. Site

Cliff Dwellers Lodge

FOREST

Vermillion Cliffs Lodge

COLORADO

RIVER

Soap Creek Canyon

Badger Canyon

Marble Canyon Lodge

Lees Ferry Campground

Paria River

Marble

The Gap

Bitter Springs

Canyon

89

89A

Navajo Bridge

Lees Ferry

To Page/ Lake Powell

To Cameron/ Flagstaff

To Tuba City

HAMBLIN RIDGE

ECHO CLIFFS

160

89

W

S   N

E

96

44 miles (71 km) from Jacob Lake to the North Rim

ARIZONA STATE HIGHWAY 67 Kaibab Plateau-North Rim Highway

Usually open May 15 through Oct. 31, the Arizona Dept. of Transportation warns visitors every year that after Nov. 1 the road could be closed on short notice because of heavy snowfall. This highway is a National Forest Scenic Byway and an Arizona State Scenic Parkway. Highway 67 is the same route formerly used by the stagecoach to transport visitors to the North Rim. It parallels the Kaibab Plateau Trail that makes up part of the 750 mile (1,209 km) **Arizona Trail**, a primitive, non-motorized way to traverse the state of Arizona from the Mexico border to Utah. The trail uses old stage coach routes, logging trails and some new trails. Once finished, the trail will be used by hikers, mountain bikers, horse enthusiasts and cross-country skiers. Help is needed to complete the trail. If you are interested in donating your time or money contact the Arizona Trail Association, P.O. Box 36736, Phoenix, AZ 85067.

KAIBAB CAMPER VILLAGE

Head south on Highway 67 about a mile, turn west at the sign. The park has 43 RV sites with full hook-ups ($22) and 24 sites with only electric and water. There are 50 tent sites ($12). Reservations: (520) 643-7804. Closes Oct. 15 to May 15 every year.

JACOB LAKE (One mile south of Kaibab Visitors Center)

Named for Mormom explorer Jacob Hamblin, this tiny lake is an example of a sinkhole formed through the Kaibab Limestone. The water on the Kaibab Plateau runs through underground limestone passageways and most of the "lakes" formed on the surface of the plateau are made from the collapse of the underlying limestone layer. (Chronic, 1986) Directly across from Jacob Lake is a historic ranger station built in 1910 listed on the National Register of Historic Places.

FOREST ROAD 429 (West)

This primitive road leads to Big Springs where President Theodore Roosevelt stayed while hunting with Jimmy Owens. "Uncle" Jimmy Owens was a famous hunter and guide of the Kaibab Forest and a participant in the failed attempt to develop the "cattalo" in House Rock Valley. (See pages 92-94.)

In the early 1900s, cattlemen used the Kaibab Plateau to graze their herds but did not like cougars eating their calves. To accommodate these interests, the U.S. government hired Owens to exterminate the cougar from the plateau. He alone may have shot more than 500 cougars. Unfortunately, it was not long afterward that the mule deer population began to skyrocket because of the elimination of its only predator, leaving the deer to die off from mass starvation.

To fix the problem, the cattlemen decided that 75,000 Kaibab Plateau mule deer should move to the South Rim. The government offered $5 per relocated deer, but how does one lead a herd of wild animals to its new homeland? One cattleman came up with the idea of staging a "deer drive." According to his plan, cowboys would round up deer on the Kaibab Plateau and herd them down one of the trails on the North Rim into the Grand Canyon. The herd would then swim across the Colorado River and travel up the trail to the South Rim.

Cowboys came from all around with guns and pots and pans to scare the deer but when they got to the rim, they didn't have one deer to herd down the trail. Wild animals do not behave the way domesticated animals do, and so the effort failed. Eventually the government stopped listening to the cattlemen and reintroduced the cougar into the delicate balance of life on the Kaibab Plateau. (Parker, 1957)

MM 604 MEADOWS

Different types of grasses and wildflowers compose this biotic community, making this an excellent grazing area for cattle and, at one time, buffalo.

Along the edge of the meadows are small, short blue spruce trees that look out of place next to the large trees of the Kaibab National Forest. These "baby trees" are smaller clones of the larger blue spruce that normally grow to a height of 80-to-100 feet (24-31 m). The smaller trees are attempting to colonize the meadow but because of the high water table, caused by the spring snow melt and 22 inches (55.9 cm) of rain fall annually, the meadow is usually too wet for the spruce to thrive. (Smith, 1962)

Old Road Kaibab Plateau, North Rim, ca. 1920s
Emery Kolb Collection, Cline Library, Northern Arizona University, NAU PH 568-7014

MM 605 KAIBAB LODGE (West)

Gaylord Staveley, the present owner of the lodge, isn't exactly sure who built it but he's pretty sure it was built in 1926. He's heard from locals that David Rust, famous for promoting tourism to the Grand Canyon in the early 1900s, may have been the builder. Regardless of its history, it is a charming place to relax and enjoy the beauty of the Kaibab Plateau. Reservations (520) 526-0924; outside AZ (800) 525-0924. **Kaibab Lodge Dining Room:** Breakfast buffet served from 6 a.m.-9:30a.m., dinner 5:30 p.m.-9:30-p.m. Reservations recommended but not required.

North Rim Nordic Center at Kaibab Lodge: The North Rim is closed from Nov. 15 to May 15 each year because of the heavy snowfall. To accommodate the avid cross-country skier, the Kaibab Lodge has developed more than 80 miles (128 km) of machine-groomed and tracked ski trails for classic and skate skiing, plus 30 miles (48 km) of marked backcountry trails. Transportation is provided to the snowbound lodge by heated snow vans. Contact Gaylord and Joy Staveley, P.O. Box 2997, Flagstaff, AZ 86003 (520) 526-0924 (Ariz.) (800) 525-0924 (outside Ariz.)

North Rim Country Store (East) Open 7 a.m. to 7 p.m. Sells the only diesel fuel available on the North Rim.

KAIBAB NATIONAL FOREST DEMOTTE CAMPGROUND (West)

25.8 miles (41.6 km) from Jacob Lake just past the Kaibab Lodge on the west side of Arizona State Highway 67. This campground bears the name of a member of John Wesley Powell's 1872 survey team. Harvey DeMotte was a professor at Illinois Wesleyan University at the same time Powell was a professor of geology. (Stegner, 1992) The campground is open May 15 to Nov. 1 (depending on snowfall). Twenty-three camping sites with picnic tables and grills. Drinking water and toilets in the campground. Fee: $10 per vehicle per night; first-come, first served.

NORTH RIM ENTRANCE STATION

The entrance fee is $20 per car and is good at both the North and South Rim for seven days. Golden Eagle, Golden Access and Golden Age passes are accepted. It is a good four-hour drive and over 216 (348 km) highway miles from the South Rim to the North Rim of the Grand Canyon. For those who do make the trip, the canyon view and surrounding vistas make the additional travel well worth the effort. The North Rim is 1,000-to-1,500 feet (305 m-457 m) higher than the South Rim and gets much more precipitation, usually in the form of snow.

Native Roads

The earliest known people to live on the North Rim, some 4,000 years ago, were the Desert Archaic People, creators of the mysterious, animal-shaped split-twig figurines. The figurines were first found in Luka Cave by a Civilian Conservation Corps work crew in the 1930s while building a trail from Phantom Ranch at the bottom of the Grand Canyon to Clear Creek on the North Rim.

Archeologists think these caves were shrines for hunters of the Desert Culture. In their rituals and prayers, the Desert people used the figurines to bring success and good fortune to their hunt.

Around 500 A.D., the Anasazi moved into the canyon and built pueblo homes of stone, mud, logs and brush. The lived in the canyon as farmers for almost 700 years but may have left the area because of a severe drought and poor soil conditions. Some anthropologists think they may have relocated to the Hopi mesas, along with other Southwestern people, where they farmed around the spring-fed terraces.

Around 1300 A.D., the Cerbat Indians, whose descendants may be the Havasupai Indians who still live in the Grand Canyon, came to live here. These people adapted to the harsh living conditions by farming in the canyon in the summer and hunting and gathering on the rim during the fall and winter. Around the same time, the Southern Paiute Indians began making visits into the canyon to hunt deer but continued to roam throughout the Colorado Plateau. (Jones, 1979, Euler, 1990)

GRAND CANYON LODGE

Perched on the very edge of the canyon, this beautiful old log lodge was built around 1926 by the Union Pacific Railroad. Stephen Mather, the first director of the National Park Service, commissioned the Union Pacific Railroad to build a hotel to accommodate the increasing number of tourists. Gilbert Stanley Underwood, the architect who designed Ahwahnee Hotel in Yosemite, designed this lodge. Constructed of native limestone during the harsh winter of 1927, the lodge was finished in 1928 at a cost of $350,000. But in 1932 a fire destroyed the original lodge. Four years later, the Utah Parks Co.,rebuilt the lodge ,again under the direction of Underwood, but it did not replace the original second story or the three story tower.

A bronze statue of **Brighty**, the famous burro that lived and played on the North Rim in the 1930s, used to sit in the corner of the sun room but Brighty now sits in front of the new visitor center. Marguerite Henry chronicles Brighty's exploits in her book, *Brighty of the Grand Canyon,* written for children in 1953.

Grand Canyon Lodge, North Rim, no date.
Emery Kolb Collection, Cline Library, NAU PH 568-5616

Rooms in the historic lodge are no longer available but you can sleep close by in a cabin or motel room. A few cabins have a view of the canyon. The motel units are in the forest. Rates vary depending on the view and room amenities. Call for current pricing. Contact Amfac Parks & Resorts for reservations: (303) 297-2757. Some cabins are handicap–accessible and there is a wheelchair lift in the dining room and lower patio.

MULE RIDES: *You can enjoy the canyon by mule. One-hour rides ($15), half-day ($40) and full-day into the canyon ($95 includes lunch). Make arrangements at the desk in the lodge or for advanced reservations write or call Grand Canyon Trail Rides, P.O. Box 128, Tropic, UT 84776, (435) 679-8665, (435) 679-8709 Fax.*

The Grand Canyon Lodge Dining Room: It is difficult to get a reservation for dinner unless you plan ahead. Hours are 6:30 a.m. to 10 a.m. full menu; continental breakfast, 10 a.m.-11a.m.; lunch, 11:30a.m.-2:30p.m.; dinner, 5:00 p.m.-9:30 p.m.every day and reservations are required for dinner. (520) 638-2611, ext. 160. Should you find yourself without a reservation in the restaurant, there is also a snack bar that serves pizza and fast food from 6:30 a.m. to 9 p.m. daily.

NORTH RIM CAMPGROUND

Located 1.5 miles (2.4 km) north and west of Grand Canyon Lodge. Open mid-May to mid-Oct., $12 per night. Eighty-two camp sites, no hook-ups. Coin operated showers, laundromat and a store are located next to the campground. Reservations for group sites and families can be made eight weeks in advance by calling DESTINET (800) 365-2267. If you don't have a reservation, arrive at the campground before 10 a.m. for the best chance of getting a campsite.

BRIGHT ANGEL POINT

This vista is a half mile (0.8 km) from the corner of the east patio behind Grand Canyon Lodge. At an elevation of 8,153 feet (2,487 m), you are at the best vantage point to see and hear **Roaring Springs**. This is one of the most prominent places where the water, filtered through the Kaibab Limestone, empties into the canyon.

NORTH KAIBAB TRAIL

You must have a permit for all overnight hiking in the Grand Canyon. Contact the Backcountry Reservations Office for permit well in advance of your trip to the North Rim. If you wait until you get to the rim, it may be possible to put your name on a waiting list from 8 a.m. to 12 noon (MST) and 1 p.m to 5 p.m. every day for a permit the following day. Permits now cost $20 and are given out at 9 a.m. and you must be present to get one, if there are any available. Backcountry Reservation Office, P.O. Box 129, Grand Canyon, AZ 86023 (520) 638-7875. Camping in the backcountry is now $4 per person, per night.

The North Rim, like the South Rim, has had its share of business tycoons interested in developing the tourist trade. E.D. Wooley developed the Grand Canyon Transportation Co. in 1903 to bring tourists from Kanab, Utah, to the canyon. To make trips possible from the North to South Rim, Wooley invested $5,000 in the Bright Angel Trail and his son-in-law, David Rust, built a cable car across the river. This is the site of the present day Kaibab Suspension Bridge that makes it possible for hikers to cross the river.

Rust set up some tents, built buildings and planted trees at a site close by the river but tourists never really used the site during his lifetime. Teddy Roosevelt stayed in the campground in 1913 while cougar hunting and so everyone began calling it Roosevelt Camp. Mary Colter renamed it Phantom Ranch in 1922 when the Fred Harvey Co. took over the campground. (Cleeland, 1986) (See page 45 for more on Phantom Ranch.)

To get to Phantom Ranch, the Colorado River and the Bright Angel Trail, you must take the **North Kaibab Trail**. It is 14 miles (22.5 km) one-way to the river and the trail descends more than 6,000 feet (1,830 m), making this a very difficult climb back up. *Do not* attempt this in one day. Take adequate water — about a gallon (4 liters) per person — and wear appropriate clothing and foot wear. This is a very arduous trip and should not be approached lightly. Several people die every year in the canyon from dehydration, hypothermia or from falls.

Rust Camp, 1913
Emery Kolb Collection, Cline Library, Northern Arizona University, #526-4689

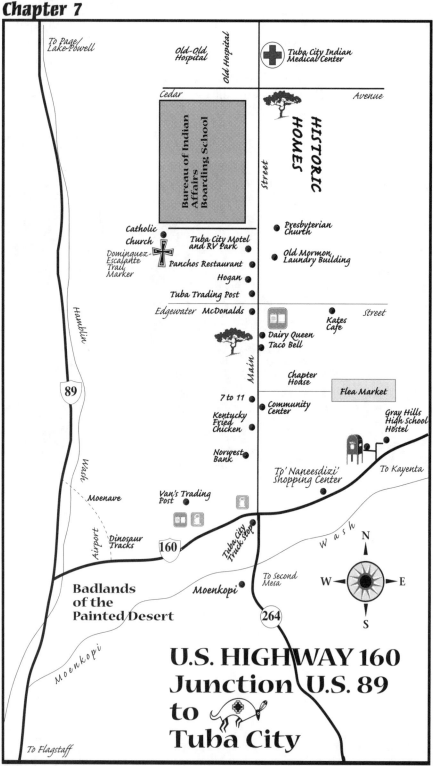

Chapter 7

To Page/Lake-Powell

Old-Old Hospital

Old Hospital

Tuba City Indian Medical Center

Cedar Avenue

Bureau of Indian Affairs Boarding School

HISTORIC HOMES

Street

Presbyterian Church

Catholic Church

Tuba City Motel and RV Park

Old Mormon Laundry Building

Dominguez-Escalante Trail Marker

Panchos Restaurant

Hogan

Tuba Trading Post

Edgewater McDonalds Street

Kates Cafe

Main

Dairy Queen

Taco Bell

Chapter House

Flea Market

7 to 11

Community Center

Kentucky Fried Chicken

Gray Hills High School Hostel

Norwest Bank

Tp' Naneesdizi' Shopping Center

To Kayenta

Van's Trading Post

Moenave

Dinosaur Tracks

160

Tuba City Truck Stop

Wash

N

W E

S

To Second Mesa

Hamblin

89

Wash

Airport

Badlands of the Painted Desert

Moenkopi

264

Moenkopi

To Flagstaff

U.S. HIGHWAY 160 Junction U.S. 89 to Tuba City

11 miles (22.5 km) from the junction of U.S. 89 to Tuba City

MM 480.5 JCT. OF U.S. 89 AND U.S. 160 TO TUBA CITY

This desolate stretch of road is wavy because the earth under the asphalt is a soft layer of shale made up of volcanic ash. When the layer gets wet it expands causing the road to heave under heavy loads. (Rigby, 1976)

MM 312 HAMBLIN WASH (North)

Usually a dry streambed, this wash follows the base of the Echo Cliffs north along U.S. 89. It is named for Jacob Hamblin, a well-known Mormon explorer and missionary who first came to the Tuba City area in 1858. Hamblin explored this region at the request of Mormon Church President Brigham Young who wanted to colonize northern Arizona and develop a good relationship with the local natives. Hamblin Wash became part of the first route south from Utah's Mormon enclaves.

In 1870, Hamblin served as a guide for John Wesley Powell, the renowned explorer of the Grand Canyon and the Colorado River, taking him over the Mormon settlers' route from Lees Ferry, south along Echo Cliffs, then east to the Hopi mesas. After visiting the Hopis, Hamblin and Powell traveled on to Fort Defiance. There Hamblin met with Navajo leaders to negotiate a peace treaty between the Navajos and Mormons. (McNitt, 1962)

MM 312.5 TUBA CITY AIRPORT (North)

This airport is little more than a paved airstrip used primarily to transport Navajo and Hopi patients for any emergency medical care not available at the Tuba City Indian Medical Center 11 miles (22.5 km) up the road. Its inconvenient and improbable location is the result of compromise reached by the Navajo and Hopi tribes which spent more than 26 years disputing ownership of thousands of acres of land surrounding this site.

MM 313 BADLANDS OF THE PAINTED DESERT

Topping the multi-colored, banded plateau at 5,500 feet (1,677 m), the highway opens to a vast, treeless expanse. Here the land changes from tawny whites to burnished red. The soil is made up of ancient silts and volcanic ash formed during the dinosaur age which combine to form bentonite. Once wet, bentonite swells and then cracks as it dries, making it easily eroded and unable to support any vegetation. (Chronic, 1986)

The Navajos call the Painted Desert *halchíítah,* or "among the colors." An incredibly beautiful place, especially at sunrise and sunset, because of the brightly-colored shades of pink, gray and green of the mesas. This colorful collection of siltstone and shales is from the Owl Rock member of the

Chinle Formation, formed more than 150–to–250 million years ago. (Rigby, 1976; Breed, 1968)

MM 313.5 PHOTO OPPORTUNITY (North)

Decide quickly! The road rises up between the narrow sides — a huge gully, really — of the eroded edge of the plateau and quickly bends to the east. By then, you've probably missed the undeveloped turnoff (a left turn if traveling easterly) that takes you off the road onto the top of an isolated mesa, a "little sister," at the top of the hill. This is a great place to pull off, explore the desert and take pictures of the lunar-like vistas of the northern Painted Desert.

MM 314 TUBA BUTTE (North) An igneous intrusive formation.

MM 316.25 BALANCING ROCKS (North)

About 200 million years ago, a warm-water ocean covered most of the western United States. On the edge of the water were marshes, swamps and jungles. Dinosaurs thrived here until about 65 million years ago when the western mountain ranges formed, blocking most of the moisture. The balancing rocks are the result of wind and water erosion of the softer sandstone.

MM 316.5 DINOSAUR TRACKS (North)

Follow the signs to the roadside stands. Usually, an enterprising Navajo entrepreneur from the area will come to your car to offer services as a guide. Shake hands, introduce yourself and the guide will show you to the tracks. A small gratuity of a couple dollars is appropriate. These tracks, found in the Tuba City and Kayenta area in 1942 and in China in the 1980s, are the worlds only evidence of "running dinosaurs" which lived during the late Triassic, early Jurassic era. The *Dilophosaurus* was a medium-sized dinosaur weighing approximately 1,000 pounds (453 kg) and standing 8–to–10 feet (2.4-3.1 m) tall. They had powerful hind legs for running and forefeet that resembled a bird's foot with four toes. The front arms were short with clawed fingers used for grasping. Although it had very sharp teeth, it probably used its hind legs and front claws to rip its prey.

The Dilophosaurus was depicted in the movie *Jurassic Park* as a venom-spitting creature that poisoned its victims before eating them. There is no evidence that the Tuba City Dilophosaurus poisoned its prey like its Hollywood cousin. To learn more about dinosaurs that lived in the Tuba City area, visit the Natural History Museum at the Tuba City Public High School. Call science teacher Gary Kmett at (520) 283-6291 for a personal tour .

Dinosaur Tracks, ca. 1930s
Fred Harvey Collection, Museum of Northern Arizona Photo Archives #301-3-149

MM 316.5 MOENAVE (North)

From Dinosaur Tracks to the north you can see a green oasis at the base of Hamblin's Ridge made up of Moenave Sandstone. Prior to 100 years ago, the abundant springs from the sandstone supported generations of Hopi farms, and, before them, prehistoric Indians. Between 1870 and 1904, a few Mormon settlers occupied the little canyon and developed its irrigation system. Since then, Navajos have lived and farmed in the canyon.

Mormon trailblazer Jacob Hamblin began farming here after making friends with Chief Tuuvi at the Hopi farming area of Moenkopi, today the Hopis' western-most village. In 1874, Hamblin sold his homestead to John D. Lee who used it to hide from authorities because of his part in the Mountain Meadows Massacre. Lee's stay in Moenave was only a short reprieve. Five months later lawmen caught him on a trip to Utah to visit his family. Taken back to Panquitch for trial, a firing squad executed him standing in his own coffin. For more information about the massacre see pages 85-87. (Brooks, 1950)

MM 318.5 IGNEOUS RIDGE AND SAND DUNE (South)

The ridge indicates that at one time there was some volcanic activity in this area pushing lava to the surface to form this ridge.

MM 319 KAYENTA FORMATION (North)

These red rocks are part of the Glen Canyon Group formed during the late Triassic, early Jurassic era around 180 to 230 million years ago. It consists of bright-colored red sandstone, mudstone and some limestone. Most of the dinosaur tracks in northern Arizona are preserved in the Kayenta Formation.

MM 319.5 VAN'S TRADING POST (North)

The Vankeuren family is one of the oldest trading families still operating a store in the Tuba City area. This location, at the foot of the mesa, is known to locals as Kerley Valley, named for John Kerley, another trader who was a partner in the Babbitt Bros. Trading Post in Tuba City. Finding the community of Tuba City too large for his liking, he moved to the "valley." Built in 1921, the old post sits right next to the gas company behind the new Van's Trading Post.

Kerley Trading Post Bus, 1925
Warren Family Collection, Cline Library, Special Collections and Archives, NAU PH 4 12.2.88

MM 322 TUBA CITY TRUCK STOP

Southeast side of the junction of 160 and 264. This restaurant is famous for its Navajo taco, voted the State Dish of Arizona in a 1995 poll conducted by the *Arizona Republic*. A Navajo taco is an amalgamation of beans, chopped lettuce, sliced tomato, shredded cheddar and an optional green chile sitting atop a piece of crispy fry bread, and eaten open-faced. Fry bread cooked on the Navajo Reservation simply *must* be made with Blue-

bird Flour from the Cortez Milling Co. to be considered authentically Navajo. The precise reason is ineffable but it's believed its higher gluten content holds the dough together better than other flours when flipped between palms to achieve the round, tortilla shape for cooking. Then the dough is fried in Crisco or lard in a heavy iron skillet. Now thought of as a "traditional food," fry bread actually came from the Bosque Redondo era when some 8,000 Navajos spent four years imprisoned and were given little more than white flour and lard to eat.

Blue Bird Flour, 1994 Photograph by Christine Stephenson

The truck stop is a favorite of locals with its classic small town ambiance and menu. Curiously, the truck stop and everything on the east side of U.S. 160 for several miles is on Hopi land. Everything to the west is on Navajo land. The boundary is the center stripe down the highway.

HISTORIC DETOUR OF TUBA CITY

Turn left at MM 322 and travel up Main Street to the first stop light. The historic section starts at the Tuba Trading Post. It was the first Mormon settlers of the area who gave this little town its moniker, naming the place after the Hopi called Tuuvi. He was from the village of Oraibi and leader among the Moenkopi Hopi farmers. Tuuvi and his wife were the first Hopis to venture to Salt Lake City, meet Brigham Young, then-president of the Church of Jesus Christ of Latter Day Saints, and convert to the Mormon religion. It was he who gave the first 14 Mormon families a place in the area Hopis knew as "white sands" to build their town, away from the Hopi village, on the condition that they protect the Hopis and their fields from Navajo and Paiute raids. In his honor the Mormons named it Tuba City.

Relations between the Mormons and natives were not always placid, especially after one of the dams built by the Mormons in 1877 broke, flooding the Hopis' crops. With the increased number of settlers moving into the Tuba area, the chief told the Mormons that his people wanted to live in peace but that the settlers must stop building farms next to every available spring.

Tuba City was a half–way station for Mormon settlers traveling south from Utah to develop communities along the Colorado River. In 1871, John D. Lee was "called" by LDS church president Brigham Young to establish a crossing on the Colorado. Situated 60 miles (97 km) north of Tuba City, Lees Ferry became the only reliable crossing of the river for hundreds of miles in either direction, easing an already hazardous journey for Mormon pioneers and other travelers.

In 1878, Erastus Snow platted the town of Tuba City, patterning it after a typical Mormon community with wide streets lined by Lombardy Poplars. By 1900, there were 150 settlers living in the community. Farming was the Mormons' primary interest and much of the area where the Indian Health Service hospital sits today was an apple orchard.

Mormon occupation was short-lived, however, after the Tuba City area was added to the Navajo Reservation. The government pressured the Mormons to sell their homes, farms, orchards and other improvements for a total of $48,000, and in 1904 they left for good. They re–established themselves in places like Snowflake and Woodruff, Ariz., and Farmington and Gallup, N.M.

A NATURAL OASIS

The Navajo name for Tuba City is *Tónaneesdizi*, which means, "many springs" or "tangled water" for the desert rivulets discharging from an underground aquifer.

The Charlie Day spring is the most famous water source in the area. It is named for Mr. Day whose hogan was next to the spring and who once served as an Army scout. In 1928, Bureau of Indian Affairs Superintendent Walker ordered the development of the spring. While digging, the construction crew found fossils of extinct mammals. The University of Pennsylvania and the American Museum of Natural History identified the findings. Among the skeletons recovered were *camelops* similar to the South American llama, bison larger than those of present day, *equus*, a type of horse that became extinct in North America during the Ice Age, and *elephas columbi*, a mammoth that was about the same size as an African elephant. (Museum Notes, 1931)

WHY ARE THERE SPRINGS IN THE DESERT?

Rain water falls on the porous sandstone and seeps into the underlying clay layers. Tuba City is especially blessed because it is south of the Kaibito Plateau, a large mass of sandstone that collects water and carries it in its natural underground clay layers to Tuba City where it bubbles up as cool, naturally pure drinking water. (Museum Notes, 1931)

Tuba Trading Post, ca. 1930s
Fred Harvey Collection, Museum of Northern Arizona Photo Archives 301-3-328

TUBA TRADING POST

This famous landmark was first opened in 1870 by Charles Algert who hired store clerk Samual Preston to run the post for him. Preston later became a partner with the Babbitt Brothers who bought out Algert in 1902. Preston built the big, beautiful, hogan-shaped portion of the post after becoming a partner. It's constructed of locally-quarried blue limestone, with logs hauled in from the San Francisco Peaks near Flagstaff.

The Babbitt family, which also owns the CO Bar Ranch on U.S. 89, has played a major role in the Indian trading business for a century. They got into Indian trading inadvertently; acquiring ownership of the Red Lake Trading Post in 1891 after its previous owner was shot and killed by a jealous lover. (See page 164 for more about Red Lake.)

The Babbitts developed 10 other trading posts throughout northern Arizona. Still a successful trading company, the Babbitt Bros. corporation owns stores in Grand Canyon, Red Lake and Tuba City.

Like other traders, the Babbitts were attracted to the reservation because of the country's need for wool at the time. In exchange for one sackful worth about $3 to $4, they traded food, clothing, tobacco, medicine, tools and kerosene to Navajo sheepherders.

Teddy Roosevelt stayed at the Tuba Trading Post with the Prestons in 1913 on his return from a mountain lion hunt on the north rim of the Grand Canyon. Zane Grey also was a frequent visitor. Several films based on his books were shot in and around the Tuba City area.

Still a working trading post, it offers many items traded or bought from local native artists: silver jewelry, sandpaintings, kachina dolls and Navajo rugs. The post also has a wonderful assortment of T-shirts and books about the Southwest. Because the post caters to a growing number of out-of-town visitors, it remains on Mountain Standard Time like most of Arizona. It's open 7:30 a.m. to 7 p.m., Monday through Saturday. (520) 283-5441 or (800) 644-8383.

NAVAJO HOGAN Just north of the Trading Post

Hooghan, pronounced in Navajo as "ho-whan" is the word for "home" and has come to also mean the traditionally round or octagonal dwelling used for living or ceremonies. Whether mud-covered, built of logs or stone or made from 2x4s and plywood, a hogan is a hogan to Navajos. Common to them all, however, is that their doors always face east to the rising sun.

Inside the hogan, life is organized in a specific way. Food is prepared and stored in the northeast corner. Tools for making a living are on the southeast corner. Spiritual paraphernalia are kept in the northwest corner and beds are stored in the southwest corner. Today, many Navajo families live in modern houses or trailers, using the hogan for primarily ceremonial purposes.

Most trading posts had guest hogans available for Navajo families who traveled long distances to trade at their particular post. To encourage business, many traders sponsored horse races, chicken pulls and ceremonials. In the past a "chicken pull" was exactly what its name implies. A rooster is buried in the sand up to its neck and two horsemen, riding bareback, compete to see who can pull the rooster out of the sand first. Since the 1920s this practice has been replaced with the more humane use of a gunny sack instead of a rooster.

ST. JUDE CATHOLIC MISSION

Turn left past the Tuba City Motel and the church is on the left about a half mile (0.8 km) down the road. John Kerley sent a request in the early 1900s to the Franciscan Friars at St. Michaels located west of Window Rock to start a mission in Tuba City. The reason given by Kerley was that "they are tired of preachers." Kerley at the time of the request was still a partner with the Babbitt Brothers who offered an acre (.004 sq km) of land and $50 to cover the friars' expenses to travel to Tuba City. Kerley and his partners felt that the community of Tuba City needed a more liberal-minded religious leader who smoked and would not condemn "drinking, picnics, card parties, picture shows, etc."

Kerley further explained that this restrictive approach to Christianity had "put the so-called Christian workers to the bad with the Indians and most of the whites on this part of the reservation." (Butler, 1991) The Franciscans couldn't honor the traders request at the time because of the cost of housing a priest in such a remote location. It wasn't until 1951 that Father Elmer Von Hagel, Superior at St. Michaels, made the 330-mile (532 km) round trip to Tuba City over dirt roads to deliver mass once a month. Finally, in 1962 funds were made available to build a permanent church.

Located next to the rectory is a **Domínquez-Escalante Marker** commemorating the priests' historic trip through Tuba City.

Historic Krenz-Kerley Trading Post

Photo ca. 1917, courtesy of Lindell Cornelison, former Tuba City Postmaster

Across the street to the north of the Quality Inn, on the east side of Main Street, is an historic trading post built by Fred Krenz. Fred was an accomplished builder who played a part in constructing many of the BIA schools on the reservation. But when he decided to try his hand at trading, the *Coconino Sun,* which frequently wrote about Indian Traders' social life, described Krenz as "the ubiquitous Indian trading poster of Tuba City." It seems that Fred was never at his post, always traveling to Flagstaff, Phoenix and Albuquerque. According to Fred's four sons, who are alive and well living in various parts of California, John left his post frequently to court their mother. Once he won her hand, he sold his post to the Babbitt Brothers and took up the life of a rancher in southern Arizona.

John Kerley gained control of the post in the early 1920s as part of the Babbitt company and used it while the Tuba Trading Post was being refurbished. Because Kerley was such an outgoing and likeable guy, everyone began refering to the Krenz building as "Kerley's Trading Post."

MOVIE LOCATION

Fictional Navajo police officer Jim Chee, one of mystery writer Tony Hillerman's two principal protagonists, is transferred to Tuba City from Shiprock at the opening of *The Dark Wind.* His assignment is to determine who is vandalizing an important windmill. Through his legwork, he comes to learn how important desert springs are to the Hopi people, as well as the motives behind the murder of a Navajo and burglary of the Burnt Water Trading Post. The basis of the story centers around the Anglo concept of revenge which is foreign to the Navajo. It is this "dark wind" that makes the white men behave in illogical ways, out of harmony with the natural order of things.

The Dark Wind was Robert Redford's first attempt to bring a Hillerman novel to the screen. For authenticity, Redford filmed the production in the Tuba City/Red Lake area. Redford's Wildwood Productions leased the "laundry" from the BIA to house a paper maché set of a Hopi village. When the film was wrapped, the crew left the set behind, complete with a life–like fireplace. Children got into the building and started a fire in the fireplace, burning off the second floor and roof. Tuba City Cultural Projects, Inc, a local historic preservation group, has renovated the building for re-use as a regional public library.

FIRST PRESBYTERIAN CHURCH

East side of Main Street, directly across from the Tuba City Boarding School. This is the first of six Presbyterian churches built on the Navajo Nation. Located right across from the boarding school, this limestone block church was part of the 1869 Grant Peace Policy. The Presbyterians were assigned to the Navajo Reservation by the government to provide religious instruction and to "civilize" the Indians. Their presence in Tuba City predates the 1905 construction of the boarding school. In 1896, they established a mission in Kerley Valley.

The San Juan Southern Paiute Tribe set up its health department in the basement of the church annex. Because the Paiutes do not have a land base of their own, they are forced to lease space from existing agencies. Their administrative offices are in Grey Hills Academy High School. See pages 64-65 for more on the San Juan Southern Paiute Tribe.

BUREAU OF INDIAN AFFAIRS BOARDING SCHOOL COMPOUND

The compound starts to the north of the Quality Inn and extends all the way to East Cedar Avenue. Construction of this large school began in 1905, one year after the federal government bought the homes, farms and improvements of the first Mormon settlers and forced them to leave.

As you drive north up Main Street past the Tuba City Motel, old sandstone buildings come into view to the west. Among the oldest are three huge, red sandstone, two-story structures with all of their windows boarded over. These were the school's original dormitories but were abandoned more than 20 years ago. Even today they remain among the largest natural sandstone buildings ever constructed on the Navajo Reservation.

Navajo and Hopi stone masons quarried sandstone from the nearby Moenkopi Wash and hauled it to the boarding school site for 50 cents a load. When finished, the school accommodated only 75 students because the design included space for classrooms, a cafeteria, an infirmary and a place for the staff to live.

The BIA's educational philosophy of the early 1900s emphasized Christianizing and assimilating Indians into mainstream America. Students had to wear uniforms, cut their hair, march military style and work at manual labor. They were ordered never to speak their own language nor to use corn pollen to pray to the Holy People, the Navajo deities. Students were taught how to farm and master skills like carpentry to enable them to work successfully in the "Anglo" world once they graduated from school.

By 1910, the Tuba City Boarding School was completely self-sufficient. It operated a 200-acre (0.8 sq km) farm with cows and chickens, a bakery, laundry and carpentry shop. Students attended school half the day and worked in the fields for the remainder. Days were very long and joyless, with the bugle awaking them in the morning and announcing the end of the day at sunset.

By 1911, there were more than 1,500 Navajo families living around Tuba City but only 100 students enrolled in school. In 1912, approval came from Washington to build the assembly hall in the center of the campus so more students could be enrolled.

Understandably, Navajo families hid their children from school authorities in an attempt to keep them at home. Methods used by the BIA to enroll

students were less than honorable. At times, school agents kidnapped children found away from their parents. To many children, living in a huge sterile room with high ceilings far from the warmth and security of their large families and womb-like hogan, school was not at all a positive learning or living experience. Dorm aides and teachers were no replacement for their own parents, aunts and uncles. Many children grew up in boarding school without nurturing or knowledge of their traditional heritage. Some could no longer speak Navajo to their grandparents when released from school.

Tuba City Boarding School student sitting in front of dormitory, ca. 1918-1920
Marie Olson Collection, Cline Library, Special Collections and Archives, NAU 516-105
Marie Olson was a nurse in Tuba City from 1918-1920.

In 1920, the country's attitude about the education of American Indians began to change. The Indian Citizenship Act of 1924 gave them the right to vote. The Meriam Report, commissioned by the Secretary of the Interior to study the quality of education and health care provided to Native Americans, urged the involvement of family and community in education. The report, prepared by the Institute for Government Research, now known as the Brookings Institution, was published in 1928. For the first time, the Indian point of view became important in the classroom.

The federal Commissioner of Indian Affairs, John Collier, attempted to implement the suggestions of the Meriam Report in the 1930s. His goals were to: 1) Provide a modern, scientific education to every Indian, and 2)

To replace the boarding school system with day schools so students could go home to their families at night.

In 1950, the Johnson O'Malley Act made it possible for Navajo children to attend public school with funding from the BIA. It is because of this law that Tuba City and other communities on the reservation have both BIA day and boarding schools as well as state–funded public schools.

Since the historic dormitories' closure and condemnation around 1970, the BIA has sought to have the buildings torn down. Lack of federal funding has prevented this, and in recent years a local community group, Tuba City Cultural Projects, has sought to save the buildings and have them restored.

TUBA CITY INDIAN MEDICAL CENTER

Just past the four-way stop sign, a half-mile (.8 km) north of the trading post, on the west side of the road is the "old" Tuba City Hospital, which today houses a tribally-run alcohol rehabilitation program.

In 1914, the oldest Tuba City hospital, which sits directly behind the "old" hospital, began to serve the boarding school students. It was an eight-bed hospital with no electricity. The first physician was Dr. Campbell who frequently made hogan visits on horseback or by wagon.

Today, the Indian Health Service, under the United States Public Health Service, is responsible for providing health care to the 185,000 Navajos living in an area the size of the state of West Virginia.

Tuba City Indian Medical Center is an 85-bed hospital with a service population of approximately 26,000 people. It operates a very busy ambulatory care and emergency room department as well as a large Community Health and Disease Prevention/Health Promotion Program.

All Indian Health Service (IHS) hospitals on the Navajo and Hopi Nations are strictly for the care of tribally-enrolled Native Americans with a census number, as well as IHS commissioned officers and their dependents. Non–natives may be seen on an emergency basis only. Health insurance is accepted. In an emergency, non–natives are admitted to the Intensive Care Unit until they are stable enough to be transferred by airplane or ambulance to the nearest private hospital. The Emergency Room number is **(520) 283-6211. There is also a 911 number in the Tuba City, Kayenta and Chilchinbito area.**

REGIONAL RUG DESIGN-STORM PATTERN

The "storm pattern" design, developed in the Tuba City area, is a vivid representation of the weather in this part of the reservation. Its design holds symbolic meaning for the Navajo people. The center of the rug represents the center of the universe or the hogan. The squares or triangles in the four corners of the rug are the four sacred mountains and the zigzag lines represent lightning bolts. The border of the rug usually has numerous symbols like clouds, beetles and feathers but the rug shown below has a more Christian theme. See the insert for a color picture of this storm pattern rug.

Storm Pattern, ca. 1920-1940
Photograph by Gene Balzer, Museum of Northern Arizona

SERVICES IN TUBA CITY

LODGING

Quality Inn A new 80-room motel decorated in a Southwestern style. Rooms are moderately priced. It fills up fast in the summer. Reservation number: (800) 644-8383;(520) 283-4545. Rates:double occupancy April-May $69; June-Oct. $89; Nov. - March $55; plus a 8.1 percent Navajo Lodging Tax and 6 percent Coconino County Sales Tax.

RV Park: Register at the Quality Inn. Full hook-ups, shower, bathroom, pay phone, laundry room, cable. $20 per night plus 10 percent tax.

Greyhills Inn: *Located on Warrior Drive off U.S. 160. Head northeast, take a left at the post office, then the first right, and the Inn office is through the gate on the left.* The academy converted one dormitory into a 32-room hostel for tourists. Most rooms have full beds or queen, some king beds available. Every room has a television. Dormitory style bathrooms. Prices are in the budget range, around $48 from May 1st to Oct.31st; $28 rest of year for two people. You can make reservations by calling the Grey Hills High School switchboard, (520) 283-6271, 24 hours, every day. Ask for the Inn. The Inn does not accept credit cards but they will hold your room until 7 p.m.

RESTAURANTS

Hogan Restaurant: Located next to the Quality Inn. Offers a lunch buffet, Mexican food and Navajo tacos. The menu is extensive. Open from 6 a.m.-9 p.m.(MST) summer; 7 a.m.-8 p.m. (MST) winter.

McDonald's: 6 a.m.-11 p.m. Sunday through Thursday; 6 a.m.-12 p.m. Friday and Saturday (DST)

Taco Bell: Open daily 7a.m-10 p.m. (DST)

Kate's Café: On Edgewater Street. Excellent specials, homemade soups, hamburgers. Open: 8:30 a.m.-8:45 p.m. (DST)

Kentucky Fried Chicken: Open daily 10 a.m.-10:30 p.m. (DST)

Dairy Queen: Open daily 10 a.m.-9:30 p.m. (DST)

Tuba City Truck Stop: Open daily 5:30 a.m.-11 p.m. (DST)

Bashas' Deli: Open 8 a.m.- 8 p.m. Monday through Saturday; 8 a.m.-8 p.m. Sunday. (DST)

FLEA MARKET: Every Friday from about 9 a.m.-3 p.m. on the north side of Hwy 160 next to Davis Chevrolet. You can get home–made mutton stew and fry bread and good prices on jewelry, Navajo pottery, herbs and unusual items.

GROCERIES: Bashas' is the major food store on the reservation. Prices are higher than off-reservation but they have a good selection of foods and an excellent produce section. Bashas' has stores in Tuba City, Chinle, Kayenta and Window Rock. Open 8 a.m.-10 p.m. Monday through Saturday, and 8 a.m.-8 p.m. on Sunday.

AUTOMOBILE SERVICES

Cal's Collison Repair and Front End Service:	(520) 283-5394
Davis Chevrolet Service Department:	(520) 283-6244
El Gran Wholesale Tires:	(520) 283-4622
Tuba City Motors Towing Service:	(520) 283-5330 Days; (520) 283-5300 Nights

BANKING SERVICES

Norwest Bank: *Located in the middle of the four-lane part of Main St., next to Kentucky Fried Chicken.* Open Monday -Thursday 9 a.m.-4 p.m.; Friday 9 a.m.-1 p.m. and 2 p.m.- 6 p.m. 24-hour Automatic Teller Machine.

TUBA CITY NAVAJO POLICE

Located on the east side of Main Street next to the tribal courthouse. (520) 283-3111. Jim Chee, Tony Hillerman's fictitious police officer, transferred to this station from Shiprock.

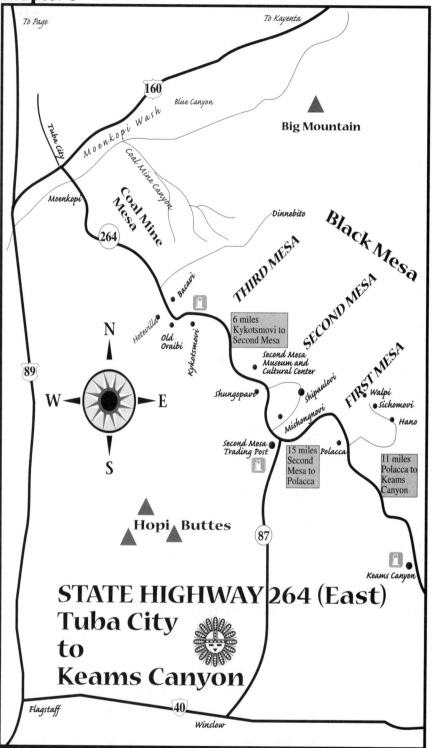

Chapter 8

To Page

To Kayenta

160

Blue Canyon

Tuba City

▲ **Big Mountain**

Moenkopi Wash

Coal Mine Canyon

Moenkopi

Dinnebito

Black Mesa

Coal Mine Mesa

264

THIRD MESA

SECOND MESA

Bacavi

6 miles
Kykotsmovi to
Second Mesa

89

Hotevilla

Old Oraibi

Kykotsmovi

Second Mesa
Museum and
Cultural Center

FIRST MESA

Shungopavi

Shipaulovi

Walpi

Sichomovi

N

W ⊕ **E**

Mishongnovi

Hano

S

Second Mesa
Trading Post

15 miles
Second
Mesa to
Polacca

Polacca

11 miles
Polacca to
Keams
Canyon

87

▲ **Hopi ▲ Buttes**

Keams Canyon

STATE HIGHWAY 264 (East)
Tuba City
to
Keams Canyon

Flagstaff

40

Winslow

160 miles (258 km) from Tuba City to Window Rock

The Hopi Nation stays on Mountain Standard Time throughout the year.

THE HOPI NATION

The Hopi (pronounced Ho pee) have always lived in the Four Corners area of the Colorado Plateau. Even though the legal boundary of today's reservation has confined them to a relatively small land mass in comparison to the Navajos', evidence of their influence via trading and clan symbols are found at the ruins of Betatakin, Keet Seel, Mesa Verde and as far east as Chaco Canyon.

The Hopis' aboriginal boundaries, or *tutsqua,* established by tradition and history, are Navajo Mountain to the north, down the Colorado River to Bill Williams Mountain to the west, over to the San Francisco Peaks or *Nuvatukya'ovi,* along the Mogollon Rim to the Zuni's Blue Lake for the southern boundary, and north to Canyon de Chelly and the Four Corners area for the eastern boundary. (Waters, 1960)

The Hopis emerged from the underworld through a *sipapu,* an opening, in the Grand Canyon. They came into this, the Fourth World, with the help of a small bird known as the shrike, which brought them into the world of light. Here they made their vow of righteous living to *Sootukwnangwu,* the Supreme Creator. *Maa'sau,* the guardian spirit over the land, told the Hopis that they were to serve as the earth's steward once their mandated four migrations to the north, south, east and west in search of *tuuwanasave,* or "earth center," had come to an end. According to legend, the Hopis traveled to the Aztec temples in Mexico, on into South America, north to the Arctic Circle and to the east and west coasts of the United States. The center point of the cross formed from their four directional routes is the Hopi mesas. This was the chosen place because it was a harsh environment where adherence to the laws of the Supreme Creator must be followed exactly to ensure the survival of the clans.

It is believed that the Bear Clan, *Honwungwa,* was the first to arrive on the remote, barren Hopi mesas. As the many different clans began to arrive from their migrations, the Bear Clan asked what they could contribute to the benefit of all of the Hopi people. Each clan contributed a different skill or ceremony to ensure the survival and prosperity of all people on earth.

One of the more important ceremonies contributed by the Bear Clan was the *Soyal*, an annual winter solstice ceremony. (Waters, 1963) The Greasewood clan of Apache descent gather sacred wood for ceremonies as their special contribution. (Berggren, 1995)

A sophisticated ceremonial calendar was developed and strictly adhered to. Specific holy men in each village continue to determine the timing of individual ceremonies by the position of the sun, making it difficult for outsiders to know exactly when a ceremony will take place.

Katsinas, or Kachinas as they are popularly called, are the very important spirit beings in Hopi cosmology who assure rain for the Hopis and all people on earth. The kachinas visit the Hopis and bring gifts. At the end of a dance, prayer feathers are given to the kachinas so that the prayers for rain and good things will be carried in all directions.

The Home Dance, or *Niman,* is the last kachina dance in the ceremonial calendar. This is when the kachinas leave the mesas to return to their home on the San Francisco Peaks. These dances are the way of communicating the Hopis' needs to the Supreme Creator. (McGibbeny, 1959)

Kachina dances are no longer always open to non-Hopis. For years, traders, and most recently tour companies, have brought tourists by the hundreds to view the ceremonies. But the villages

and ancient roof tops were not designed to handle large crowds. More seriously, visitors have violated the Hopis' rules about not photographing or videotaping anything in the villages. This has resulted in the posting of "closed" signs at the road entrance during a dance. Do not enter a village if you see one of these signs.

Each village has a number of kivas, or underground chambers, entered through a hole in the roof. Specific societies use the kiva for meditation, prayer and preparation for their own important ceremonies.

Antelope Kiva, Walpi, First Mesa, ca. 1904-1906
Jo Mora Collection, Cline Library, Special Collections and Archive, NAU 281.
Jo Mora was an artist who lived with the Hopis from 1904 to 1907. He learned their language and was permitted to photograph the Hopi villages, people and ceremonies.

The Hopis knew through prophesy that they would be visited someday by a strange and powerful people who would be their white brother, *pahaana.* Hopi legend explains that all people, including white people, came from the underworld with the Hopis. Their white brother became separated during the migrations but promised to return as the savior.

The Spanish were the first to visit the Hopis around 1540, led by gold-hungry Coronado. During this time, many Spanish adventurers sought the "Seven Golden Cities of Cibola." The legend tells of a bishop who, during the Moors invasion of Spain, escaped to the west on boats with more than 1,500 people. He allegedly established a community so lavish that its inhabitants used golden implements. (Granger, 1983)

After finding the Zuni villages in New Mexico not to be the fabled seven golden cities he sought, Coronado sent Don Pedro de Tovar to investigate the Hopi villages. Indian informants had described a golden land where the Hopis lived. Coronado, not realizing that Indians had never seen gold, took their description literally. Perhaps what Coronado actually heard was a description of the yellow pottery made in the Jeddito area. (James, 1994; Malotki, 1993)

To recoup the expense of their expedition to this new country, the Spanish saw value in making the Hopi people slaves and converting them to Christianity. Franciscan monks descended upon the Hopi villages and began to build churches, often right over sacred springs and shrines. One was believed to have been built over a kiva. In addition to enslaving the Hopi people, the Spanish almost wiped them out with an epidemic of smallpox in 1634. Within a few years, 7,000 Hopis — three quarters of the entire tribe — would be dead from this disease.

It wasn't long before the Hopis realized this was not the prophesied white savior. Tired of subjugation by the Spanish, and to protect their own beliefs and spiritual practices, all of the pueblo villages along the Rio Grande joined with the Zunis and Hopis in 1680 to secretly rise up and forcefully expel the Spanish from their land. Missionaries were killed and their churches destroyed. Totally beaten, the Spanish withdrew. Yet it was only a short 21 years after the Pueblo Revolt that, in 1701, the Spanish returned to Hopi land to establish another mission at Awat'ovi, intent on their goal to "convert the pagans." (Today this village is in ruins.)

Again, to the traditional majority, this encroachment on Hopi life and beliefs was intolerable. In 1703, the Hopi villages conspired to destroy the Franciscan monks and converted Hopi men living in Awat'ovi. The women and children were dispersed to other villages.

NATIVE ROADS

In 1810, the Mexicans fought the Spanish for independence and won, ending Spanish domination of this area. This transfer of power placed the Hopis under Mexican rule but Mexico was unable to protect the Hopis from constant and damaging attacks by Navajo, Apache and Ute raiders. With the signing of the Treaty of Guadelupe de Hidalgo in 1840 between Mexico and the United States, the Hopis fell under the jurisdiction of the United States. In 1882, President Chester A. Arthur signed an executive order to create a 2.5-million-acre (10,156 sq km) Hopi reservation. But the new reservation boundaries took into consideration neither the Hopis' traditional use of the surrounding land nor the geography of the region.

Although the founders of the U.S. Constitution believed in the concept of religious freedom, they were thinking of Christian values, not centuries-old Native American religions and cultures. Government officials believed it was their responsibility to impart to the Indians the blessing of civilization. To do this, the Grant Peace Policy was passed in 1869 to allow the Office of Indian Affairs to facilitate placement of ministers among the Indians. Christian missionaries of all denominations began to arrive in Indian country but the ones to have the most impact on the Hopi people were the Mennonites and The Church of Jesus Christ of Latter Day Saints, or the Mormons.

In 1830, *The Book of Mormon* was published. God had revealed to Joseph Smith, founder of the religion, that American Indians were the lost tribe of Israel which traveled from Palestine only 600 years prior to his revelation. For neglecting the true religion, Smith believed Indians, whom he called "Lamanites," were cursed with dark skin. If the Indians could hear the word of God and convert to Mormonism, their dark skin would become "white and delightsome" and their transgressions in the past would be forgiven.

RULES ABOUT VISITING VILLAGES
1. Disruption of shrines or removal of articles is not allowed. All archaeological sites located on the Hopi Reservation are protected by federal law and Hopi tribal ordinance.
2. Photographing, recording and sketching villages and ceremonies is strictly prohibited.
3. Overnight camping is allowed for a maximum of two nights at designated camping areas only.
4. Alcoholic beverages and drugs are strictly prohibited.
5. Before spending any length of time in any village, permission should be obtained from the village leader.

6. Each village is autonomous and has the authority to establish its own governing policies supported by the Hopi Tribal Council. It is advisable to check with village community development offices before going into the village to visit or watch a ceremony.

ATTENDING A HOPI CEREMONY

All Hopi ceremonies are highly spiritual in content and should be viewed and respected as such. Dance participants are required to prepare extensively to accomplish the spiritual mission of the ceremony. Likewise, spectators are expected to provide their heartfelt prayers during the public viewing. In this way the collective positive energy will benefit all of the people on earth.

Dress is important and visitors should pay attention to this detail because of your important role in the success of the ceremony. Men should wear long pants and shirts. Women should wear clothing that completely covers the body. Hats and umbrellas are discouraged. During the ceremony do not ask questions or discuss the events. Do not follow the kachinas or ceremonial participants out of the plaza. Choose a place to observe the ceremony and do not walk around the plaza or the village.

MOENKOPI VILLAGE Hopi: *Munqapi*

(Head east on Hwy. 264 about one mile.) When Mormon explorer Jacob Hamblin met the Hopis in 1858, there was no permanent village here. Hopis gradually built the village beginning around 1870. Hopi farmers from the village of Oraibi, more than 30 miles (48 km) away by trail, managed large cotton farms in the very fertile Moenkopi Wash Canyon, running several times a week from home to their fields.

In 1879, Hamblin met Tuuvi, the Oraibi chief of the Water and Corn Clans, farming at Moenkopi. They developed a close relationship which eventually led to the establishment of the first Mormon colony at Moenave, eight miles farther west.

Hopi Weaver, ca. 1913-1934
Leo Crane Collection, Cline Library, Special Collections and Archives, NAU PH 658.220

Tuuvi and his wife, Katsinmana, agreed to be Hamblin's guests in Utah for a year to learn about the Mormon way of farming and religion. The Mormons' high speed loom greatly impressed Tuuvi.

Brigham Young's son, John, probably encouraged by Tuuvi's impression of the looms, built a woolen mill at Moenkopi. But the Hopi weavers, who had woven cotton on hand looms for generations, were not interested in a new vocation.

On the south side of Highway 264, overlooking Moenkopi, is a Arizona historical marker placed here in 1957 by the Arizona Economic Development Board. Although the face-piece is missing it should say: *"Near here in 1879 Mormon colonists built Arizona's first Woolen Mill. Hoping to utilize Hopi and Navajo wool and labor, the Mormons intended to build a new industry to supply the early settlers. The 192-spindle mill operated only a short time, its abandonment signaling failure of the missionary movement among the Hopi."* (Fireman, 1957) The last statement may be true but technically the Mormons were forced to abandoned the mill in 1903 because of the government's demand that they leave the newly–expanded Navajo reservation. (Barnes, 1960)

One of Hamblin's original reasons for developing a relationship with the Hopis was to encourage them to move north of the Colorado River. Brigham Young thought that friendly Indians could serve as a buffer against more hostile groups like the Utes and the Navajos. Speculation is that Hamblin strongly encouraged the development of a permanent Hopi settlement in Moenkopi for the same reason; to provide protection to the Tuba City Mormon settlement.

Present day Moenkopi actually consists of two villages. Upper Moenkopi is the more modern, built around the Bureau of Indian Affairs Day School, and Lower Moenkopi is more traditional in its lifestyle.

Moenkopi Community Development Office: (520) 283-6684.
Office Hours: 8 a.m.-5 p.m. Monday through Friday. Closed weekends.

 MM 324.5 MOENKOPI WASH

Moenkopi Wash is one of five washes that drain Black Mesa. This major drainage, made primarily of Chinle Sandstone, forms the lower section of Blue Canyon. An older name for this wash, found on the Domínguez-Escalante map of 1776, is *Cosonias*. Cosonias was the Hopi word for the Havasupai Indians who lived in the area prior to losing their land rights after the expansion of the Navajo Reservation in 1903. (Barnes, 1960)

 MM 336.5 COAL MINE CANYON (North)

Head north on the dirt road leading to the windmill, right beside the rodeo grounds. This magnificent canyon is easily missed if you don't have the right map or are looking the wrong way as you drive by. It's known to the Navajo as *hááhonoojí*, meaning "jagged," which describes the erosion patterns in the canyon. Its top layer is Dakota Sandstone overlying Cow Springs Sandstone.

Coal Mine Canyon
Photograph by Christine Stephenson

NATIVE ROADS

Everyone in the local communities of Tuba City and the Hopi villages know about the existence of the canyon ghost seen only during a full moon. In an article in *Outdoor Arizona*, the author tells the story of a ghost figure named *Quayowuuti,* or Eagle Woman, from Old Oraibi. She allegedly became mentally ill and wandered away from the village on the path to Moenkopi. Along the way, she stopped to rest on the rim of the canyon and decided to end it all. Ever since, when the conditions are just right, her spirit will appear during the full moon.

The Mormons began to mine coal here in the late 1800s to heat their new homes in Tuba City. After the Bureau of Indian Affairs built the boarding

school, the old coal mine was reopened around 1908 to fuel the steam generators to heat the entire complex. Because of the poor quality of the coal, however, it was never mined commercially, saving this beautiful canyon from the removal of its more than eight feet (2.4 m) of coal. (Anderson, 1958)

Entrance to a coal mine at Coal Mine Canyon, ca. 1918-1920.
Marie Olson Collection, Cline Library, Special Collections and Archives, NAU PH 516-17

Coal Mine Canyon turns into Blue Canyon along the Moenkopi Wash heading east toward Red Lake on U.S. Highway 160.

Blue Canyon, 1927
Philip Johnston Collection, Cline Library, Special Collections and Archives, NAU, 413-53

REGIONAL RUG DESIGN-COAL MINE

In the 1970s, Dr. Ned Hatathli, once the manager of the Navajo Arts and Crafts Guild, who later became the first president of Navajo Community College, encouraged weavers to add threads to outline the geometric designs in their rugs. Unfortunately, many important weavers of the Coal Mine Mesa area have relocated because they were on the wrong side of the 1979 boundary separating the Navajo and Hopi reservations. (See MM 362)

MM 344 COAL MINE CHAPTER

This is one of 110 community units, called chapters, that govern local matters on the Navajo Reservation. Hours: 8 a.m.-5 p.m. Monday through Friday.

MM 350 PANORAMIC VIEW

If you are heading east look straight ahead. In your line of vision, from left to right is Preston Mesa, White Mesa, Wildcat Butte and Navajo Mountain. See Chapter Ten for more information on these geologic features.

MM 362 TO DINNEBITO (North)

In Navajo, *diné bitó* means "Navajo water." This community got its name because of the many springs that are fed from Third Mesa on the east and from the Moenkopi Plateau on the west, making this a prime agricultural and grazing area. The famous Navajo leader, Narbona, moved his family here from the Chuska Mountains sometime during the severe drought of 1820. He successfully farmed side by side with the Hopis for nine years. Two of his sons and one daughter married Hopis. When the drought lifted, he moved his family back to their ancestral home in the Chuska Mountains. See Chapter 18 for more information about Narbona. (Newcomb, 1964)

Big Mountain

About 20 miles (32 km) north of the Dinnebito Trading Post on an unimproved dirt road is the sacred and controversial Big Mountain. This area has long symbolized Navajo resistance to federally-mandated relocation resulting from the Navajo-Hopi land dispute and the 1974 Navajo-Hopi Relocation Act.

In 1882, when President Chester A. Arthur set aside 2.5 million acres (10,156 sq km) of land for the Hopi Reservation, he used the words stipulating that the new reservation was for the Hopis "and such other Indians as the Secretary of Interior sees fit to settle thereon." Prior to that, and following their release from imprisonment in 1868, Navajos migrated into the area looking for good grazing land and were residing there when the land became part of the Hopi Reservation.

However, after a century, the Hopis were increasingly unhappy with what they saw as encroachment onto their land. In 1958, the federal government authorized a lawsuit between the tribes to determine which one actually held title to the land. The 1962 case of *Healing vs. Jones* created the Navajo-Hopi Joint Use Area, popularly known as the JUA. It gave the Hopis exclusive rights to the District Six grazing area surrounding their villages. But because the Hopis alleged that the Navajos still would not allow them to use the land, they took the situation to Congress for resolution.

In 1974, the Hopis succeeded in getting Congress to pass P.L. 93-531, the Navajo-Hopi Relocation Act. Ultimately, the law called for the division of the former JUA, leaving each tribe with 911,000 acres (3,701 sq km) of the land. It also called for the removal of families living on the other tribe's land, meaning the relocation of some 12,000 Navajos and 100 Hopis.

Since the beginning of this tribal land dispute (which most authorities now agree was created and exacerbated by the federal government), there has been Navajo resistance to the law and relocation. Today, about 250 Navajos continue to resist and in 1989, these Navajos — independent of the Navajo Nation — filed a First Amendment religious freedom lawsuit, arguing that forced relocation impinged on their right to practice their traditional, land-based religion. The case was dismissed by a federal district court but, on appeal, the Ninth Circuit Court of Appeals ordered one last round of mediation, which has lasted more than two years.

THIRD MESA

Because early explorers entered the Hopi villages from the east, the mesa sitting on the southernmost tip of Black Mesa became First Mesa with Second and Third Mesa following.

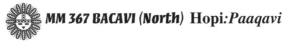

MM 367 BACAVI (North) Hopi:*Paaqavi*

(For visitors traveling east, skip ahead and read about Old Oraibi (MM 371) first, then Hotevilla (MM367.25) then Bacavi to better understand the history behind the founding of these three villages.) In Hopi *Paaqavi* means "place of the jointed reed." While "hostile" leader Yukioma of Hotevilla was imprisoned at Fort Wingate, his people suffered terribly from lack of food. The first winter was particularly difficult. Hoping for reconciliation, a small group returned to Oraibi but were no longer welcome. In 1907, this displaced group started the community of Bacavi.

Even though the founders of this village were considered hostile to the U.S. government, they did consent to a BIA Day School, built here in 1911, and allowed the Mennonite church to build a mission in 1916. For a complete history of the founding of Bacavi, read *Bacavi: Journey to Reed Springs* by Peter Whiteley.

Community Development Office: (520) 734-2404. Office Hours: 8 a.m.- 5 p.m., Monday through Friday. Closed weekends.

Corn Planter from Bacavi Village, ca. 1914
Leo Crane Collection, Cline Library, Special Collections and Archives, NAU PH 658.309
Leo Crane was Indian Agent at Keams Canyon beginning in 1911.

MM 367.25 HOTEVILLA (South) Hopi: *Hotvela*

A common translation for Hotevilla is, *hota,* "a back" and *veli*, "to peel," referring to villagers frequently scraping their backs upon entering or leaving the low cave where the spring was located. But according to a longtime residents, this is an old joke told by Second Mesa people about Hotevilla. The village name actually comes from *hotski* meaning "cedar tree" and *atpela,* or "slope." This location had both cedar wood for fuel as well as a spring making it a good site for Yukioma's displaced group.

Founded in 1906, Hotevilla became the refuge for Yukioma and his followers after his defeat in a pushing match at Old Oraibi with "friendlies." This was the name given to Hopis who accepted and worked with the Indian Service. Yukioma was the leader of a faction known as "hostiles" who wanted no services provided by the United States and resisted all intervention from the Indian Service and missionaries into the Hopi way of life. After the scuffle, Yukioma was arrested by the military and imprisoned at Fort Wingate. This led to a great deal of hardship for his people in their new home. (James, 1974)

Community Development Office: (520) 734-2420
Office Hours: 8 a.m.- 5 p.m. Monday through Friday. Closed weekends.

 MM 371 OLD ORAIBI (South) Hopi:*Orayvi*

Orayvi means place of the Oray Rock, and to the people of Third Mesa this is *Tuwanasavi*, or "earth's center." Although contested by some villages, Oraibi is considered the oldest, continuously-inhabited village in the United States. The logs used to build many of the homes are from 1260 to 1344 A.D. according to tree-ring dating. It is thought that the logs came from the San Francisco Peaks, more than 100 miles (160 km) away. You may walk through the ancient streets but cannot go past the old village where the ruins of a church stand.

Loololma was one of the strongest Hopis against the U.S. government and missionary transgression in Oraibi. In 1880, he opposed Hopi children attending government schools, and wanted Hopis to live their lives as the Creator instructed them to live. Somehow, Thomas Keam, then the Indian agent, persuaded Loololma to visit Washington as his guest. When Loololma returned, his opinion had completely changed. When asked why, he said he saw that there were so many white people. Like "disturbing an ant hill," he believed that the Hopis had no choice but to cooperate with the government. (Whiteley, 1988)

Lomahongyoma, another powerful member of Old Oraibi, disagreed with Loololma's conversion. This led to a severe split between the Bear and the Spider Clans in 1906. When Loololma died, Tawaquaptewa became chief and was like-minded in believing that it was possible to allow children to attend government schools while maintaining Hopi spiritual life. To end the increasing hostility between the "friendlies" (people cooperative with the government) and the "hostiles" (people opposed to the government), Tawaquaptewa ordered the hostiles to leave. He further demanded that the families from Shungopavi who moved to Oraibi in support of the hostiles also leave.

Yukioma, ca. 1913

Leo Crane Collection, Cline Library, Special Collections and Archives, NAU PH 658.299

Lomahongyoma had turned the responsibility of leading the hostiles over to Yukioma who challenged Chief Tawaquaptewa to a contest. Yukioma drew a line in the sand and the chiefs' men were to push him over it. If they could, Yukioma and his followers agreed to leave the village. Placing their hands on each other's shoulders, with their individual faction members pushing from behind Yukioma went on to lose the fight. As he had promised, he moved his group to the mesa near the spring known as Hotevilla.

Inscribed in sandstone below the village is a recording of the event. It reads:

> Well it have to be this way not,
> pass me over this LINE
> it will be DONE.
> Spt. 8, 1906

MM 372 PUMPKIN SEED POINT (North)

A great place to stop for a picnic and enjoy the tremendous view of the Hopi Buttes. (See page 142 for a discussion of the Hopi Buttes.)

MM 373 KYKOTSMOVI (New Oraibi) Hopi: *Kiqotsmovi*

This is the location of the modern Hopi government. The modern-day politics and bureaucracy that the Bureau of Indian Affairs brought to the "People of Peace" has been a constant source of irritation between villages and clans. Hopis do not differentiate between life and religion. Their sole purpose and the source of their strength is found in the adherence to centuries-old teachings and a plan for life. To this end, each village traditionally has a *kikmongwi*, or "father of the people," who makes decisions for his village based on prayer and meditation.

Hoping to modernize the relationship tribes had with the federal government, Congress passed the Indian Reorganization Act in 1934. Two years later, the commissioner of Indian Affairs, John Collier, decided that all tribes must have a tribal council. He believed this would help bring about changes in the administration and treatment of Indians under the BIA. Oliver LaFarge, an anthropologist and Pulitzer Prize-winning author of the novel *Laughing Boy*, was an advisor to Collier. He was responsible for writing the Hopi Constitution and Bylaws. The constitution stated that village chiefs were allowed to certify their village's representatives to the tribal council and that the spiritual leaders would be consulted on important matters. This process did not work as well as it sounded on paper. The Hopis abandoned the first tribal council in 1943.

In 1951, the Hopis began their fight for land with the federal government. To proceed with the case, the government would recognize only one representative of the Hopi people and that would have to be the tribal council. (Matthiessen, 1984)

The Mennonite Church has had a strong presence in this community since Henrich R. Voth built a chapel sometime around 1901 on a path to the "Kachina Resting Place Point." This, of course, upset many Hopis but Voth claimed he had permission to build on the site from the kikmongwi. Interestingly, the church was struck by lightning, not once but twice. (Whiteley, 1988)

The Mennonites were a German religious group that emigrated to Russia in 1786 to practice their religion freely. But in 1874 they left Russia for the United States and joined the established Mennonite congregation already living in Newton, Kan. In 1892, Henrich Voth and his wife traveled to Hopi land. Although very helpful to the Hopis during a severe measles epidemic and supportive of the hostiles' effort to maintain their tradition, the Hopis don't remember him warmly. Voth actively recorded and disseminated sacred and secret knowledge about ceremonies and displayed this information along with religious artifacts in museums. According to anthropologist Peter Whiteley, Voth went so far as to display an important religious altar in the Hopi House at the Grand Canyon. (Whiteley, 1988)

Community Development Office: (520) 734-2474. Office Hours: 8 a.m. - 5 p.m. Monday through Friday. Closed weekends.

The **Kykotsmovi Village Store** for many years was part of the Babbitt Bros. Trading Co. Recently, the village chose not to renew the trading company's lease and decided to operate the store themselves.
Open 8:00 a.m. to 6:00 p.m. (MST).

MM 373.5 ORAIBI WASH PICNIC AREA (North)

SECOND MESA

At an elevation of 6,000 feet (1,829 m), this mesa divides into two distinct sections. To the east, are the villages of Shipaulovi and Mishongnovi. To the west is the village of Shungopavi. Artists living on this mesa are well-known for their coiled baskets, kachina dolls and overlay jewelry.

 ## MM 375 HOPI COOPERATIVE GUILD (North)

Fred Kabotie, the famous artist from Shungopavi, started the guild. He is known for painting the Hopi Room in the watchtower at Desert View in the Grand Canyon and three murals at the Painted Desert Inn. More than 300 Hopi artists display their handcrafted items at the guild and Hopi silversmiths work on-site. Open 8 a.m. - 5 p.m. (MST) every day.

MM 379.5 HOPI CULTURAL CENTER AND MUSEUM (North)

The cultural center is a non-profit corporation with the goal to present accurate cultural and historical information to visitors traveling through Hopi country. It contains shops and one of the three restaurants on the reservation. Open from 8 a.m. - 5 p.m. Monday through Friday; Saturday 9 a.m.-3 p.m. Admission $3.00 adults; $1:00 children ages 1-13. (520) 734-6650.

To Hopis, no food is as important as corn, or *Qaa'o*. Not only is it a dietary staple, its role in Hopis spiritual life is incalculable. To the Hopi, corn *is* life. Every special event has corn associated with it. A perfect ear of white corn represents the spiritual mother of a newborn. At death, a cornmeal path leads the spirit of the deceased to its new home.

Hopi elder with grandchild, ca. 1930s
Fred Harvey Collection, Museum of Northern Arizona MS 301-5-118

WHAT IS PIIKI? You will have the opportunity to buy piki, or *piiki*, bread throughout your travels on the Hopi reservation, usually for about $2 a roll. Try it. It's an ancient food that Hopi women have made for centuries. First, boiled water is mixed with blue corn flour and a small amount of juniper ash or saltbush ash (to enrich the color). A flat, seasoned stone is heated hot enough to burn the hand. Melon seeds are spread on the stone and their oil is allowed to bake in. Then batter is spread lightly on the stone with fingers, baking very quickly. Several tissue-thin sheets are made this way and then rolled and stacked.

Hopi Cultural Center Motel: One of only two motels on the reservation, this lodge has 33 rooms and fills up quickly in summer. For reservations call (520) 734-2401. While here, try the blue corn pancakes and *noqkwivi*, traditional Hopi stew with lamb and corn. The restaurant also makes a very good Hopi taco, much the same as its Navajo counterpart. Open from 7 a.m. - 9 p.m. (MST)

Dominquez-Escalante Trail Marker

Located in the parking lot of the Second Mesa Cultural Center, this marker commemorates the trail that Sylvester Vélez de Escalante and Francisco Atanasio Domínguez took in 1776 in their attempt to find a route from Santa Fe, N.M., to Monterey, Calif. (See pages 76-78 for more on this famous expedition.)

TSAKURSHOVI STORE

Located 1.5 miles (2.4 km) east of the Hopi Cultural Center on Highway 264. This small but interesting store belongs to Janice and Joseph Day. It could be one of the more educational stores you will visit on your travels. Because the Days supply Hopis with traditional items needed for their ceremonies, you will have an opportunity to see handmade rattles, turtle shells, fox furs, moccasins, herbs, sweet grass and other paraphernalia needed by ceremonial participants. The concept of selling or trading completed items to dancers is not a new one. No one was able to make every required item or trap every animal skin needed for a particular ceremony. Specialists developed to supply different items and this practice continues today.

MM 381.5 SHUNGOPAVI Hopi:*Songoopavi*

In Hopi, *songoopavi* means "sand grass spring place." It was named for a nearby spring. By tradition, "Old Shungopavi" is the oldest village, established by the Bear Clan; the first clan to arrive on the Hopi mesas after the peoples' migrations. The older village is at the base of the mesa, where more than 2,000 people lived until fear of retribution from the Pueblo Revolt of 1680 caused them to move the village to the mesa top.

Tourists may not attend ceremonies at this village without an invitation or as a guest of one of the residents.

Community Development Office: (520) 734-2570. Office Hours: 8 a.m.-5 p.m., Monday through Friday. Closed weekends.

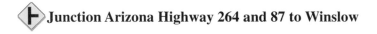 **Road to Second Mesa Villages**

Turn north by the Texaco station across the street from the Second Mesa Day School.

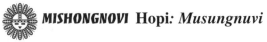 **MISHONGNOVI** Hopi: *Musungnuvi*

The Crow Clan came to the Hopi mesas looking for refuge. Their contribution was to be guardian of the sacred Corn Rock for the people of Shungopavi. (Barnes, 1960; Waters, 1963; Nequatewa, 1967)

Community Development Office: (520) 737-2520. Office Hours: 8 a.m.-5 p.m., Monday through Friday. Closed weekends.

Mishongnovi is the home village of Tony Hillerman's fictitious character Officer Cowboy Dashee of the Hopi Tribal Police. He is a character in *Sacred Clowns*, *Dark Wind* and *Talking God*.

 **SHIPAULOVI** Hopi:*Supawlavi*

Supawlavi means "place of the mosquitoes." This name stuck when villagers fled Homol'ovi to escape the mosquitoes. Homol'ovi refers to the area around Winslow on the Little Colorado River. See page 255-256 for information about Homolovi Ruins State Park. (Van Valkenburgh, 1941) As you enter the village, on the west side of the main road there is an old abandoned store before you go farther up the mesa. This is the original Secakuku Trading Post. The same family owns a modern trading post at the junction of Highways 264 and 87. *Continuing on past the trading post will take you back to the Second Mesa Cultural Center.*

Junction Arizona Highway 264 and 87 to Winslow

SEKAKUKU TRADING POST (South)

Hours: 8:00a.m.-8:00p.m. (MST) Summer
        8:00a.m.-7:00p.m. (MST) Winter

FIRST MESA

Artists on First Mesa are known for their pottery, kachina dolls and weavings. If you wish to visit the First Mesa villages, you must stop at Ponsi Hall at the top of the mesa on the right, at the end of the road. Tours of Walpi are offered Monday through Friday, 9:30 a.m. - 4 p.m. The tours are free but donations are welcomed. This is the only mesa that offers tours. (520) 737-2262.

MM 392 POLACCA

Tom Polacca, a Tewa and former resident of Hano, started this village in 1890. Encouraged by Polacca's move and looking for ways to disrupt the Hopis' ceremonial life, the Indian Service tried to lure people down off the mesa by building individual houses by the day school. Completed in 1900, no one wanted to move into the homes. By 1935, only seven percent of the residents of First Mesa lived in Polacca. (Van Valkenburgh, 1941) Today, the residents of Polacca have maintained their affiliation to political and ceremonial activities on First Mesa.

Hopi Polewyma Travel and Tours: A great way to visit the Hopi Nation and meet many of the artists and crafts people is with a Hopi tour guide. Contact Hopi Polewyma Travel and Tours, P.O. Box 210, Polacca, AZ 86042. Phone/Fax (520) 525-9490.

MM 392 Road to First Mesa Villages (North)

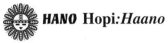

HANO Hopi:*Haano*

This is the first village you will drive through when climbing up the steep road to Walpi. Hano is a Tewa village, established by people who came from the Rio Grande area near Albuquerque after the Pueblo Revolt of 1680. As was customary, each arriving clan was asked by the Bear Clan what they could contribute to the good of the people. To this the Tewas of Hano contributed their ability to be guardians of First Mesa.

Nampeyo firing pots, ca. 1904-1906 with E.A. Burbank looking on.
Jo Mora Collection, Cline Library, Special Collections and Archives, NAU PH 86.1.463
(E.A. Burbank was an artist who painted the rug designs for Lorenzo Hubbell that hang in his home in Ganado. See page 149.)

Hano was the home of the famous potter **Nampeyo**, born in 1860. She developed her world-renowned pottery after two anthropologists, J.W. Fewkes and F.W. Dodge from the Smithsonian Institute, excavated Sikyatki, a ruin on First Mesa. Nampeyo used the ancient pot shards they brought to her as a guide for her geometric designs, maintaining the ancient techniques that developed into a pottery style known as the Sikyatki Revival. (Van Valkenburg, 1941)

Nampeyo became so popular that Fred Harvey commissioned her to perform pottery exhibitions at the Grand Canyon. As her fame spread, she traveled on the newly-completed Santa Fe Railroad to the Chicago Railway Exhibition, and even to the east coast to display her skills. Over the years she became blind but taught her daughters how to copy her intricate earth tone designs. This skill has passed from one generation of the Nampeyo family to the next, making it possible for you to still buy a Nampeyo pot. (Waters, 1960)

Nampeyo Pot, purchased by the Babbitt family in the early 1920s.
Museum of Northern Arizona Photo Archives, #10098

Hano is also famous for hand-coiled pottery. You may stop at homes with "Pottery For Sale" signs to buy these beautiful pieces directly from the potter.

Traditional Hopi pottery is not fired in a kiln but hand-fired over an open fire of sheep dung or coal, as was the custom at Awat'ovi in prehistoric times. (Berggren, 1995) You can tell the difference between open fire and kiln pottery. Kiln pottery has a more consistent coloring than the hand-fired pot.

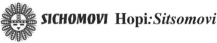 **SICHOMOVI** Hopi:*Sitsomovi*

This means "place of the mounds where wild currants grow." Located between Walpi and Hano, members of Walpi founded Sichomovi in 1750. The village has running water, electricity and garbage pickup. At the end of the road is **Ponsi Hall** where you can make arrangements for tours of Walpi.

Your chances of being allowed to visit Walpi on a Saturday or Sunday are minimal in summer, the busiest time of the Hopi ceremonial calendar. Tourists may not attend these ceremonies without an invitation as a guest of one of the local villagers. **Ponsi Hall**: Tours of Walpi Monday through Friday 9:30 a.m. - 4 p.m. (520) 737-2262.

First Mesa Community Development Office: (520) 737-2670. Office Hours: 8 a.m. - 5 p.m., Monday through Friday. Closed on weekends.

WALPI

Walpi, ca. 1930s
Fred Harvey Collection, Museum of Northern Arizona Photo Archives, MS 301-3-160

Walpi means "the gap," referring to the opening in the mesa just below Hano. The village sits on the narrowest part of the mesa and is only 150 feet (46 m) across at its widest point. Just below this village on the northwest side of the mesa is the original village of Old Walpi where the Hopis lived until they moved their village to the top of the mesa. They did this because they feared Spanish retribution after the 1680 Pueblo uprising. There is a ruin of a small catholic mission, built during the Franciscan period, near the old village but it is off-limit to tourists.

On your tour of Walpi, you may notice the **Hopi Buttes** far off in the southern distance. They are located 40 miles (64 km) away near Dilkon on the Navajo Reservation. In the 1900s, these buttes were known as the Moqui Buttes. The Hopis were forced to suffer with the name *moqui,* given to them by the Spanish and carried on by the Indian Service as their official tribal name. To the Hopi, it was an insult to be called moqui, meaning "dead" in their language. The name stuck until the tribe officially petitioned the government to change their name back to Hopi, meaning "peaceful people" or "people who live in the proper way."

MM 396.5 Hopi Police Station and Junior-Senior High School (South)

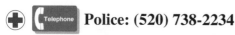 **Police: (520) 738-2234**

COAL MINES: There are two abandoned coal mines along this road before Keams Canyon. Hopis have mined coal from Black Mesa since 900 A.D. Well-known for its vast deposits, the first mine may have been in the Jeddito Valley. It is estimated that the Hopis mined as much as 450 pounds (204 kg) of coal a day until the 1700s. When the Bureau of Indian Affairs began building boarding schools, the method of choice for heat was steam produced by coal-burning generators.

 ## MM 403.5 KEAMS CANYON

This remains a government town, named after Thomas Keam, a former trader and Indian agent. Before 1860 it was known as Peach Orchard Springs. To the Hopi, this natural oasis, is called *Pongsikya*

After the Navajos signed a treaty with the Spanish in 1819, they began to settle in Hopi territory. Prior to this, there had been a long history of conflicts between Hopi farmers and some Navajo clans, although the Navajos gave many Pueblo refugees safe haven from Spanish cruelty over the years.

Nonetheless, in 1863 when the United States decided that the Navajos were causing too much trouble for white settlers and Hopi, they sent in the Army. Col. Kit Carson, with the aid of 100 Hopi, Utes and white volunteers from New Mexico waged a fierce and cruel campaign to force the Navajos to surrender and remove them from the area.

Carson assembled his legion in Peach Orchard Springs, or Volunteer Canyon as he referred to it. Scored on the canyon wall behind the BIA Agency building is an inscription that reads: "1st Reg't N.M. Vol's., Aug 13, 1863, Col. C. Carson, Comm."

Kit Carson Inscription, 1863
Philip Johnston Collection, Cline Library, Special Collections and Archives, NAU PH 413-1225

Thomas Keam was born in England and came to this country around 1861. He rode with Gen. James Carleton and was one of the soldiers in charge of the Navajos' Long Walk to Bosque Redondo. While in Indian territory, he learned to speak both Navajo and Hopi fluently and worked in Fort Defiance as an interpreter after his discharge from the army. It was here he met and married his Navajo wife, Grey Woman, in a traditional Navajo ceremony.

In 1872, Keam became temporary special agent to the Navajos and developed the first Navajo police force with Chief Manuelito as its head. A year

later, the permanent special agent arrived and Keam went back to England to visit his sick mother. Sometime during his year–long absence, Grey Woman, thinking that Keam was not coming back, married another man.

When he did return, he moved to Peach Orchard Springs and opened Keam's Tusayan Trading Post. In 1886, the government bought his property for $1,500 to build the new BIA Boarding School. Keam moved his trading post to the mouth of the canyon where the Keams Canyon Shopping Center stands today.

Thomas Keam, not dated.
Portrait by Prince Artistic Portraits, Washington, D.C
Museum of Northern Arizona, Photo Archives, 68.1188

In 1899, Keam started to experience real trouble from the new BIA superintendent, Charles Burton. Burton demanded that the Hopi ceremonial dances stop, that Hopi children cut their long hair and that all children attend boarding school even if it required the use of force.

Keam publicly disagreed with Burton's beliefs and practices. This caused Burton to retaliate by charging Keam with defrauding the government in the sale of his property and for allowing gambling at his trading post. Burton also disliked Keam's marriage to a Navajo woman. Keam could not stand the allegations any longer and traveled to Washington to answer the charges where he was found innocent. Now Burton's style of management was in the spotlight. Along with Keam, many Hopi people complained

about Burton's cruel treatment resulting in his removal from office.

Emotionally damaged by this episode, Keam decided his days as a trader were over. He sold his post to Lorenzo Hubbell in 1902 and went back to England where he died two years later. (Bailey, 1961)

Hubbell's Trading Post, Keams Canyon, ca. 1920
Leo Crane Collection, Cline Library, Special Collections and Archives, NAU PH 658-98

SERVICES IN KEAMS CANYON

Motel: Newly-remodeled but a basic motel with two double beds, bath with shower, TV, no telephones. Open year-round. (520) 738-2297.
Restaurant: Monday through Friday 6:30 a.m. to 8:30 p.m. (MST); Saturday and Sunday 7 a.m. to 6:30 p.m.. Closed on Sunday in the winter.
Union 76 Gas Station: The only gas station and the only available pay phone. Open 7 a.m. to 8 p.m. (MST)

✚ KEAMS CANYON INDIAN HEALTH SERVICE HOSPITAL

Follow the signs to Keams Canyon, the hospital is located at the end of the canyon. It is operated by the Phoenix Area Indian Health Service. Non-Indians may be seen here on an emergency basis only. **Telephone: (520) 738-2211.**

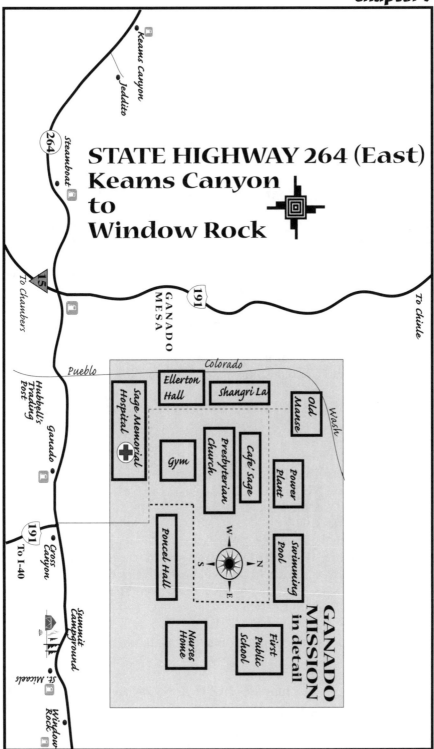

Chapter 9

STATE HIGHWAY 264 (East)
Keams Canyon
to
Window Rock

Keams Canyon

Jeddito

264

Steamboat

15

To Chambers

191

GANADO MESA

To Chinle

Pueblo

Hubbell's Trading Post

Ganado

191

To I-40

Cross Canyon

Summit Campground

St. Micaels

Window Rock

Colorado

Ellerton Hall

Shangri La

Old Manse

Wash

Sage Memorial Hospital

Gym

Presbyterian Church

Café Sage

Power Plant

Poncel Hall

Swimming Pool

W

S

N

E

Nurses Home

First Public School

GANADO MISSION in detail

70 miles (113 km) from Keams Canyon to Window Rock

MM 407.5 JEDDITO SCHOOL (North)

An Arizona state public school with headquarters in Holbrook.

Entering the Navajo Nation, change to DST from April through October.

MM 427.5 STEAMBOAT CANYON (North)

About one mile (1.6 km) from this community, on the north side of Highway 264, is a sandstone formation that looks like a steamboat, hence the name. This area was actually a very important watering place to the Navajos who call it *Tóyéé* or "scarce water." The Hopis stopped at this spring for water on their journey to the Zuni Salt Lake near St. Johns, Ariz.

The Spanish came through here on their many incursions into Hopi land and called this area *"La Mesa de las Vacas," or* "the mesa of the cattle." On one of the canyon walls is the inscription:
"A 20 Abril, Ano de 1666. P de Montoya."

Montoya might have been a guardian of the cattle for the Franciscans who established a mission at the Hopi village of Awat'ovi, not too far from Steamboat.

Another inscription found in this vicinity says:
"SHALL I NOT DRINK IT?"
St. John.
Colyer 1868
Centered beneath the inscription were carved two clasped hands with an arrow beside one hand and an American flag beside the other hand. It probably was carved by a soldier from Fort Wingate who was referring to the Treaty of 1868 signed that year between the United States and the Navajo people. (Van Valkenburgh, 1941)

MM 438 View of the Chuska Mountains to the north

Junction of AZ Highway 264 and U.S. Highway 191
Taco Bell Express open Sunday-Thursday 10 a.m.- 10 p.m.; Friday and Saturday 10 a.m. to midnight.

MM 441 GANADO

This settlement was originally named Pueblo Colorado for the wash that runs by the Hubbell Trading Post. Lorenzo Hubbell changed the name to Ganado to honor his close friend and ally, Navajo leader Ganado Mucho. Hubbell also worried that people might confuse his town with Pueblo, Colo., also a thriving community of the time. (Barnes, 1960; Brugge, 1993)

Ganado Mucho was the western leader of the Navajos and the twelfth signer of the Treaty of 1868 which led to the release of the Navajos from Bosque Redondo. He was a short, stocky man of Pueblo ancestry and was responsible for leading his people back to the Pueblo Colorado to develop large farms, cattle and sheep herds from the animals given to the Navajos by the military. (Brugge, 1993; Barnes, 1960)

Warehouse at Hubbell Trading Post, ca. 1890
Photo by Ben Wittick
Courtesy School of American Research Collections in the Museum of New Mexico, 16037

HUBBELL'S TRADING POST (South)

Charles Crary built the original trading post in 1871 and sold it to Lorenzo Hubbell in 1876. Hubbell was to own many trading posts in his lifetime and become an important political figure in Arizona's history. He even ran for the U.S. Senate in 1914 but lost and was indebted to the first Navajo Tribal Chairman Chee Dodge for $30,000 in campaign expenses. (Brugge, 1993)

Hubbell began to make his fortune in 1875 when the price of wool was very high. He formed a partnership with C.N. Cotton of Gallup and together they purchased and sold more than 40,000 pounds (18,144 kg) of wool. (Brugge, 1993)

Don Lorenzo Hubbell looking at a rug in front of his trading post, ca. 1890
Photo by Ben Wittick, School of American Research Collection, Museum of New Mexico, Santa Fe

When the Navajo Reservation was enlarged by executive order in 1880, Hubbell's Trading Post was sitting inside the new reservation boundary. To keep the land his successful post was on, he went to the U.S. Congress. With the help of Cotton and the Arizona governor, he requested an exception of land from the Navajo Reservation based on his prior claim as a settler. He was ultimately successful and received the claim to the land in 1908.

Hubbell was also friends with the eastern leader of the Navajos, Manuelito. A fierce warrior, Manuelito had won many wars against the Mexicans and many believed him to have supernatural powers because of his great courage in battle. Highly intelligent, he was able to hold out longer than any other group against Kit Carson and surrendered only when his people were close to starvation. (Brugge, 1993)

After Manuelito was released from Fort Sumner, he was in charge of the first Navajo police department and was responsible for preventing renewed hostilities in the area. (Brugge, 1993)

In back of the Hubbell home is a hill named for the family. It now serves as the family graveyard with Lorenzo Hubbell and his closest friend Manyhorse, Ganado Mucho's son, buried beside him. (Brugge, 1993)

The trading post still operates as it once did with Navajos coming to trade for supplies. The only difference is that the post is run by the Southwestern Parks and Monuments Association as a nonprofit business. The trader, Bill Malone, is truly authentic. Before coming to Ganado, Malone was a trader at the remote trading post in Pinon, Ariz., for 20 years.

Hubbell's Trading Post is now a National Historic Site managed by the National Park Service. It's open seven days a week from 8 a.m. to 6 p.m. (DST) in summer and 8 a.m. to 5 p.m. (MST) in winter. It's closed on Thanksgiving, Christmas and January 1. Guided tours of the Hubbell home are offered on a daily basis. Check at the visitors center for the daily schedule or call ahead at (520) 755-3475. This free tour is limited to 15 people. You can borrow, or purchase for $1.00, a self-guided tour book for the exterior grounds and there is a slide show about Lorenzo Hubbell available for viewing upon request at the visitors center. Navajo rug weavers and silversmiths demonstrate their arts daily in the visitors center.

REGIONAL RUG DESIGN- GANADO RED

Ganado Red, ca. 1900-1930
Photograph by Gene Balzer, Museum of Northern Arizona

Hubbell was influential in helping Navajo weavers of the area develop the Ganado Red rug style. He promoted it through his successful mail-order catalog. This design always has a red background with a diamond or cross pattern in the middle. On the edges of the diamond are geometric designs and shapes such as zigzags and crosses. Hubbell encouraged the use of large, heavy Navajo rugs on the floor. You can see copies of Hubbell's original floor rugs during the tour of his home. The Fred Harvey Co.

was one of the larger consumers of Ganado Reds, displaying them in their hotels and on trains, making them the most well-known of all of the Navajo rug designs. (Lamb, 1992, James, 1976)

Like J.B. Moore at the Crystal Trading Post, Hubbell hired artists traveling through Ganado to paint new rug patterns which he framed and hung in his office. One of his favorite artist was E.A. Burbank from Illinois. Over his life time, Hubbell collected over 300 of Burbank's oil paintings and sketches. (On page 139 there is a picture of Burbank watching Nampeyo fire a pot.)

GANADO MISSION AND SAGE MEMORIAL HOSPITAL

Heading east on Hwy 264, about one mile from Hubbell's Trading Post on the north side of the road. The largest Presbyterian Mission to the Navajos started in Ganado in 1903 with the help of Lorenzo Hubbell, a Roman Catholic. Hubbell saw the many advantages the Presbyterians could bring to the area and welcomed Charles Bierkemper, the first missionary, providing him a place to stay while his house was under construction.

The goal of the new minister was not just to preach the gospel but to provide a formal education and health care services to the Navajo people. The first hospital, built in 1911, was a one-man operation. Dr. James Kennedy frequently made house calls on foot to visit the sick and to take them medicine.

In the 1960s, the Presbyterians began to move out of education and health care on the Navajo Reservation. They turned the school over to the College of Ganado, run by a Navajo board of directors, and the hospital was given to Project Hope, then called the Hope Foundation.

Project Hope ran the hospital until 1974 when the Navajo Nation Health Foundation, with an all-Navajo board, was organized to oversee the operation of the hospital and its community outreach programs.

HISTORIC DETOUR

Turn north off Highway 264. At the stop sign directly in front of you is the newly-remodeled **Poncel Hall,** named after Dr. Joseph Poncel, one of the past superintendents of the mission.

Poncel Hall housed the first **Sage Memorial Hospital,** named for Olivia Sage who, along with the Navajo Tribe, contributed money to build the hospital in 1929. It was state-of-the-art when it opened, boasting an operating room and obstetrics unit.

Take a left at Poncel Hall. On your left is the current Sage Memorial Hospital–due for replacement within a few years. Because this is a private hospital, unlike Indian Health Service hospitals, there are no restrictions on who can be seen here. **Emergency Room: (520) 755-3411.**

On your right is the gym. At the next road take a right. On your left is **Ellerton Hall,** built in 1929 to house the mission's administration offices and the Industrial Arts Program.

Next to Ellerton Hall is **Shangri-La** named by Dr. Clarence Salisbury. He was a surgeon who came to Ganado on a one-month assignment during a diphtheria epidemic in 1927 and stayed for 21 years. Salisbury had just come from a 17-year mission to China and called his home Shangri-La to remind him of where he would like to be. He kept hoping for a transfer back to China but it never came because he was indispensable in Ganado.

The classic book, *Sagebrush Surgeon,* by Florence Means is about the life of Clarence Salisbury in Ganado. When he arrived, modern medicine was foreign to the Navajo people. Hospitals were a place to die. Not surprisingly, when Salisbury's first surgical patient did die of an embolism, the Navajo community was outraged. Some considered killing him in retribution. After hearing of the death, many family members met at Hubbell's Trading Post down the road to discuss the danger this newcomer brought to their traditions. But it was a medicine man, Red Point, who persuaded the crowd to reconsider. He pointed out that even though the medicine man does everything in his power to help the patient, some do not recover. He told them that he was sure that this doctor also did everything to save his patient and did not want her to die. (Means, 1956)

Gradually the community began to trust Dr. Salisbury. In 1930, the first registered nurse training program in the state of Arizona opened its doors in Poncel Hall. At one time, many of the Navajo nurse administrators employed by the Indian Health Service and the Navajo Tribe graduated from this program.

Salisbury's wife, Cora, was responsible for planting most of the cottonwood, willow, spruce and elm trees on the campus.

Directly across the street is the **Presbyterian Church.** It was constructed in 1941 using local sandstone quarried by masons from the Ganado area.

Behind the church is a two-story adobe building constructed in 1920 as a dormitory and infirmary. It has been refurbished by the Navajo Nation Health Foundation to house **Café Sage**, a cafeteria-style restaurant that offers two or three entrees, an excellent soup and salad bar and wonderful desserts. The prices are probably the lowest you will find on your travels. Open from 7 a.m. to 8 p.m.

From the Café turn north heading toward the Pueblo Colorado Wash. Straight ahead at the end of the road, over the wooden bridge, is the "**Old Manse.**" This was Mr. Bierkemper's home, built in 1903. It is the first and oldest building on the mission grounds.

Turn east on the dirt road directly behind Café Sage to continue around the campus. On your left is the **Power Plant** built around 1920. This building housed the coal power generator, replaced in 1960 by two surplus submarine turbines donated by the Navy.

An interesting story about the Ganado Mission has to do with the water supply. When you entered the mission grounds, you probably thought it a natural oasis like Tuba City. Not so, and according to geologists, the sandstone under the mission extends 1,000 feet (305 m) down, making it next to impossible to drill a productive well. Needing a dependable source of water for the hospital and school, the superintendent contracted with a Bureau of Indian Affairs drilling crew to try drilling a much deeper well than the shallow one they had. After coming up dry three times, the Presbyterians held a prayer vigil. On the fourth attempt, the cable on the drill snapped at 450 feet (137 m) releasing 4,500 gallons (19,080 liters) of water an hour. It is known as the Presbyterian miracle.

Turn right at the **swimming pool**, built in 1930 to provide recreation and a ready pool of water in case of fire. The pool is now closed because of funding shortages and liability issues.

Facing east from the swimming pool is the first **Public School Building** built in northern Apache County in 1929.

Leaving the circle, you will pass by the **Nurses Home,** behind Poncel Hall on the left, where student nurses in Salisbury's nursing school lived while attending school. It now houses nurses and staff who work at Sage Memorial Hospital.

Turn east to continue on to Window Rock. The road ascends through the Petrified Forest member of the Chinle Formation.

MM 448.5 GANADO LAKE North on I.R. 27 about one mile (1.6 km)

Listed on most current maps, this was a man-made lake formed from a dam. Currently empty, there are plans are to refill the lake sometime in 1995.

MM 455 CROSS CANYON

Named for a Navajo trail that crossed this canyon. Highway 264 begins climbing the Defiance Plateau to the Ponderosa Pine forest at 7,719 feet (2,353 m).

MM 451 Fields of sagebrush on the north and south sides of road

MM 466 SUMMIT CAMPGROUND AND PICNIC AREA.

On both sides of the road. Permit required for camping, see page 40 for permit instructions. No water; outhouses, picnic tables only.

MM 472 TWO STORY TRADING POST (North)

Still a working trading post.

ST. MICHAELS MISSION (South)

This 440-acre (1.78 sq km) Franciscan mission was started in 1896 by Rev. Mother Katharine Drexel, founder of the Sisters of the Blessed Sacrament for Indians and Colored People.

The daughter of a wealthy investment broker who, upon her father's death in 1885, became heir to a fortune. She purchased squatter's rights to a small piece of land to the north of the present mission. One year later she bought 160 acres (.65 sq km) of land from squatter Bill Meadows where the Mission Museum and church stand today. The original Navajo Reservation boundary of 1886 was seven miles (11.3 km) north of the mission.

(See page 19 for map.) Much of the land in St. Michaels was in a checker-board pattern with some land owned by the railroad and some designated as public lands. It was possible in 1896 for a settler to obtain title to rail-road land through squatter's rights requiring a person to live on the land one night each year.

The Spanish Franciscans called this area in the late 1500s *Cienega Ama-rilla* because of its masses of wild sunflowers. The Navajos called it *tso hootso*, meaning yellow meadow. After purchasing the land, Mother Katharine changed the name to St. Michaels after her childhood home in Pennsylvania.

Father Juvenal Schnorbus and Father Anslem Weber from the Franciscan Order of the Province of St. John the Baptist in Cincinnati, Ohio, were enticed by Mother Katharine to come to Arizona to run the mission. Many Navajos accepted the Ohio Franciscans for two reasons. First, the timing of the priests' encounter with the Navajos was just after their return from Bosque Redondo and the Navajos needed the Franciscans' help to defend themselves against the bureaucracy of the Indian Service and hostile neigh-boring ranchers. Secondly, these Franciscans were willing to learn the Na-vajo language and incorporate Navajo traditions and ceremonials into their Catholic services. This distinquished them from the Spanish Franciscans of the 1500s who were not successful in their dealings with the Navajo; primarily because of their disregard for the highly-developed Navajo be-lief system and language.

Luckily for the Ohio priests, they had help in learning the language from the first trader in the Cienega Amarilla area, Charles Day. He was very happy to see the mission established so his two sons, who spoke fluent Navajo, could learn reading, writing and arithmetic. The Days agreed to serve as interpreters and help the priests learn Navajo in exchange for the education of their children. In 1902, the St. Michael's Indian Boarding School opened on the mission's grounds.

One of the more famous Franciscans to come to the region was Father Berard Haile. Credited with developing the Navajo written alphabet using the international phonetic alphabet, he published the first Navajo ethno-graphic dictionary in 1910. A prolific writer and anthropological researcher, he also helped with the reorganization of the Navajo Tribal Council under the Collier Administration in the 1930s.

Father Anslem Weber voting in the first Arizona territorial election, 1912.
St. Michaels Photo Collection of the Franciscan Friars at St. Michaels, Ariz., Museum of Northern Arizona Photo Archives, MS 119-104-81 *(From left to right: seated. Sam Day; the person behind Day is not known; Frank Walker, interpreter for the Friars from 1900-1945, and Brother Simeon Schwemberger who was responsible for taking many of the photographs in the Saint Michaels' collection. Standing from left to right: Father Anselm Weber and Daniel Holmes Mitchell.)*

The most important function the Franciscans performed for the Navajos was to negotiate with Washington for additional land for the growing population. Father Anslem learned how to survey from the team that came through St. Michaels to determine the boundaries of the new Arizona Territory. This skill was to become invaluable in the settlement of land disputes between Navajo clans and in Father Anslem's successful attempt to increase the size of the Navajo reservation. He is said to have written over 3,000 letters on behalf of the Navajos and made yearly visits to Washington to fight for the increased land base. Because of his efforts over 1,400,000 acres (5,687 sq km), to the east and south of the 1868 reservation boundary, were added to the Navajo Nation. He was also successful in obtaining more than 122,000 acres (497 sq km) for off-reservation Navajos. *You can visit the Saint Michaels Historical Museum from Memorial Day (last Monday in May) to Labor Day (first Monday in September), Monday through Friday from 9 a.m.-5 p.m. (DST) (520) 871-4171. No admission fee but donations are welcomed.*

Tay Notah and John Foley delivering mail by burro
St. Michaels Photo Collection of the Franciscan Friars at St. Michaels, Ariz.
Museum of Northern Arizona, Photo Archives, MS 119-167-2585

 **NAVAJO AREA INDIAN HEALTH SERVICE HEADQUARTERS**

North side of highway 264, just past St. Michaels Mission. This area is considered the town of St. Michaels. It has its own post office and zip code.

WINDOW ROCK

Window Rock is named for the large window in the Cowsprings Sandstone behind the Navajo tribal government offices. John Collier, the federal commissioner of Indian Affairs, centralized the headquarters for Navajo Indian Affairs here in the 1930s. Collier understood the importance of including the Navajo people in the decisions made about their children's education and health care. He implemented changes such as starting day schools to replace the isolating and lonely boarding school system of education.

Window Rock is the home of Lt. Joe Leaphorn, Tony Hillerman's first important character who appears in the *Blessing Way*, *A Thief of Time*, *Dance*

Hall of the Dead, *Listening Woman* and *Skinwalker*. Hillerman has been named a "Special Friend of the Diné" by the Navajo Nation for his positive portrayal of the Navajo people.

MM 475 NAVAJO NATION FAIRGROUND (South)

The Navajo Nation Fair is held the first weekend after Labor Day each year and features an intertribal powwow, a Miss Navajo Nation contest, and a rodeo. For more information call (520) 871-6478.

NAVAJO ARTS AND CRAFTS AND TRIBAL MUSEUM

North through stop light. Founded in 1941 by the Navajo Nation to promote and market Navajo handmade items. The quality and authenticity of items purchased here is assured. Located in the same building is the Navajo Tribal Museum which houses more than 4,000 items that trace Navajo history from the 1600s to the present. A replica of the dinosaur *Dilophosaurus,* found near Tuba City, is on display. Open 8 a.m.– 5 p.m., Monday through Friday, (520) 871-4095.

TSO BONITO PARK

Follow the pink bear signs; located directly behind the new museum and library off Highway 264 on the north side directly in front of the Parks and Recreation Office. The Navajo Nation Zoological and Botanical Park opened in 1962 to care for a bear abandoned by its owners while it was on display at the tribal museum. The zoo has grown to include cougars, Mexican wolves, coyotes, deer, elk, bobcats, Navajo churro sheep, rabbits and a pony. Birds of prey, wild turkeys and roadrunners are also on display with an assortment of snakes, lizards and turtles. Open from 8 a.m.-5 p.m., Monday through Friday.

THE HAYSTACKS *Behind the Navajo Museum*

Made of Entrada and Cowsprings Sandstone, these formations look like haystacks and are known as *Tséghálhoodzáni* or "wind going through the rocks." Near here is *Tseyaato*, or "spring under the rock," that served as a watering stop for the 8,000 Navajo on the "Long Walk" to Fort Sumner.

"A View in the Haystacks," Window Rock, Arizona, ca. 1890
Photograph by Ben Wittick
Courtesy School of American Research Collection of the Museum of New Mexico, 15551

NAVAJO LIBRARY , MUSEUM AND VISITOR CENTER

Opened in 1998, this 58,000 sq.ft. museum is the largest museum dedicated to Native American history in the country. It has a library, a childrens museum and Miss Navajo Nation's office. In the future, it will house thousands of valuable and sacred artifacts waiting for repatriation from museums all over the country. The museum and library is open Monday through Friday, 8 a.m. to 5 p.m. For more information call (520) 871-6436 or 871-7371.

SERVICES IN ST. MIICHAELS/WINDOW ROCK

LODGING

Days Inn: Just opened in 1998, this motel sits almost directly across from St. Michaels Historical Museum. It has an indoor pool,sauna and cable television. Rooms run around $75 for a double in winter and much higher in summer. National Reservations 1-800-DAYSINN; local (520) 871-5690.

Navajo Nation Inn: Moderately priced, this motel is decorated in a Southwestern style. The curtains and bedspreads have Navajo pastoral scenes. This is the only motel in toWindow Rock. A drive to Gallup, about 30 miles (48 km) away, is the only second option if the new Days Inn in St.

Michaels is full. Because this is the capital of the Navajo Nation, it is often difficult to reserve a room here. Room rates: Two double beds, cable TV, shower, $64.80 plus an 8.1 percent Navajo Lodging Tax. Reservations: (520) 871-4108.

RESTAURANTS

Denny's to be located in front of the Days Inn in St. Michaels. Not yet constructed at the time of printing.

Navajo Nation Inn Dining Room: This is the place to have lunch if you want to see many of the members of the Navajo Tribal Council and the president having lunch. Open from 6 a.m.-9 p.m.

Hong Kong Restaurant: located in the Window Rock Shopping Center. Chinese food. Open from 11 a.m.-9 p.m., Monday through Friday; closed Saturday and Sunday.

Los Verdes Mexican Restaurant: Excellent homemade food but a little hard to find. Located on the north side of the four-lane highway sitting back on a dirt road. Watch for it across from St. Michaels Mission.

Tullers Cafe: Actually located in St. Michaels, just west of the Navajo Area Indian Health Service headquarters. Specializes in Navajo tacos, hamburgers, pork chops, mutton stew, fry bread. Open from 7 a.m.-9 p.m.

Church's Kentucky Fried Chicken: In the Ch'i' hootso Shopping Center. Open 11 a.m.-10p.m

Bashas' Deli: Open 8 a.m.-10 p.m. Monday through Saturday, and 8 a.m.to 8 p.m. on Sunday.

Pizza Hut Express/Taco Bell Express/TCBY

Open 10 a.m. to 10 p.m., seven days a week.

BANKING SERVICES

Norwest Bank in Window Rock: Open 9 a.m.-3:30 p.m. Monday, Tuesday, and Thursday. Hours: 9 a.m.-2 p.m.; 3 p.m.-6 p.m., Wed. and Fri.; 24 hour ATM.

AUTOMOBILE SERVICES

Legah Towing   (520) 871-5040

Window Rock Tire Center   (520) 871-4068

NAVAJO POLICE STATION: (520) 871-6113 or 911.

KTNN RADIO: If you haven't had the chance to hear spoken Navajo, tune into KTNN at AM 660. It is a very powerful radio station owned by the Navajo Tribe. Primarily a country and western station, it also plays traditional Native American chants and some of its advertising and interviews are conducted in the Navajo language.

TSE BONITO, NEW MEXICO: Starting a private business on the reservation is a project for a very patient person. Land for commercial development is scarce because many livestock owners want to keep as much of the land as possible for grazing. If an entrepreneur is lucky enough to get a site lease, there is massive tribal, as well as BIA, bureaucratic red tape. Because of this, many of the businesses have set up just across the reservation border in New Mexico.

Chapter 10

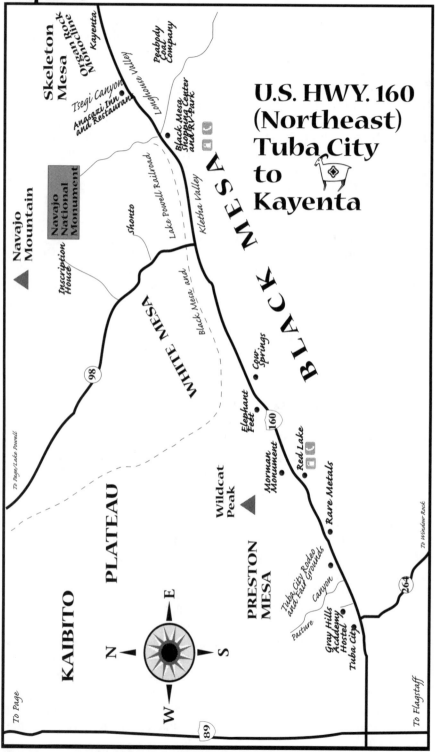

U.S. HWY. 160
(Northeast)
Tuba City
to
Kayenta

78 miles (126 km) from Tuba City to Kayenta

GREY HILLS ACADEMY HIGH SCHOOL

Turn north just east of the pedestrian overpass, the school is on the right.
This 300-student high school is one of the best examples on the Navajo
Reservation of self-determination in education at work. Grey Hills transferred from the Bureau of Indian Affairs to an all-Navajo school board in
1989 and is now a university system laboratory school.

Students accepted to the academy from other parts of the reservation and
the country stay in former BIA dormitories. A portion of the dormitory is
now a motel and youth hostel where students learn hotel management skills.
(See page 118 for reservation information.) The school also operates the
only high school radio station in Arizona, **KGHR** (91.5 FM), which broad-
casts an eclectic mix of classical, country and western, rock and Native
American music; plus National Public Radio's (NPR) "Morning Edition"
and "All Things Considered." If you're listening to NPR on KNAU (88.7
FM) from Flagstaff on your way to the Grand Canyon and lose the signal
along Hwy 64 (because of the Gray Mountain), tune to 91.5 and pick up the
signal clearly all the way to the canyon.

MM 323 PASTURE CANYON (North)

The cliffs surrounding this canyon are made of Kayenta Sandstone from
the early Jurassic Period, laid down more than 190 million years ago.

Hopi families say their ancestors lived in this area when the first Mormon
settlers began arriving in 1875. However, the Navajo story about the Mormon settlement of Tuba City is quite different than that told by the Hopis,
who say no Navajos were then in the area.

Navajos say the Mormons told them they were just passing through on
their way to settle along the Little Colorado. But because they had run out
of food, they asked to camp in Tuba City for the winter. When spring came,
the Mormons asked if they could stay for one planting season to grow enough
crops to carry them through to their new home. The Navajo families agreed.
But by the end of the planting season, permanent shelters had been built
and more and more settlers were moving into the area. Finally, the Mormons were so well-established here they obtained a court document in Flagstaff claiming the land and all of the water in Moenkopi Creek as their
own.

This caused resentment among the Navajos who had shared their land and food with the Mormons when they were in need. The situation became worse when fences kept Navajo sheep and cattle out of Pasture Canyon. The fence builder was a disagreeable Mormon leader named Lot Smith who owned a large dairy herd he grazed in the canyon. During a long drought in 1892, he allegedly refused to allow any of the neighboring Navajos to use the watering hole. One day, two children accidently herded their flock of sheep into Pasture Canyon. Outraged, Smith got his gun and began shooting wildly at the sheep and children. The Navajos claimed that Smith killed seven sheep and 23 died later from their wounds. The Mormon version is that Smith killed two sheep. To retaliate, a Navajo shot six of Smith's dairy cows. Joe Lee, the grandson of John D. Lee, was in Pasture Canyon on that fateful day and says that a sniper, whom no one could identify, shot Smith. Chach'osh Neez was blamed for mortally wounding Smith because he had made many threats against him in the past. (Tanner, 1977; Correll, 1966; Richardson, 1974)

A military officer traveled to the scene from Fort Wingate, near Gallup, N.M., to investigate the shooting. Before Smith died he admitted that he should have stopped shooting when the Navajo shot his cattle but he didn't think they would shoot at him. Not wanting to go to Fort Defiance for a trial, Chach'osh Neez, protected by many family and friends, hid in Blue Canyon, sending messages back and forth to the military investigator. Finally in 1895, he gave himself up to stand trial in Flagstaff where he was acquitted in the death of Lot Smith.

Pasture Canyon is today part of the Hopi Reservation as a result of a federal court ruling. The Mormon settlers developed the series of reservoirs within the canyon now used to irrigate Hopi cornfields. It is also home to various species of water birds such as the blue heron.

MM 323.5 TUBA CITY RODEO AND FAIR GROUNDS (North)

Every year, the Western Navajo Fair is held here during the first weekend after Columbus Day in October.

MM 327.5 RARE METALS URANIUM MILL (South)

Five miles north of Tuba City you will notice trees growing on both sides of the road. Beneath their branches are the foundations of homes built here in the late 1950s to house workers of the uranium mill that processed 300 tons (272,727 kg) of vanadium and uranium ore every day. Ore, or "yellowcake," came by truck from mines in Cameron, Monument Valley and the Orphan Mine in the Grand Canyon. In 1968, the Rare Metals Corp. of America went bankrupt and abandoned the site, leaving thousands of tons of low-level radioactive waste in huge piles to blow away in the wind. In 1981, a local group in Tuba City pressured the U.S. Dept. of Energy (DOE) to clean up the site. The waste was gathered into a pile, shaped to shed water, and covered with rock. What remains today is a huge, gray-

colored pile with the radioactive waste buried beneath it. That two-year, $13 million project ended in 1992. In 1996, DOE will return to ensure that an underground aquifer is not contaminated.

Rare Metals Uranium Processing Plant, ca. 1950s
Museum of Northern Arizona, Photo Archives

MM 328 PRESTON MESA (North)

Seen to the north of Tuba City in the distance is a large red mesa made of Navajo Sandstone. The mesa is named in honor of Sam Preston, the first store clerk who worked for Charles Algert at the Tuba Trading Post in the late 1870s and who later became partners with the Babbitt Brothers. Preston's original reason for coming to Arizona was to work for the Union and Pacific Railroad.

MM 336 COWSPRINGS SANDSTONE (South)

Part of the San Raphael Group formed during the Jurassic era, 135- to-180 million years ago.

MM 338.5 WILDCAT PEAK (Northwest)

Formed by a volcanic intrusion with surrounding dikes.

MM 344 TONALEA GENERAL STORE AND COMMUNITY

This community is built around the BIA Day School. The Babbitt Bros. Trading Co. moved their store from the historic Red Lake Trading Post down the road to this new facility just a few years ago.

⬧ MM 344 RED LAKE TRADING POST

Also known as Tonalea Trading Post because Tonalea is a close approximation of the Navajo word for lake, *tónteel*. Although smaller now, there once was a large lake below the trading post.

George McAdams built the first trading post, really a four-room fort, on the shore of the lake around 1880. Sam Preston, an employee of the Babbitt Brothers Trading Co., built this two-story trading post in 1891 with living quarters upstairs. (Richardson, 1974)

McAdams' sister, Jane, married John Richardson. Their sons, S.I., C.D and Hubert, owned and operated many trading posts throughout northern Arizona, including the Cameron Trading Post. (Richardson, 1986)

Red Lake Trading Post
Warren Family Collection, Cline Library, Special Collections and Archives, NAU 412-2-94

The Babbitt Brothers started in the trading business here in 1891 out of necessity when the owner, Sam Dittenhoffer, heavily in debt to the Babbitts for his store merchandise, was killed in a poker game. According to Joe Lee, who worked at the post for a few months after McAdams sold it in 1889, Dittenhoffer was having an affair with a Mrs. Matthews, a widow from Flagstaff. A few days after he brought her to Red Lake, a strange man showed up. He talked Dittenhoffer into playing poker and at the start of the first hand accused the trader of cheating. Angered, Dittenhoffer jumped to his feet. The stranger, actually a secret admirer of Mrs. Matthews, took this as an attempt to draw on him and shot him dead but Dittenhoffer didn't have a gun. The stranger took off for Colorado but was apprehended and brought back to Arizona where he was found guilty of second degree murder. (Richardson, 1974)

An interesting feature of this post is that the upper story and warehouse are made of Arbuckle Brothers coffee boxes. According to Floyd Boyle, the trader at Red Lake in 1948, Arbuckle "Ariosa" coffee was *the* most popular coffee sold all over the reservation. It came packed in sturdy wooden cases each containing 100 one-pound packages of coffee. The coupons on

the back of the coffee bags were redeemable for catalog items so the traders bought back Arbuckle coupons from their customers for a penny a piece and redeemed them for "luxury" items. According to Boyle, many of the traders furnished their kitchens, bought clothes and pots and pans through the Arbuckle catalog. One Indian Health Service dignitary, visiting the reservation from Washington, commented to the Boyles about how popular their silver pattern was on the reservation; he had seen it at every trading post he visited.

Arbuckle Coffee-Box Wall,
Red Lake Trading Post, 1992
Photograph by Gene Balzer

The Mormon explorers established a trail through Red Lake in 1869. (See page 197 for map.) (Richardson, 1948)

 MOVIE LOCATION

The Red Lake Trading Post became the set for the fictitious Burnt Water Trading Post in the movie, *The Dark Wind*, based on the Tony Hillerman novel. Produced by Robert Redford, the movie was filmed in the Tuba City/Red Lake area in 1992. It was during renovation of the post for the movie that the Arbuckle coffee wall was discovered.

MM 344.2 MORMON MONUMENT (North)

On the north side of the road, midway up in the sandstone bluff, is a stone monument placed here by the Mormon Church in 1938. This spot marks the place where, in 1860, Jacob Hamblin's party met up with an unfriendly band of Navajos. The Navajos said they would leave the Mormons alone if they would give them their Paiute scout as a captive. The Mormons refused but did give the Navajos ammunition and supplies. Not happy with the negotiations, the Navajos attacked the party the next morning, killing George A. Smith, Jr.

Native Roads

 MM 345 ELEPHANT FEET (North)

Made of Cow Springs Sandstone, these giant formations look like a pair of elephant's legs and feet. They are the result of wind and water erosion. (Breed, 1968)

MM 346 WHITE MESA (North)

This heart-shaped mesa consists primarily of Dakota Sandstone from the Cretaceous period formed more than 65 to 135 million years ago. The mesa is about 8.5 miles (13.7 km.) wide and 16 miles (25.7 km.) long, running north and south. There are many traditional Navajo sheep camps beneath White Mesa. To get to the mesa you must drive through and disturb many private camps. Please do not trespass here.

MM 359 PYGMY FOREST

This forest consists of Utah juniper and pinyon pine on both sides of U.S. Highway 160.

MM 361.5 Turn-off to Shonto/Page, Junction State Highway 98

MM 369 SAGEBRUSH *on both sides of the road.*

MM 373 ELECTRIC TRAIN (North)

If you're lucky, you'll spot the Black Mesa and Lake Powell train, an 88-mile-long (141.6 km) railroad with one destination and one freight: the Peabody Coal silo in the Klethla Valley, and coal. This electric train travels from the Navajo Generating Station, a coal-fired powerplant on the shores of Lake Powell. It crosses the Navajo desert and runs several miles along Highway 160. It makes three trips a day, carrying 24,000 tons (21,772,800 kg) of coal per trip. The BM & LP train is one of the longest electric coal trains in the world.

This is also the infamous electric train that George Hayduke, a fictitious character in *The Monkey Wrench Gang,* written by environmentalist Edward Abbey, plots to blow up, along with the Glen Canyon Dam, to protest the destruction of the Colorado River and Plateau.

SCENIC DETOUR

NAVAJO NATIONAL MONUMENT: *Turn north off U.S. Hwy. 160 on to Arizona Highway 564, 10 miles (16.1 km). Hours: May to early September.: 8 a.m. - 6 p.m. (DST); Early Sept. to mid-Dec. and March through May: 8 a.m. - 5 p.m. (DST & MST); Mid-Dec. to March: 8 a.m.-4:30 p.m. (MST). Admission is free but donations are welcomed. Operated by the National Park Service. Camping is also free, on a first-come, first-served basis. A maximum of seven nights is allowed in this very nice campground. Shade is provided by Utah juniper and pinyon pine in each of the 30 camping sites. There are toilets and running water but no showers or RV hook-ups. An RV longer than 25 feet (7.6 m) is not recommended because of the narrow, winding road through the campground. There is one handicapped camp site with toilet.*

The road entering the monument travels on top of the Organ Rock Monocline with Navajo Sandstone lining both sides of the road. This is one of the more beautiful of all of the managed ruins because of its location in Tsegi Canyon and the many springs that feed the area. Towering ponderosa pine grow on the canyon floor because the vertical height of 700 feet (213 m) diffuses the sunlight, producing moderate temperatures at the bottom of the canyon. Take the short but steep **Aspen Forest Trail** behind the visitors center to see the beauty of the canyon interior. A grove of quaking aspen grow in the bottom of the canyon along with ponderosa pine. It is not possible to see Betatakin ruin from this trail.

SANDAL TRAIL (Behind the Visitors Center)

A one-mile (1.6 km) round-trip, paved trail leads to the overlook for *Bitát'ahkin*, which means "ledge house" in Navajo. Built in a large cave around 1250 A.D., it had 135 rooms and a kiva. Approximately, 125 Anasazi lived in Betatakin and farmed in this fertile valley until 1300 A.D. when they left the area after a serious drought changed the farming conditions in the canyon.

During the peak tourist season, from May 31 through August 31, Navajo National Monument rangers lead groups of 25 hikers to visit the ruin starting at 9 a.m. (DST) and again at noon (DST) daily. In the off-season (MST), early May and during the fall months beginning in October, the guide leads one tour a day, at 10 a.m. This strenuous five-mile (8 km) round-trip hike takes between five-to-six hours. Time is allowed for an interpretive discussion of the ruin and its environment and to hike the 700-foot (213 m) ascent from the bottom of the canyon. To join the free tour, you must obtain a ticket at the visitor center on the morning of the hike. No reservations are accepted and the tickets are given out on a first-come, first-served basis. Because temperatures approach the 100 degree (38° C) mark in the summer, carrying at least one quart of water per person is recommended. (You can buy water bottles at the visitors center. But bring a daypack so you can have your hands free.) Solid footwear like hiking shoes or good sneakers are recommended because the trail is rocky.

Betatakin Pueblo , ca. 1930-1940
Philip Johnston Collection, Cline Library, Special Collections and Archives, NAU PH 413-77
Philip Johnston was born in 1892 the son of a missionary to the Navajos. During WW II he started the famous Navajo Code Talkers.

KEET SEEL RUINS

Kits' iiilí means "broken pieces of pottery" in Navajo. Although the pueblos were built around 1250 A.D., the Anasazi were known to have used the cave as early as 900 A.D. Keet Seel is located in a large cave in Tsegi Canyon and is one of the best preserved cliff dwellings in the monument.

The first custodian of Navajo National Monument was John Wetherill, trader and explorer from Kayenta. He was responsible for overseeing the building of trails from Marsh Pass to Keet Seel Pueblo and for the stabilization of the ruin in 1933. (See page 177-178 for more about Wetherill.) (Anonymous, 1934)

Wetherill brought many famous visitors to Keet Seel. One of them was Zane Grey who used the scenic beauty of Keet Seel as the backdrop for his book *Riders of the Purple Sage*. (Babbitt, 1990)

You can visit this ruin by horseback with a free National Park Service permit from May 31 through August 31. Navajo families provide the horses and a park ranger accompanies the group. The trip costs $55 per person for an entire day, from 8 a.m. to around 7 p.m. Children under 12 are not permitted on the ride. You must make reservations at least two months in advance. If you have a fear of heights, this ride is not for you because the trail drops more than 1,000 feet (305 m). Call the visitor center to make reservations at (520) 672-2366 or 2367.

WHAT MAKES A CAVE? Water spilling over the edge of the sandstone cliffs works its way into the many cracks and crevices, freezing in winter. Over millions of years, sections of sandstone break loose from the larger mass, leaving a beautiful cave. (Hargrave, 1934)

INSCRIPTION HOUSE

It is no longer possible to visit this ruin because of its fragile condition. Also, local Navajo families who live close to the ruin do not want visitors.

The history of the people who "found" Inscription House is interesting. The ruin gets its name from an inscription that reads:

"S_____Hapeiro Ano Dom 1661"

Because there was no recorded history of the Spanish visit to this area, many people thought the inscription was written by pothunters playing a joke. But Navajos who lived in the area knew that many unauthorized Spanish gold explorers came through Tsegi Canyon looking for riches.

A Museum of Northern Arizona team researched the ruins in 1953 and concluded the inscription could have read "1861" because of a nearby Mormon inscription dated 1861.

Elizabeth Compton Hegemann talks about the validity of the 1661 date in her book *Navajo Trading Days*. Hegemann was owner of the Shonto Trading Post from 1929 to 1939. She was good friends with John Wetherill, who, with Byron Cummings, first saw the ruins in 1909. Wetherill's 10-year-old daughter was on the expedition with her father and Cummings. As an adult, she told Hegemann that she and Cummings' son Malcolm had found the inscription while playing. Hegemann, an accomplished photographer, took a picture of the inscription. In her book, the picture clearly shows 1661. (Richardson, 1948; Hegemann, 1963)

Inscription House Ruins, ca. 1930-1940
Philip Johnston Collection, Cline Library, Special Collections and Archives, NAU PH 413-77

 **END SCENIC DETOUR**

MM 374 BLACK MESA SHOPPING CENTER (South)

RV Park: Limited space, $7/night, showers, dump station and electricity. (520) 677-3212

MM374 BLACK MESA AND PEABODY WESTERN COAL COMPANY (South)

If you are traveling east, you have followed Black Mesa on the south side of Highway 160 since leaving the Red Lake Trading Post. Black Mesa is the largest single landmass in northern Arizona, embracing almost 20 percent of the entire Navajo Nation. It rises to an elevation of 8,210 feet (2,502 m) and extends from Red Lake, to Kayenta, around to Chinle. Its southern escarpment includes the three mesas of the Hopi Nation, reaching like fingers into the plain. Because of its large, underground sandstone strata, it holds the primary water source for the Hopi villages and surrounding Navajo communities. Next to Navajo Mountain, this mesa is one of the more remote and isolated areas in the Southwest. Roads are primitive and the people living on the mesatop remain some of the more traditional on the reservation.

The Peabody Western Coal Co. operates two of the largest open pit strip mines in the country on Black Mesa. Large deposits of coal are found here because 65 to 135 million years ago this area was a coastal swamp where massive amounts of vegetation accumulated to form coal now found in the Dakota, Torvea and Wepo formations that predominate this area. (Nations, 1981)

Coal from the Kayenta Mine travels to the Navajo Generating Station near Page on the second largest coal train in the world and the only railroad operating on the Navajo Reservation. Coal from the Black Mesa Mine goes to the Mohave Generating Station on the Nevada-Arizona border through the Black Mesa Pipeline. Each year, it uses one billion gallons of some of the country's most pristine water from deep subterranean wells to slurry the coal more than 273 miles (439 km) around the Grand Canyon. The journey takes three days.

The Navajos and Hopis receive royalties from Black Mesa coal. But many, particularly Hopis, are angry that mining takes place at all. They believe the coal slurry pipeline's use of water is depleting many of the natural springs that farmers have traditionally relied upon. Peabody contends that the amount of water used every day for the slurry is not enough to affect the water table and that the springs are recharged from other sources. Resolution of this dispute, which has held up the issuance of Peabody's Black Mesa Mine "life-of-mine" federal permit for years, is now in the hands of the secretary of the Interior.

MM 374 LONG HOUSE VALLEY (North and South)

This valley extends all the way from the turnoff to Navajo National Monument to Tsegi Canyon. It was named for a ruin found here.

MM 381.5 TSEGI CANYON (North)

The Navajo word *Tséyi'* means canyon. The sheer walls are primarily made of Navajo and Wingate Sandstone and were sculpted by Laguna Creek to make this incredible gorge. The creek was given its name because of the lagoon–like conditions Captain John Walker found while on a survey of the area for the military in 1860. He reported many pools and rich marshy growth in the canyon. Fresh water shells are commonly found along Laguna Creek. It is no wonder that so many important Anasazi sites have been found here. In summer you can see numerous Navajo cornfields along the creek.

NAVAJO DRY FARMING

Most of the small, green cornfields you pass along the highway are "dry farms." Crops are nutured only by the falling rain, which is minimal in most parts of the Navajo Nation, especially in the spring when crops need it most. The majority of rain falls in summer from July through September. The Navajos, like the Hopis, have adapted their ancient farming methods to take advantage of every drop of available moisture. Most fields are planted at the mouth of a canyon to capture the winter snow melt or rain that may fall far away and run through the canyon. Using a planting stick made of greasewood, seeds are planted deep in the earth to take advantage of the moisture in the ground. The time to plant is critical. To determine the correct time, the farmer watches for the disappearance of the constellation Pleiades. Easily seen in the winter sky, these stars gradually disappear as the weather gets warmer and spring approaches. (Bingham, 1979)

MM 382 MARSH PASS

The pass between Black Mesa and Tsegi Canyon is known as Marsh Pass. It describes the swamp-like environment that existed during the building of Highway 160, formerly known as **Navajo Route 1**.

Anasazi Motel at Tsegi Canyon: Basic accommodations but an incredible location. Two double beds, TV, shower, no phones in the rooms. June through October, double occupancy $75 plus an 8.1 percent Navajo Lodging Tax. (520) 697-3793.

Restaurant: Open from 5 a.m. - 11 p.m. in the summer and 5 a.m. - 10 p.m. in the winter. They serve everything but their most popular item is fry bread.

Marsh Pass along old Navajo Route 1 and Organ Rock Monocline, 1920
Philip Johnston Collection, Cline Library, Special Collections and Archives, NAU, PH 413-514

MM 385 ORGAN ROCK MONOCLINE (North)

Also known as Skeleton Mesa, this monocline formed about 75 to 80 million years ago. It is an excellent example of geologic uplift along vertical faults caused during a period of large-scale earth movements. A monocline is a one-sided fold where the sedimentary rocks on top are draped over the displaced rocks exposed through the fault. At the bottom of the fault is Chinle Sandstone with a solid wall of Wingate Sandstone above it. (Nations, 1981)

MM 387 The elevation here is 6,000 feet (1,830 m).

If you are traveling east, you have climbed more than 1,000 feet (305 m) in elevation since leaving Tuba City. Notice the change in vegetation from desert scrub land to pinyon-pine and Utah juniper forest.

MM 390 AGATHLA PEAK (North)

Traveling east on Highway 160, you can see Agathla Peak to the north. This is a volcanic monolith near the entrance to Monument Valley and will be discussed on page 179.

MM 393 BURGER KING (North)

Owned by Navajo businessman Richard Mike, this restaurant has an excellent photographic exhibit on the Navajo Code Talkers. Mike's father, King Mike, was a Navajo Code Talker in WWII. Because Navajo was not a written language and has many complexities and nuances, it was the only military code the Germans and Japanese were unable to break.

KAYENTA VISITORS CENTER

Located just east of the Burger King on the north side of U.S. 160 is a new store built by the Navajo Tribe. Designed in the shape of a hogan with its entrance to the east, the center provides an opportunity for Navajo vendors to sell their wares to tourists in an environment less affected by the weather than the roadside vendor stands. The center has 40 vendor booths, a visitor information booth, an outdoor amphitheater, a museum and a food court specializing in traditional Navajo food.

COMMUNITY OF KAYENTA

The Navajo name for Kayenta, *Tódínéeshzheé*, means "water spreading out like fingers" referring to a seasonal spring that flows from the hill behind the old Wetherill Trading Post. This town has grown to provide housing for workers at the Peabody Coal mines and to accommodate the thousands of visitors to Monument Valley who come every year from all over the world. In the 1950s and 60s, there was also a booming uranium mining business in Monument Valley.

SERVICES IN KAYENTA

LODGING
Holiday Inn: May to October, high season rates of $109 plus a Navajo tax of 8 percent for a room with two double beds, $129 for a family suite. Winter rates are $69 plus tax. Office open 24 hours. (520) 697-3221

Wetherill Inn: From April 15 to Oct. 15 a room for one person is $72; double $78; triple $84; and for four people $90. From Oct. 16 to April 14, a room for one person is $45; double $49.50; triple $54.50; and for four people $59.50. Office hours: 7 a.m. - 10 p.m. in summer; 8 a.m. - 9 p.m. in winter. (520) 697-3231

RESTAURANTS
Burger King: (Highway 160 west of Hwys. 160-163 intersection) - Fast food burgers, breakfast, lunch and dinner. 6:30 a.m.-11 p.m. (520) 697-3534

The Blue Coffee Pot Restaurant: (Intersection of Hwys. 163 and 160) Navajo tacos, steaks, burgers, local food. 6 a.m-9 p.m. (520) 697-3396

Pizza Edge: Pizza, calzone, frozen yogurt. Ten minute personal pan pizza specials for lunch. Located in the *Tódínéeshzheé* Shopping Center. 11 a.m.-10 p.m. (520) 697-8427

Holiday Inn-Wagon Wheel Restaurant: (Intersection of Hwys. 163 and 160) Breakfast, lunch and dinner. 6 a.m. to 10 p.m. (520) 697-3221.

Amigo Café: (Highway 163) Mexican/local, breakfast, lunch and dinner. 7 a.m.-10 p.m.; weekends 8 a.m.-10 p.m. (520) 697-8448

Golden Sands Restaurant: (Highway 163, just before Wetherill Inn) Navajo tacos, burgers, steaks. 6 a.m.-9:30 p.m. (520) 697-3684

Bashas' Deli: (*Tódínéeshzheé* Shopping Center) Sandwiches, salads, deserts, drinks. (520) 697-8176

Flea Market: Next to the Community Center on U. S. Highway 163 every Wednesday from 9 a.m. to 3 p.m. Local stands specializing in Navajo tacos, burritos, fry bread, pop.

Bashas' Grocery Store: Open 8 a.m.-10 p.m. Monday through Saturday and 8 a.m.-8 p.m. Sunday.

⊕ HEALTH SERVICES

Navajo Area Indian Health Service Clinic: Emergencies only, unless Native American with a census number. Located on Highway 163 just past Wetherill Inn on the west side of the road. **(520) 697-3211 or 911.**

BANKING SERVICES:
Norwest Bank: Open 9 a.m. to 2 p.m. and 3 p.m. to 5 p.m. Monday through Friday. Drive through window open 9 a.m. to 6 p.m. ATM in lobby available everyday.

AUTOMOBILE SERVICES
Kayenta Discount Towing:	(520) 697-3200
Chief Towing:	(520) 697-3763
Kayenta Discount Auto Parts:	(520) 697-3200

KAYENTA NAVAJO POLICE STATION: (520) 697-8669

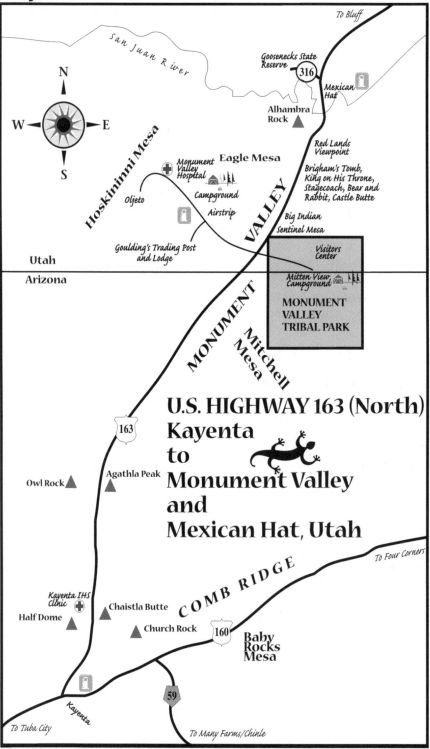

Chapter 11

To Bluff

San Juan River

N
W — E
S

Goosenecks State Reserve
316
Mexican Hat

Alhambra Rock ▲

Red Lands Viewpoint

Brigham's Tomb, King on His Throne, Stagecoach, Bear and Rabbit, Castle Butte

Hoskininni Mesa

Eagle Mesa

Monument Valley Hospital ✚

Oljeto

Campground

Airstrip

Goulding's Trading Post and Lodge

Big Indian Sentinel Mesa

VALLEY

Visitors Center

Utah

Arizona

Mitten View Campground

MONUMENT VALLEY TRIBAL PARK

MONUMENT

Mitchell Mesa

U.S. HIGHWAY 163 (North)
Kayenta
to
Monument Valley
and
Mexican Hat, Utah

163

Owl Rock ▲

Agathla Peak ▲

To Four Corners

COMB RIDGE

Kayenta IHS Clinic ✚

Chaistla Butte ▲

Half Dome ▲

Church Rock ▲

160

Baby Rocks Mesa

Kayenta

59

To Tuba City

To Many Farms/Chinle

26 miles (42 km) from Kayenta to Monument Valley

MM 395 WETHERILL INN (West)

John and Louisa Wetherill were two famous traders in Kayenta, contemporaries in time and repute to the Richardsons of Cameron. John Wetherill was from Mancos, Colo., and part of the large Wetherill family famous for their "discovery" of Mesa Verde. Louisa Wade's father was a hopeful miner who had traveled to Colorado to find his fortune. John married Louisa in 1896 and tried to make a life as a farmer in Mancos but the first year was a complete failure. After their children Ben and Ida were born, the Wetherills moved to Oljeto, about 33 miles (53 km) from Kayenta and eight miles (13 km) past the present Goulding's Lodge in Monument Valley. Here they opened the first trading post in hostile country controlled by Hoskinnini. Even though Hoskinnini resented the intrusion, over the years he became a close personal friend of the Wetherills and, according to Louisa's autobiography, gave her the responsibility of dividing his wealth among his children when he died. In 1910, the Wetherills moved their trading post to Kayenta. John used to enjoy telling visitors that they were the "farthest point from a railroad in the United States." (Clark, 1993)

John Wetherill was best known for his exploration of Mesa Verde, Keet Seel, Inscription House and Betatakin ruins. He served as a guide in 1909 for Byron Cummings, dean of arts and sciences at the University of Utah, in his quest for Rainbow Bridge. (See pages 70-71 for more on this expedition.)

The Navajos called Louisa Wetherill, 'Anísts'óózi Ts'ósí, or "Slim Woman." She spoke fluent Navajo and accompanied her husband on most of his expeditions, serving as interpreter. She was well-known for her depth of knowledge and respect for the Navajo lifeways. (Clark, 1993)

Zane Grey, America's most prolific western writer from 1908 to his death in 1939, spent a great deal of time in the Kayenta/Navajo Mountain area. He used Tsegi Canyon and Rainbow Bridge as the setting for *The Rainbow Trail*, a story about a tenderfoot, named Shefford, who comes west to find himself and his own true love.

Wetherill House in Kayenta, 1934
L. to R. a Mrs. Coston and Louisa Wetherill
Photo by Milton Snow, Museum of Northern Arizona, Photo Archives, #74.1198

Grey uses John Wetherill as the basis for his character Trader Withers. Grey describes him:

> He was muscular and weather-beaten, and appeared young in activity rather than face. A gun swung at his hip and a row of brass-tipped cartridges showed in his belt. Shefford looked into a face he thought he had seen before, until he realized the similarity was only the bronze and hard line and rugged cast common to desert men. The gray searching eyes went right through him. (Grey, 1915)

He also describes Louisa Wetherill as Trader Wither's wife,

> He (Withers) had lived at Kayenta for several years–hard and profitless years by reason of marauding outlaws. He could not have lived there at all but for the protection of the Indians. His father-in-law had been friendly with the Navajos and Paiutes for many years, and his wife had been brought up among them. She was held in peculiar reverence and affection by both tribes in that part of the country. Probably she knew more of the Indian's habits, religion, and life than any white person in the West. (Grey, 1915)

MM 396 HALF DOME (East) Igneous intrusive rock.

WHAT IS AN IGNEOUS INTRUSIVE ROCK?

An intrusion is like a volcano that never broke the earth surface. It solidifies in place because of the cooling effect of the rock layer into which it has intruded. Over eons, erosion wears off the top layers covering the intrusion, exposing the harder volcanic core.

MM 397 Kayenta Sandstone on both sides of the road.

MM 398 CHAISTLA BUTTE (East) Igneous intrusive rock.

MM 399 COMB RIDGE (East) See page 195 for a discussion of Comb Ridge.

MM 402 AGATHLA PEAK (East)

Considered the center of the Navajo volcano field, an underground explosion formed this volcanic neck millions of years ago.

According to Navajo legend, this peak is the center of the world. Because the sky was too low, the earth people were suffering from the intense heat of the sun. To help them, the Holy People placed this peak here to create a little more distance between the sky and the earth. It is also thought to be a transmitter to send prayers to the Holy People. (McPherson, 1992)

'Aghaałá means "much wool" in Navajo. This name comes from a Navajo story about an endless snake that became tired after traveling a great distance and made its home at the base of Agathla Peak. His wife the owl stayed with him and made her home close by (see Owl Rock). The snake lived very well here because of the plentiful supply of antelope. After eating his fill, the snake would throw the fur outside and thus the name "much wool." (McPherson, 1992)

Kit Carson renamed Agathla Peak **El Capitan** because of its commanding presence over the valley.

MM 402.5 OWL ROCK (West)

Seen from the right angle, this incredible monolith, composed primarily of Wingate Sandstone, looks just like an owl surveying the valley below. It is 6,547 feet (1,996 m) in elevation.

MM 412 BEARS EARS

Directly in front of you on the horizon if you are traveling north on U.S. 163. These two identical buttes are in the Manti-La Sal National Forest in Utah at an elevation of 9,058 feet (2,761 m).

The bear plays an important part in Navajo legends and ceremonial healing. One of the stories about the bear teaches about the triumph of good over evil. Coyote desired a beautiful Navajo maiden but she was repulsed by him because he was such an evil being. To put him off, she agreed to marry him if he could accomplish a series of seemingly impossible tasks. Through deceit and cunning, Coyote, the trickster, was able to perform every task she demanded. Forced to marry him because of her promise, the maiden began to take on the evil ways of her husband. She gained the ability to turn herself into a bear. When in a bear state she lost control of her human functions and her own identity. One day she killed two of her brothers but the third brother escaped. Guided by the Wind, he found her human body parts (hidden while she was in a bear state), and threw them in different directions. Each part was turned into things of good. One part of her became the pinyon pine nut, another became the acorn and her head became the Bears Ears. (McPherson,1992)

MM 412 MITCHELL MESA (East)

In 1883, when Kit Carson was searching for Navajos to send to Fort Sumner in New Mexico, a small band led by Chief Hoskinnini was able to hide

from Carson's troops. Chief Hoskinnini, "the angry one," was the ruler of Monument Valley from 1862 until 1912 and was particularly hostile toward white prospectors and settlers.

At the time Hoskinnini moved into Monument Valley, it was Ute territory. Agathla Peak marked the boundary between Navajo and Ute country.

When word came that Carson and his troops were on the way, Hoskinnini and 17 others ran for Navajo Mountain where they lived beside a stream for six years undiscovered except for one Ute who did not give away their hiding place.

Hoskinnini and Ida Wetherill (Detail), 1909
Stuart M. Young Collection, Cline Library, Special Collections and Archives, NAU 643-1-27

One day, while Hoskinnini was riding on Navajo Mountain, he found silver. All of the male members of his group dug out all of the silver they could find and fashioned plain silver jewelry. When the band heard of the Navajos' release from Bosque Redondo, they moved back to Monument Valley a very rich group. Eventually, word began to leak to the outside world that Hoskinnini had found a rich silver mine, attracting many prospectors to remote Monument Valley. Hoskinnini and his band never revealed where they found the silver but miners Merrick and Mitchell allegedly found the mine. Both volunteer soldiers with Kit Carson, they came to Monument Valley after the Navajo wars were over because of rumors of

Hoskinnini's rich silver mine but didn't live long enough to enjoy their discovery.

It is thought that Mitchell and Merrick might have been successful in secretly removing one load of silver from the mine before their death. In *Traders to The Navajo*, now a 1934 classic, Louisa Wade Wetherill claims that her father knew Mitchell and Merrick and saw the assay for their silver mine valued at $800 a ton (4,400 kg). Wade looked for the mine himself in 1882 but without success. (Gilmore, 1934)

According to Hoskinnini's son, Hoskinnini-Begay, interviewed by reporter Charles Kelly in 1953, he had come upon Utes dividing up the miners' possessions. The Utes told him they killed the miners when they refused to share their tobacco. Another version is that when the Paiutes found Mitchell's burro laden with silver, they became outraged at his abuse of Mother Earth and killed him. His partner Merrick escaped but the Paiutes caught up with him at the base of the butte that bears his name. (***Merrick Butte** can be seen from the viewpoint at the visitors center in between the **Right and Left Mittens**.*) Chief Hoskinnini denied any knowledge of, or involvement in, the miners' deaths.

Another white man attempted to find the location of the silver mine by befriending Hoskinnini. Cass Hite, a Mormon settler who established a ferry across the Colorado River not too far from Monument Valley, just rode into Hoskinnini's camp one day, sat down and asked for food. As it would be the height of bad manners to kill a guest in your camp, Hoskinnini had no choice but to feed this man who spoke very little Navajo. Hite gave Hoskinnini and his family presents and gradually developed a friendship with the group. After a respectable period of time he asked the family if they knew where he could find valuable minerals in the area. Hoskinnini was kind enough to tell Hite where to find gold in the Colorado River. In 1883, Hite built a trading post and a house near the river to begin panning for gold. This is where **Hite Marina** on Lake Powell stands today.

You are probably wondering what happened to the silver mine. According to Hoskinnini's son, the mine was completely exhausted and most of the silver is buried with his father who died in 1912. The rest was divided among Hoskinnini's family. Hoskinnini-Begay's silver is buried with his eight wives. (Kelly, 1953)

 **MM 416 RIGHT AND LEFT MITTEN (East)**

SCENIC DETOUR

Merrick Butte, not dated.
Photo by T. Harmon Parkhurst, Courtesy Museum of New Mexico, #71068

MONUMENT VALLEY NAVAJO TRIBAL PARK VISITOR CENTER

Turn east and travel three miles (4.8 km) to the Monument Valley Tribal Park Visitor Center. Half way, there will be a place to pay an entrance fee. $2.50/person, $1 senior citizens 60 years or older, free to children under six years. National Park Service passes are not accepted at any tribal park. Park hours: May through Sept., 7 a.m. to 7 p.m.; Oct. through April, 8 a.m. to 5 p.m.; closed Christmas, New Year's and Thanksgiving Day. During the summer, the visitor center offers Indian dances on the patio from 8 p.m. to 9:30 p.m. Check at the desk to confirm the day and time for the performance.

Right Mitten, Monument Valley, 1994
Photograph by Christine Stephenson

MITTEN VIEW CAMPGROUND: *Register at the visitors center. The campground is across the street. There are 99 sites, 37 tent spaces, 36 RV sites, nine pull-throughs and nine day-use picnic areas. The fee is $10 per night on a first-come, first-served basis. The campground has men's and women's bathrooms, coin-operated showers but no phones or hookups for RVs. There is a filling/dump station. A metal awning at each camp site provides the only shade. Summer temperatures at Monument Valley are usually over 100 degrees (38° C).*

Once Paiute aboriginal land, the northwest section of the valley became part of the Navajo Reservation through the Treaty of 1868. The western and northern sections were added in 1884. In 1934, some of valley was converted to public domain land but the protest was heard in Washington and the land was reinstated to the Navajos by an act of Congress. (Van Valkenburg, 1941) The Navajo Tribe opened the park in 1960.

The Navajos view the whole of Monument Valley as a huge hogan. Its door, facing east, is near the visitors center. The fireplace, or the center of the hogan, is the butte behind Goulding's Trading Post. (McPherson,1992)

You can hire a tour guide at the visitors center to take you through the valley or you can drive your own car. The road is unpaved and changes condition after each rainstorm. Sand traps and high road centers can cause problems for low-clearance vehicles. The self-guided tour is 17 miles (27 km) along the valley floor. There are information signs that correspond to a map you can purchase in the visitor center for $1.

TOUR GUIDE OPERATORS

The superintendent of the park controls all of the tour guide fees. Occasionally some prices will be lower but are not allowed to go any higher than the prices advertised. Most of the tour companies are Navajo-owned.

JACKSON TOUR: *(435) 727-3234 message*
P.O. Box 360375, Monument Valley, UT 84536
Owner: Betty Jackson started this company in 1970. The Jackson family has lived in Monument Valley for generations. She offers jeep tours, Mystery Valley tours, hiking tours, photography tours and private tours.

ROLAND'S NAVAJOLAND TOURS: *(800) 368-2785 or (520) 697-3524*
P.O. Box 1542 Kayenta, AZ 86033 **Owner:** Roland Cody Dixon
Offers: One-hour, two-hour or three-hour open air jeep tours. Also offers a three-hour tour with a cookout (requires 15-person minimum).

BENNETT TOURS: *(435) 727-3283*
P.O. Box 360285,Monument Valley, UT 84536 **Owner:** Tom Bennett
Offers: Four-wheel or hiking, group, private, cookout, commercial, photography, overnight camping tours.

FRED'S ADVENTURE TOURS
(435) 739-4294 (evenings)
Box 310308, Mexican Hat, UT 84531-0308
Owner: Fred Cly. According to his brochure, Cly Butte in Monument Valley was named after his grandfather. His father, Gie Cly, was a stunt rider in one of the John Wayne movies shot in Monument Valley and his mother is a well-known rug weaver.
Offers: Hiking and jeep tours of Monument Valley back country, Hunts Mesa, Mystery Valley, Wetherill Mesa, customized photo tour and winter photo workshop in December and February.

Three Sisters, Monument Valley, not dated.
Atchison-Topeka-Santa Fe Collection, Kansas State Historical Society, Topeka, Kansas 2/514.11

BLACK'S VAN AND HIKING TOURS *(435) 739-4226*
P.O. Box 310393, Mexican Hat, UT 84531
Owner: Roy Black **Offers:** Jeep and hiking tours to Monument Valley, Hunts Mesa, Wetherill Mesa, Mitchell Mesa.

TOTEM POLE GUIDED TOURS *(800) 345-TOUR or (435) 727-3313*
P.O. Box 360306, Monument Valley, UT 84536
Owner: Vergil Bedoni **Offers:** Group or private jeep or hiking tours, commercial, photographic or overnight camping tours.

ED BLACK MONUMENT VALLEY HORSEBACK TRAILRIDES
(800) 551-4039 OR (435) 739-4285
P.O. Box 310155, Mexican Hat, UT 84531
Owner: Ed Black **Offers**: Horseback rides to The Mittens , *Yé'ii bicheii* Mesa and Totem Pole , Big Rock Door Mesa or North Window , Echo Cave Ruin , John Ford's Point, Mystery Valley, Full Moonlight Trail ride , sunrise and sunset tours , Horse Canyon tour , Rain God Mesa ; Wagon rides.

DANIEL'S GUIDED TOURS *(435) 727-3227; (800) 596-8427*
P.O. Box 360153, Monument Valley, UT 84536 Owner: Daniel Chee

BEGAY'S TOUR *(435) 697-8452* Owner: Manuel Begay
P.O. Box 360231 Monument Valley, UT 84536

BIGMAN'S HORSEBACK TOURS *(520) 677-3219* Owner: Dick Bigman
P.O. Box 360426, Monument Valley, UT 84536

HOMELAND HORSEBACK TOURS *(435) 727-3227; (800) 596-8427*
P.O. Box 360349, Monument Valley, UT 84536

MONUMENT VALLEY HORSEBACK TOUR *(520) 691-6161*
P.O. Box 360126, Monument Valley, UT 84536

NAVAJO COUNTRY TRAILRIDES *(435) 727-3210*
P.O. Box 360416, Monument Valley, UT 84536

SACRED MONUMENT TRAILRIDES *(435) 727-3218*
P.O. Box 360350, Monument Valley, UT 84536

KEYAHO HOZHONI TOUR *No phone*
P.O. Box 913, Kayenta, AZ 86033

CRAWLEY'S TOUR *(520) 697-3463/3742*
P.O. Box 187, Kayenta, AZ 86033

COUNTRY OF MANY HOGAN BED AND BREAKFAST
Located in the heart of Monument Valley, at the foot of Boot Mesa, just ten miles southwest of Monument Valley Tribal Park Visitor Center. The Bedonie family has opened its traditional hogan to allow visitors to experience the Diné lifestyle and hospitality. They also offer hiking, horseback and vehicle tours of Monument Valley. You can even experience a traditional Navajo sweatlodge. For more information and a brochure call (520) 283-4125 or 888-291-4397; e-mail at nezfoster@prodigy.com.

END SCENIC DETOUR

GOULDING'S TRADING POST MUSEUM

After leaving the visitors center, continue across Highway 163 and follow the signs. The museum is open from late March through October from 7 a.m. to 9 p.m, (DST), closed in winter. No admission fee but donations are welcomed. The lodge and restaurant are open year round.

The Navajos called Harry Goulding *Dibé Nééz* or "Tall Sheep" because of his tall stature and interest in sheep. Harry first saw Monument Valley in the early 1920s when he came here as a representative of the Lybrook Ranch in Farmington, N.M., to buy Navajo Churro sheep. By the 1920s, these sheep, imported with the Spanish in the 1500s, were almost extinct. The breed has silky, long wool and four horns that grow out of the top of their forehead and curl down into their face. Crossbred with Merino sheep, the Churro sheep was quickly losing the qualities that made it so valuable. Today the Merino sheep is the most common type of sheep you will see along the highway but the Churro sheep is gaining in popularity. (You can see a flock of Churro sheep at the Tso Bonito Zoo in Window Rock.)

As soon as Goulding saw Monument Valley, he knew this was to be his destiny. So when the opportunity arose to purchase 640 acres (2.6 sq km) of land beneath Big Rock Door Mesa for $320, he jumped at the chance. The Paiute Indians had been given a small reservation here but because of the poor farming conditions they were moved to a more fertile area in Utah and the land became state property available for sale. Goulding officially bought the property in 1937 against protest by the Indian Service. The land

had technically been added to the Navajo reservation in 1933 but the sale was allowed because the state of Utah had maintained ownership of all school property and had the right to sell it. (Markward, 1992; Clark, 1993; Moon, 1992).

Goulding's Trading Post under "Old Baldy," not dated.
Courtesy Museum of New Mexico #71078

During the Depression in the 1930s there was not much money coming onto the reservation. To make matters worse the BIA, under John Collier's administration, decided that Navajo sheepherders must reduce their herds because of severe overgrazing. Forced to sell their sheep at ridiculously low prices or slaughter them, many families became destitute. Even though Collier made positive changes in the education and health care systems on the Navajo reservation, he is not remembered kindly by the Navajo people for his callous disregard for the importance of sheep. Samual Moon, in his book *Tall Sheep,* quotes Maurice Knee, Harry Goulding's brother-in-law, as saying that if a Navajo family had a dog they didn't like they would name it "John Collie." (Moon, 1992)

When Harry heard a rumor in 1937 that United Artists was looking for a place to shoot a movie in the Southwest, he packed his bags and traveled to Hollywood hoping to attract the movie makers to the valley. With just a few pictures of Monument Valley and a lot of patience and persistence, Harry convinced John Ford to shoot his next western on location in the valley. The first film made in 1938 was *Stagecoach* with John Wayne in the lead role. Other Ford movies followed, including *She Wore a Yellow Ribbon*, *My Darling Clementine* and *Fort Apache.* (Moon, 1992; Clark, 1993)

The success of John Ford's movies paved the way for many other movie companies to make their films or commercials here. Today, no self-respecting car company would make a commercial unless its backdrop is Monument Valley. One movie made here has a touch of irony to it. The movie was *Kit Carson,* the same person who had chased Hoskinnini's clan into the valley. Now Hoskinnini's descendents, just 80 years later, would work in a movie that glorified Carson's actions. (Klinck, 1973)

When the Gouldings retired, they sold their property to Knox College in Illinois in exchange for royalties and scholarships for Navajo students. In 1981, Knox College sold Goulding's to the LaFont family which also owns the Canyon de Chelly Motel in Chinle and the Wetherill Inn in Kayenta.

SERVICES AT GOULDING'S

Lodge: A 62-room motel with each room facing Monument Valley. It also has an indoor swimming pool. Reservations: Goulding's Lodge, Box 360001, Monument Valley, UT 84536, (801) 727-3231

Prices: Add a 9 percent sales tax to all prices.

April 15-May 30	sngl/dbl $108; add $6 for each additional person
June 1-Oct. 15	sngl/dbl $128
Jan. 1-Mar.14	sngl/dbl $62
Mar. 15-April 14	sngl/dbl $92

Stagecoach Restaurant: Navajo-American, open from 6:30 a.m.-9 p.m. DST. (801) 727-3231 Ext. 404.
Limited hours in winter but breakfast, lunch and dinner are served.

Guided Tours: Price includes entrance fee to park.
Full-Day (lunch included) $60/person
Children (under 12) $45/person
Departs at 9 a.m. DST-Approximately 8 hours.
Half-Day $30/person
Children (under 12) $18/person
Leaves at 9 a.m. and 1:30 p.m. for approximately 3.5 hours.

Evening Entertainment at Goulding's

EARTH SPIRIT: A Celebration of Monument Valley is a slide presentation about Monument Valley. It shows nightly at 6:10 p.m., 7:10 p.m. and 8:10 p.m. Admission: Adult: $2; Children: $1; under 12, free.

◀ Take a left (west) at the end of Goulding road to the Seventh Day Adventist Hospital and Goulding's Campground.

MONUMENT VALLEY AIR STRIP (East)

Harry Goulding had to do some major land negotiations to get this airport. He wanted it to transport critically-ill patients to and from the hospital as well as accommodate Hollywoods' need to fly in actors, equipment and crew for a day or two of shooting. Harry first asked the governor of Utah to finance the airstrip. Then, because the land he wanted was on the Navajo Reservation, he had to get congressional approval to exchange a piece of his own land for the airstrip land. (Klinck, 1973)

Lake Powell Air Service offers scenic air tours of Monument Valley from this strip. Prices for a 20-minute flight, two passenger minimum, runs about $60/person. (800) 245-6668.

SEVENTH DAY ADVENTIST HOSPITAL (East)

Before 1950, no health care was available in Monument Valley. The Gouldings frequently drove their neighbors to Tuba City, Ariz., about 120 miles one-way, over unimproved roads. The last time they did this in 1949, the small child did not survive the trip. Harry Goulding gave the Seventh Day Adventists a 99-year lease if the church, which operated medical missions around the world at the time, would open a clinic to serve the people of Monument Valley. (Moon, 1992; Clark, 1993)

The first building constructed on the hospital grounds was made from materials from the movie set of *She Wore a Yellow Ribbon.* Today, there's a private, 18-bed hospital with dental and eye clinics which, unlike the Indian Health Service, has no restrictions on who may receive treatment. Tourists are welcome. Private insurance is accepted. (435) 727-3241.

GOULDING'S MONUMENT VALLEY CAMPGROUND

Open March 15 through October 15th. Located in Rock Door Canyon, this 66-site campground is a "Good Sam Park" that offers a grocery store, gift shop, laundry facilities and BBQs, plus an indoor pool. Prices for RVs, $22/two people, extra person $3 includes: Full hookups: water, sewer, electricity, TV. TENT: $24/two people, extra person $3. (435) 727-3231 or 3235.

Go back past the airport to U.S. Highway 163 and turn north to see the Goosenecks of the San Juan River. Twenty-five miles (40 km) to Mexican Hat, Utah.

ENTERING UTAH

MM 4 SENTINEL MESA (East)

You can see a piece of the Left Mitten Butte in front of Sentinel Mesa but you really have to go inside the park to see the Mittens from the visitors center.

MM 5 BIG INDIAN (East)

MM 6 BRIGHAM'S TOMB, KING ON HIS THRONE, STAGECOACH, BEAR AND RABBIT, CASTLE BUTTE (East) If you look closely at all of these landforms, you'll see that their names were well chosen.

MM 9 REDLAND VIEW POINT (East)

Monoliths visible from this viewpoint are shown on the map on page 190.

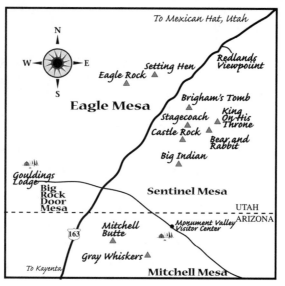

MM 10 SLEEPING UTE MOUNTAIN, CORTEZ, COLORADO (East)

See page 201 for a description of this mountain.

MM 18 ALHAMBRA ROCK (West)

This is an igneous rock formation. Like Agathla Peak, in Navajo cosmology, it, too, supports the sky. (McPherson, 1992)

MEXICAN HAT SYNCLINE

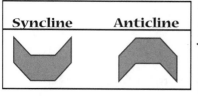

As you cross the bridge over the San Juan River, the syncline is directly in front of you. This is just one part of the combinations of synclines and anticlines that make up the Monument Upwarp. A syncline is where layered rock dips toward each other from opposite sides of a depression. An anticline is folded rock that bends downward from the crest.

MM 21 SAN JUAN BRIDGE

The construction of this bridge in 1909 ended a long history of dangerous crossings by Paiutes, Navajos and pioneers.

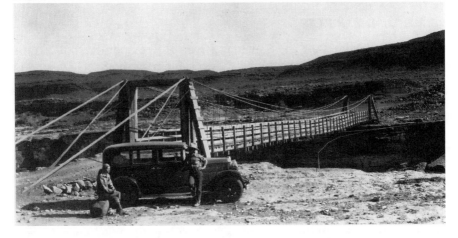

First Bridge Across the San Juan River, ca. 1930-1940
Philip Johnston Collection, Cline Library, Special Collections and Archives, NAU 413-525-526

MM 21 SAN JUAN RIVER

This is the northern boundary of the Navajo Nation. The headwaters originate above Pagosa Springs and Wolf Creek Pass in Colorado and flow into Lake Powell. Before construction of the Glen Canyon Dam, the San Juan River flowed directly into the Colorado River.

MEXICAN HAT

Named Black Hat in Navajo, this town gets its name from a rock formation about 1.5 miles (2.4 km) northeast of the bridge that looks like an upside down Mexican sombrero. This is the takeout point for many San Juan River trips that start at Sand Island Recreation Area near Bluff, Utah, and travel about 26 miles (42 km) to Mexican Hat. Because of the popularity of this river, you must obtain a permit based on a lottery system to float the San Juan privately but there are many commercial companies for hire.

San Juan River Tour Companies

Adrift Adventures *(800) 874-4483*
P.O. Box 577, Moab UT 84532
Arizona Raft Adventures, Inc. *(800) 786-7238 or (520) 526-8200*
4050 E. Huntington Dr., Flagstaff, AZ 86004
Four Corners School of Outdoor Education *(435) 587-2159, (800) 525-4456*
196 S. Main, Monticello, UT
Wild Adventures *(800) 259 RAFT or (800)RIO-MOAB*
P.O. Box 801, Moab, UT 84532
Wild River Expeditions *(800) 422-7654*
P.O. Box 118, Bluff, UT 84512

🦎 MM 22 OIL DERRICKS

While prospecting along the San Juan River, E.L. Goodridge noticed oil seeping out of the rocks about where the bridge over the San Juan stands today. Others probably noticed this black stuff but no one seemed to realize its value except Goodridge. He built a drilling rig about 100 feet (30 m) from the natural oil seep and, at 225 feet (69 m), hit a "gusher" on March 4, 1908. This started an oil boom and the bridge was built over the San Juan to accommodate the glut of oil tycoons wanting to haul equipment from Bluff to the oil fields.

The geology of Mexican Hat, at that time known as Goodridge, did not hold large reservoirs of oil because the river had already sapped most of it out of the rock over millions of years. It wasn't until 1956, when Texaco drilled a well at Aneth, Utah, on the Navajo Reservation, that the truly important oil field was discovered. The Aneth Oil Field is expected to produce more than 500 million barrels of oil over its lifetime. (Baars, 1986)

SERVICES IN MEXICAN HAT

LODGING
The San Juan Inn *(800) 447-2220*
P.O. Box 535, Mexican Hat, UT 84531
Summer rates for two people about $56, plus 9% tax.
Burch's Valley of the Gods Inn and Restaurant *(435) 683-2221*
Box 310337, Mexican Hat, UT 84531
Summer rates for two people, about $65 plus tax.
R.V. Park: $15 includes a full hookup, only three spaces available.
Canyonlands Motel *(435) 683-2230*
P.O.Box 11, Mexican Hat, UT
Summer rates for two people $42 plus tax.
Mexican Hat Lodge *(435) 683-2222*
Summer rates for two people $58 plus tax.

RV PARK
Valle Trailer Park *(800) 683-2226*
31 RV sites, full-hook-ups, shower, restrooms and dump station.
$12 for the first person, $2 for each additional person.

RESTAURANTS
The San Juan Inn: Breakfast, lunch and dinner. 6:30 a.m.-10 p.m.
Valley of the Gods Inn: Breakfast, lunch and dinner 7 a.m.-10 p.m

GOOSENECKS OF THE SAN JUAN RIVER

Just a few miles past Mexican Hat is the crookedest river in the world. This amazing geologic wonder formed about the same time as the volcanic plugs, like Shiprock and Agathla Peak, when the uplift created the San Juan canyon. Once a wide, wandering river, as the shores rose around it, the San Juan river began cutting deeper and deeper. Now entrenched in harder and harder rock, the river had no choice but to follow the meandering path it had previously cut. The San Juan River travels 135 miles (218 km) through its many twists and turns from the point where it enters the canyon to the point where it empties into Lake Powell, a distance of just 63 miles (102 km) as the crow flies. (Vokes,1942)

Goosenecks of the San Juan River, ca. 1930-1940s
Philip Johnston Collection, Cline Library, Special Collections and Archives, NAU PH 413-534

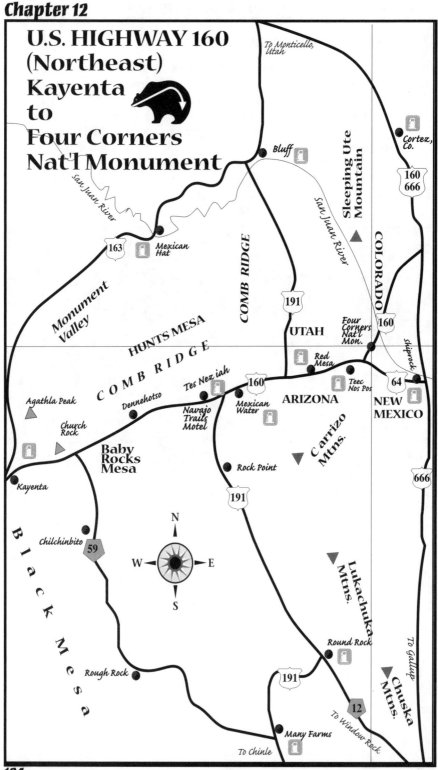

Chapter 12

U.S. HIGHWAY 160 (Northeast) Kayenta to Four Corners Nat'l Monument

To Monticello, Utah

Cortez, Co.

Bluff

San Juan River

160 666

Sleeping Ute Mountain

San Juan River

163 Mexican Hat

COLORADO

COMB RIDGE

Monument Valley

191

HUNTS MESA

UTAH

160

Four Corners Nat'l Mon.

COMB RIDGE

Red Mesa

Shiprock

Tes Nez iah

160

Teec Nos Pos

64

Dennehotso

ARIZONA

NEW MEXICO

Agathla Peak

Navajo Trails Motel

Mexican Water

Church Rock

Carrizo Mtns.

Baby Rocks Mesa

Rock Point

666

Kayenta

191

Chilchinbito

59

N

W   E

S

Black Mesa

Lukachuka Mtns.

To Gallup

Round Rock

Rough Rock

191

12

Chuska Mtns.

Many Farms

To Window Rock

To Chinle

78 miles (126 km) from Kayenta to Four Corners National Monument

MM 400 CHURCH ROCK (North)

This is an excellent example of an igneous intrusive rock formation like Agathla Peak. It formed when the sedimentary material surrounding the hardened volcanic plug eroded away, leaving the remains of a vent or cylinder eerily exposed in the general shape of a church and steeple.

MM 400 COMB RIDGE North, behind Church Rock

One of the larger monoclines in the world, this 70-mile (112 km) ridge of Navajo Sandstone extends from Kayenta to Blanding, Utah. (Barnes, 1960)

Comb Ridge shows the characteristic pink, light orange and gray colors that make up much of the beauty of the Southwest. Navajo Sandstone is simply compressed ancient sand dunes. If you look closely, you can see the way the wind was blowing from the directions of the lines on its surface. This makes it a favorite for photographers.

Many Navajos think of Comb Ridge as the backbone of the earth. They also see it as one long arrowhead, set on edge, one of four that protects the boundaries of the Navajo Nation. (McPherson, 1992)

MM 407 BABY ROCKS MESA (South)

This assortment of spires and knobs resulted from the erosion of the Entrada Sandstone formed during the Jurassic Era. Navajos use this mesa to teach their children values. One story tells of a big sister who refused to give blue corn bread to her baby sister. To end big sister's fighting and selfishness, the Holy People punished her by turning her to stone where she lives as one of the baby rocks.

This was once a Navajo farming community that was unable to continue farming after a 1912 flood cut Laguna Creek too low to allow irrigation to reach Baby Rocks. The people moved their farming community 15 miles (24 km) downstream to Dennehotso. (Van Valkenburgh, 1941)

The trading post and gas station were built by Clark Hadley, a Navajo businessman, in the 1960s. His family has lived at Baby Rocks for generations. Since Hadley's death in 1985, the businesses have been closed but his family plans to reopen the trading post. (Wicoff, 1993)

Native Roads

Baby Rocks Mesa is Tony Hillerman's fictional Navajo police officer Jim Chee's favorite place to wait for speeders along U.S. Highway 160. Who knows? Maybe the real Navajo police like this area also.

MM 408 HUNT'S MESA North, behind Comb Ridge

Locals consider this the back door to Monument Valley. Following a rugged, twisting four wheel drive trail, you arrive on top of Hunt's Mesa where you can look down upon the world famous buttes and spires. Not recommended without a guide and proper back road equipment. (See tour guides, pages 184-186.)

MM 412 RED POINT MESA (South)

MM 418 DENNEHOTSO (North)

This name comes from a Navajo word meaning "people's farms." The leader of the Baby Rocks group, named Old Crank, built an earthen dam in 1912 to promote farming along Laguna Creek. A concrete dam replaced it in the 1940s to irrigate nearly 800 acres (3.2 sq km). This area was also the site of a uranium mine. (Van Valkenburgh, 1941)

MM 422 CARRIZO MOUNTAINS (Southeast)

See MM 465 for an explanation of these mountains.

MM 428 DENNEHOTSO CANYON (South)

Cut by the Chinle Wash.

MM 429 TES NEZ IAH

In Navajo, this means "tall cottonwood grove."

NAVAJO TRAILS MOTEL: Rooms run around $44 double, $39 single plus an 8 percent Navajo tax. No restaurant but Mexican Water restaurant just down the road heading east, serves breakfast, lunch and dinner. There is only one T.V. channel and the only telephone is a radio phone. (520) 674-3618.

Junction U.S. Highway 191 south to Canyon de Chelly

MM 436 MEXICAN WATER

Called Mexican Water, or *Naakaii to' hadayiiznili*, which in Navajo means "Mexicans dug shallow wells." In 1939, a steel bridge was built over Walker Creek ending the use of the original 1879 Mormon Road. This road ran from Cedar City, Utah, crossed the Colorado River at Lees Ferry, ran through Willow Springs, Moenkopi, Red Lake, Kayenta and Mexican Water. It crossed the San Juan River at Bluff, Utah, the Colorado River at Moab and circled back around to Cedar City. (Barnes, 1960)

Mexican Water Restaurant: Open from 7 a.m.-10 p.m. According to locals they make a good Navajo taco.

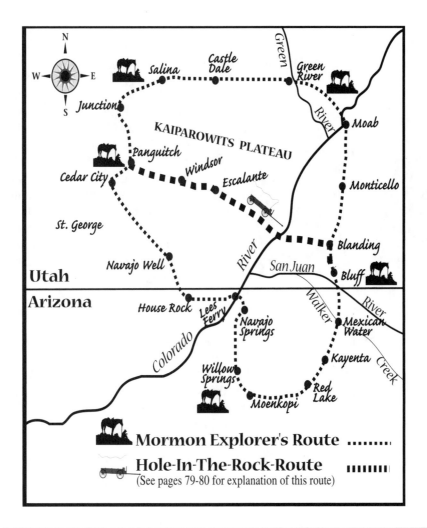

Mormon Explorer's Route ....

Hole-In-The-Rock-Route ||||||||
(See pages 79-80 for explanation of this route)

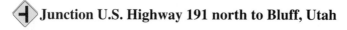 Junction U.S. Highway 191 north to Bluff, Utah

 MM 450 RED MESA

This incredibly red mesa gets its color from mud sediment found in the Carmel Formation. The Carmel Formation is part of the San Raphael Group formed during the Jurassic Era, 135-to-180 million years ago. It is mostly red, brown and grey mudstone and sandstone. (Nations, 1981)

MM 464 TEEC NOS POS

T'iis názbąs means "cottonwoods in a circle" in Navajo.

The original Teec Nos Pos Trading Post was built in 1905 by the Foutz family. They are related by marriage to the Tanner family, the first Mormon settlers of Tuba City in the 1800s. When the original trading post burned in

 the 1950s, the decision was made to rebuild closer to the rumored new Navajo Route 1 (U.S. Hwy. 160). According to Kathy Foutz, who currently works at the post, Grandpa was just a little off in his calculations. The trading post is located about 1/4 mile (.4 km) past the turn-off to Four Corners on the north side of the road. Open 7:30 a.m.-6:30 p.m. DST.

Teec Nos Pos Trading Post, 1949
Photo by Milton Snow, Courtesy Museum of New Mexico #46042

Teec Nos Pos is the childhood home of Peter MacDonald, former chairman of the Navajo Nation. His maternal great-grandparents were prisoners at Bosque Redondo. Their son, Deshna Chischillige, became the second chairman of the Navajo Tribe in 1928, the same year Peter MacDonald was born. MacDonald was given the name Peter Donald by a BIA school official who couldn't pronounce his Navajo name, a common practice in most boarding schools at the time. When his classmates heard the name they changed it to MacDonald after the song *Old MacDonald*. (Frink, 1968, MacDonald, 1993)

Once considered the most powerful American Indian in the country, MacDonald is now serving a 14-year prison term for corruption, accepting bribes and conspiracy in relation to a 1989 riot in the Navajo capital of Window Rock which led to the deaths of two of his supporters. The riot resulted from the frustration his supporters felt over his suspension from office by the Navajo Tribal Council after he was implicated in fraudulent schemes by a U.S. Senate panel looking into fraud in Indian Country. Despite convictions in tribal and federal courts, MacDonald has always maintained he was duped and had done nothing wrong from a Navajo traditional context. Though discredited in the eyes of some, his supporters remain ardently loyal to him. He is a very popular figure on the Navajo Reservation with large groups of supporters calling themselves *Diné Bóhoníih* which means "the people are our boss." Many of his supporters believe that MacDonald was the victim of a federal and tribal vendetta, stripped of power illegally and treated unfairly. In April 1995, a newly-elected Navajo Nation Council granted MacDonald a complete pardon and requested President Clinton to pardon him for his federal crimes. (Donovan, 1993; Hardeen, 1995)

Despite his legal problems, MacDonald accomplished much for the Navajo people during his almost 25-year reign as chairman. His rise to power came through his appointment as director of the Office of Navajo Economic Opportunity in 1964 by former Navajo Chairman Raymond Nakai. In that position, MacDonald obtained the tribe's first federal grant under the newly-legislated Economic Development Act of the Johnson administration.Through MacDonald's grant, a pre-school program, small business development center and neighborhood youth corps were established. (Frink, 1968)

REGIONAL RUG DESIGNS-TEEC NOS POS

Usually a very large rug, the Teec Nos Pos design has an intricate center and wide borders which many think resembles Persian rugs. Because of their intricacies and size, they can be very expensive. (Lamb, 1993)

Teec Nos Pos, ca. 1970
Photograph by Gene Balzer, Museum of Northern Arizona

◀ **Junction to Four Corners National Monument.**

Follow U.S. 160 heading north, 5.8 miles. The monument is on the west side of the road.

SERVICES AVAILABLE AT TEEC NOS POS

Frank's Groceries:	Hours 7 a.m.-9 p.m.
Teec Nos Pos Trading Post:	Hours: 7:30 a.m.-6:30 p.m.

Carrizo Mountains, 1890
Photograph by Ben Wittick
Courtesy School of American Research Collections in the Museum of New Mexico, #15568

🐻 MM 465 CARRIZO MOUNTAINS (South)

Since Red Mesa, you have been able to see these mountains rising slowly to their highest peak at an elevation of 9,420 feet (2,873 m.). The Navajos call this mountain *Dził Náhooziłii*, which means "the mountain that gropes around" or "circular mountain." Uranium is plentiful here because of the extensive Morrison Formation. Long coveted for its reported mineral wealth, the mountain has been the target of miners' attempted explorations since the late 1800s. In 1890, Indian agent C.E. Vendever heard a rumor that 50 prospectors illegally entered the reservation and were mining on the mountain. Vendever sent for troops from Fort Wingate, and along with Chee Dodge and famous photographer, Ben Wittick, accompanied the troops to the mining site where they found 15 prospectors besieged by a mob of angry people defending their sacred land. Everything ended peacefully, with the prospectors escorted off the reservation by the soldiers. (Van Valkenburgh, 1941)

When uranium miners asked Tall Bitter Water, a resident of the Carrizos, for permission to explore for oil and uranium in this mineral-rich area, he explained the significance these mountains hold for the Navajo people. He said that the mountain has arms and legs. He was referring to the belief that the mountain ranges of the Chuska, Lukachukai and Carrizo make up a male figure. The Carrizos are the figure's legs and must not be tampered with. Bitter Water continued to explain that this mountain takes care of the Navajo people and helps people get well. It cannot do that if its legs are cut off. (McPherson, 1992)

SLEEPING UTE MOUNTAIN Look to the north in the distance
This is a landmark in traditional Ute territory known as *Dzil Naajinii'*, or "black mountain sloping down" to Navajos. It's possible to see a human figure when you look at the mountain from the east. The story is told that a Ute chief is buried here. His head lies toward the north with his face to the sky. His arms cross over his chest and his feet point to the south. (McPherson, 1992)

FOUR CORNERS NATIONAL MONUMENT *Open 7 a.m. - 8 p.m. The entrance fee is $1 for adults, free for children under 6. National Park Service passes are not accepted. This is a Navajo tribal park. No camping.* If you stand in the center of the circle you will be able to tell your friends that you were in all four states at the exact same moment. In 1875, the first surveying marker was placed dividing the territories — later to become the states of Arizona, New Mexico, Colorado and Utah. But it was not until 1962 that a paved road made the monument accessible and a plaque commemorating this surveyor's dream was dedicated. Each of the four states has its seal on the monument. The inscription reads, "Here Meet, in Freedom, Under God, Four States." (Muench, 1963) There are jewelry and food vendors here.

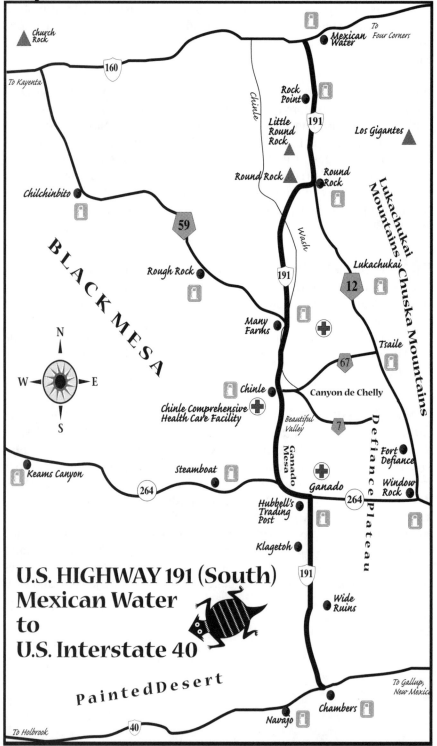

Chapter 13

Church Rock

To Kayenta

160

Chinle

To Four Corners

Mexican Water

Rock Point

191

Los Gigantes

Little Round Rock

Round Rock

Round Rock

Lukachukai Mountains Chuska Mountains

Chilchinbito

59

Wash

Rough Rock

191

Lukachukai

12

N
W   E
S

B L A C K   M E S A

Many Farms

Tsaile

67

Chinle

Canyon de Chelly

7

Chinle Comprehensive Health Care Facility

Beautiful Valley

Ganado Mesa

Defiance Plateau

Fort Defiance

Keams Canyon

Steamboat

264

Ganado

Window Rock

264

Hubbell's Trading Post

191

Klagetoh

**U.S. HIGHWAY 191 (South)
Mexican Water
to
U.S. Interstate 40**

Wide Ruins

To Gallup, New Mexico

P a i n t e d   D e s e r t

To Holbrook

40

Navajo

Chambers

136 miles (219 km) from Rock Point to U.S. Interstate 40

MM 495 ROCK POINT

Established in 1926, this community is the starting point of "Red Rock Country." This scenic area stretches all the way from here southeast to Red Rock on the east side of the Chuska Mountains. Most of the rock in this area is Wingate Sandstone, formed during the Triassic era. The bottom layer, or Salt Wash Formation, holds large deposits of uranium found primarily in the Lukachukai Mountains in the 1950s.

Throughout Red Rock Country are countless prehistoric and historic ruins, natural bridges, coves, caves and other interesting phenomenon. In 1965, Stephen Jett of Ohio State University studied potential tourist attractions for inclusion in the Navajo tribal park system. He found "...Red Rock country to be one of the most outstanding areas in the region, both from a scenic and an archeological point of view...." (Jett, 1965)

MM 486 LITTLE ROUND ROCK MESA (West)

MM 486 ROUND ROCK MESA (West)

Look for a window in Round Rock Mesa visible from the road.

MM 482.5 LOS GIGANTES East, behind the mesa. Spanish for "the giants."

This is the setting for Tony Hillerman's first Navajo detective novel written in 1970. *The Blessingway* won Honorable Mention from the Mystery Writers of America as Best First Novel. (Erisman, 1989)

Hillerman originally intended to call the book *The Enemy Way* because the plot centers around this ceremony but his publisher at Harper & Row decided to change the title to *The Blessingway*. The story is about a urban Indian who doesn't know his culture. An organized crime syndicate uses him to find a White Sands military rocket lost in the rugged Lukachukai Mountains so they can sell its secrets to the enemy. Navajo Police Lt. Joe Leaphorn deduces that the "relocation Indian" is the cause of a murder associated with the search for the missile and related "Navajo Wolf" scares to keep people away from his find. Leaphorn figures this out because of the illogical reasoning used by this man without a culture.

NATIVE ROADS

Blessingway Ceremony

The Blessingway is the cornerstone of the Navajo ceremonial healing system. This ceremony helps the patient restore a sense of harmony with his surroundings and brings happiness back into his life. The songs and prayers chanted during this lengthy "sing" describe the Navajo creation story. It tells about the emergence of the Holy People from the underworld, the birth of Changing Woman, the building of the first hogan and the creation of the four sacred mountains. The patient feels like he or she is one with the story and an important participant in the creation of the earth.

Native diagnosticians will prescribe this ceremony for people experiencing stress, anxiety, boredom, lack of confidence or fear. Many Navajos have a Blessingway annually to ensure happiness and a harmonious life throughout the year. (Dennison, 1994)

MM 485 LUKACHUKAI MOUNTAINS (East)

This is a small mountain range that runs from Round Rock to Lukachukai where the Chuska Mountains begin.

MM 485 ROUND ROCK TRADING POST (West)

This trading post once belonged to Chee Dodge and his partner Stephen Aldrich in 1881. Chee Dodge was the first chairman of the Navajo Tribe. He was appointed by a Bureau of Indian Affairs agent in 1884 because of his leadership and speaking skills. Born in 1860 in Fort Defiance, his father was a Mexican interpreter and his mother was a member of the Coyote Pass Clan. When Kit Carson carried out his scorched earth plan to subjugate the Navajos, Dodge's family fled for the safety of the Grand Canyon. On the way, his mother stopped at Walpi to ask for food but died at the hands of angry villagers tired of Navajo raiders. His family continued on to the Grand Canyon but eventually came back to Fort Defiance to surrender to Kit Carson when they heard that other Navajos had surrendered at Canyon de Chelly.

At the age of four, Dodge made the long walk to Bosque Redondo with his aunt. There he learned to speak English fluently. He became the "boy interpreter" and upon his release from Fort Sumner, returned to Fort Defiance to serve as an interpreter and Army scout. Dodge later became a very successful rancher who owned vast amounts of grazing land. He loaned Lorenzo Hubbell money and on two occasions loaned money to St. Michaels Mission. Dodge helped the Franciscans establish their mission school as an alternative to the repressive government boarding schools.

This trading post was the site of the famous Black Horse Rebellion of 1892. Black Horse and other Navajos held Indian agent David Shipley hostage to put an end to the deceitful methods he used to lure children to school, which included kidnapping and physical abuse. The people of Round Rock could stand no more and took the law into their own hands to protect their children.

A Navajo policeman barely rescued David Shipley, named *Tł'ízí nishchxon* (Smelly Goat) by the community, from being beaten to death. When a battalion of soldiers finally arrived at Round Rock, Black Horse and his followers were arrested and taken to Fort Wingate. There they testified to officials about Shipley's cruel treatment of their children, resulting in his removal from office. (Trauger, 1967)

Intersection of U.S. 191 and N.R. 12. Turn south on U.S. 191 to Chinle.

MM 470 CHINLE WASH WITH COTTONWOODS

Cottonwood thrives in areas where water is plentiful such as wash beds and around springs. They belong to the poplar family and have cotton-like hairs that grow around the seed. The Hopi use the cottonwood root to make *katsina* dolls and *paho* (prayer feather) sticks.

MM 462 MANY FARMS

It's Navajo name is *Dá'ak'ehaláni* meaning large cultivated fields.

TSEYI' SHOPPING CENTER (West)

BASHAS' GROCERY STORE: Working with the Center for Diné Studies at Chinle Public School, this Bashas' store labels more than 200 food products in the Navajo language. This is not always a simple task. For some foods, like watermelon, translators had a hard time deciding if it should be called *Ch'eehjiyaan* "to eat in vain" *or T'eehjiyaan* "raw food." The goal of the project is to promote the use of the Navajo language. If the Chinle pilot project is successful, it will be expanded to Bashas' four other stores on the reservation. (Weatherburn, 1995)

⊕ MM 445 CHINLE COMPREHENSIVE HEALTH CARE FACILITY (West)

This new hospital truly incorporates Navajo tradition into its health care system. Largely due to the influence of Ursula Knoki-Wilson, a certified nurse-midwife, the obstetrical unit takes advantage of many of the age-old Navajo beliefs and customs to make patients feel safe and comfortable during the labor and delivery experience. Cedar is burned as incense to provide a sense of calmness and to bless the room and the family. A Navajo sash belt hangs in each labor room for the pushing phase of delivery.

Once the baby is born, some traditional Navajo families take the placenta and umbilical cord back to their camp. It's buried on the south side of the hogan if the baby is a girl so that she will be a good weaver or buried in the corral if the baby is a boy so he will take good care of the livestock.

Traditional healers use the hogan built inside the hospital to conduct ceremonies for their patients. Because it's necessary to have a connection with Mother Earth, the hogan fireplace reaches down through the foundation to connect it directly to the earth beneath the building. (Hardeen, 1994)

As a visitor to the Navajo Nation, you can be seen at the hospital for an emergency only, such as an auto accident with injuries. All other health conditions will require that you see a private physician or health facility. **Emergency Room: (520) 674-5464**

🐜 MM 432 BEAUTIFUL VALLEY (East)

This is the same Chinle formation that you have seen at the Petrified Forest and the Painted Desert.

🐜 MM GANADO MESA (East)

Capped by the Bidahochi Formation that consists of sediment from ancient lake deposits.

⊕ Junction of U.S. Highway 191 and Arizona State Highway 264

Turn east to continue on U.S. Highway 191 to U.S. Interstate 40

MM 441 GANADO: See chapter nine for a full description of Ganado.

Junction Arizona State Highway 264 and U.S. Highway 191 to U.S. 40

MM 397 KLAGETOH

In 1935, Leonard Walker, a well-known trader who would own many posts throughout the reservation, was a teenager working for the owner of the Klagetoh post. It was a quiet morning with people sitting around the warm fire burning in the pot-bellied stove when a woman dressed like a hard-working cowboy walked in with two colt .45s strapped to her hips. She demanded to see the owner but Walker said he was the only one available to help her. Angered by this, she proceeded to tell him the reason for her visit. She said she had heard from her customers that he was selling flour for $1.15 a sack when the going rate was $1.25. She then pulled out her guns and began shooting at the exposed nails in the wall. When she finished, a shaken Walker told her what she had heard was wrong. He, too, was selling flour for $1.25. Upon hearing this, she turned and headed for the door, only stopping to say, "Keep it that way." The woman was Winnie Balcomb, Walker's competitor at Wide Ruins Trading Post, a post Walker later would own. (McIlhaney, 1983)

 REGIONAL RUG DESIGN-KLAGETOH

Klagetoh is famous for a rug style very similar to the Ganado Red. Weavers of both rugs use the colors red, black and grey in their design but the Klagetoh usually has a grey background instead of red. The weaver of this particular rug has chosen to use grey around the center and in the zig zag design. Natural dyes are used in most Klagetoh rugs.

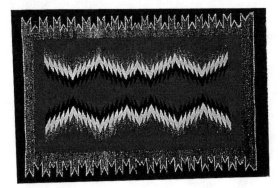

Klagetoh, 1968
Photograph by Gene Balzer, Museum of Northern Arizona

 MM 392 WIDE RUINS

The name comes from the translation of *Kinteel,* or "wide house," the Navajo name for the ancient ruin found in this area.

Wide Ruins Trading Post, ca. 1930
Leo Crane Collection, Cline Library, Special Collections and Archives, NAU PH 658-967
Leo Crane was Indian Agent in Keams Canyon starting in 1911. All of his pictures were taken between 1913 and 1934.

REGIONAL RUG DESIGN - WIDE RUINS

The Wide Ruins design developed during the classic period of Navajo weaving dating back to between 1850 to 1883. Wide bands enclose complex geometric designs on a rug without a border. A Wide Ruin rug is finely woven and usually only natural plant dyes are used.

Encouraged by the Lippincotts, traders at Wide Ruin Trading Post during the 1930s, weavers started to experiment with the development of subtle shades such as pastels of pinks, yellows, beige, tans and browns made from vegetal dyes. Natural dyes are made from tree bark, flower petals, bulb

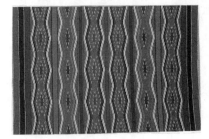 skins, wild carrots, pine needles, leaves, lichen, corn, berries, cactus fruit and walnut shells. Urine and juniper ash sets the dye. In 1940, Nonabah Bryan wrote a book describing 84 different shades of vegetal dye. Today the number has increased to more than 100 shades. (James, 1973)

Wide Ruins, 1972
Photograph by Gene Balzer, Museum of Northern Arizona

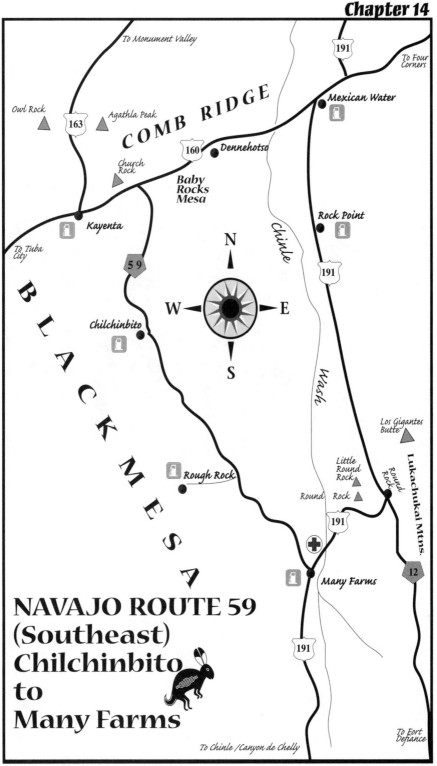

Chapter 14

To Monument Valley

C O M B   R I D G E

191

To Four Corners

Mexican Water

Owl Rock

163

Agathla Peak

160 Dennehotso

Church Rock

Baby Rocks Mesa

Rock Point

Kayenta

To Tuba City

59

Chinle

N

W ⊙ E

S

191

Chilchinbito

B L A C K   M E S A

Wash

Los Gigantes Butte

Little Round Rock

Round Rock

Rough Rock

Round   Rock

Lukachukai Mtns.

191

12

Many Farms

NAVAJO ROUTE 59 (Southeast) Chilchinbito to Many Farms

191

To Fort Defiance

To Chinle / Canyon de Chelly

46 miles (74 km) from U.S. Highway 160 to Many Farms

Tribal Highway 59 does not have mile markers, so set your trip counter to zero.

MILE 1 CARRIZO MOUNTAINS (East)
See pages 200-201 for an explanation of these mountains.

MILE 15 CHILCHINBITO (West)
In Navajo, *Chiiłchin Biító* means "water in the sumac." Navajo artists use sumac, that grows around a spring here, to create baskets.

Chilchinbito Trading Post, not dated.
Museum of Northern Arizona, Photo Archives, 10718

BLACK MESA (WEST) You will follow this mesa all the way to Many Farms.

MILE 31 ROUGH ROCK DEMONSTRATION SCHOOL (West)
Bob Roessel, a widely-known educator who has had a significant impact on the improvement of education to Navajo children, once said, "Education as the Indian knows it on the reservation can be characterized as the 'either-or' type. One is either an Indian or a white man, and the way we traditionally have weighted things, the good way always is the non-Indian way and the bad way always is the Indian way. We have told the child that he is superstitious and primitive... We try to impose our values on him and

tell him he should eat green, leafy vegetables and sleep on a bed and brush his teeth. In short, we try to make a white man out of an Indian. The child listens and looks at himself and sees that he doesn't measure up. In his own eyes he is a failure. Education can be a shattering experience when one is taught nothing but negative things about himself...."

Funded in 1965 by the Office of Economic Opportunity, Rough Rock Demonstration School attempted to teach the Indian child about his own history, language and heroes so that students would come away with a sense of who they are as individuals and collectively as Indian people. They did this by involving an active and interested community in the teaching of their children. Elders taught language and legends that children should have learned at home from their grandparents but may have missed because they were away at boarding school.

Originally built in 1930 by the Bureau of Indian Affairs, an all-Navajo school board took over control of the school in the 1960s under the Indian Self-Determination Act. Rough Rock was the prototype upon which community members lobbied Congress to charter the first Indian-run community college, Navajo Community College. (Broderick, 1968)

Struggling for support since the end of the 1960s, Rough Rock has scaled back its curriculum development and press. It is still possible to buy reprints of curriculum and research on Indian education reform at the book store. A special treat at Christmas time are cards developed by local artists and sold through the school. You can phone the Rough Rock Book Store at (520)728-3311.

Navajo Police Sgt. Jim Chee, Tony Hillerman's second major fictional character, was first introduced in *People of Darkness*. He supposedly grew up at Rough Rock and was a member of the imaginary Slow Talking Clan. His uncle, Hosteen Frank Sam Nakai, who was a well-known "singer," or medicineman, was the mentor who taught Jim Chee his knowledge about traditional healing. Chee was learning the Nightway Chant and the Enemy Way ceremony.

ENEMY WAY: Also known as the Squaw Dance, this is an important ceremony for people who have been living off the reservation among "enemies." Many Desert Storm veterans had this ceremony when they returned from Saudi Arabia. In summertime, it's common to see signs along reservation highways announcing a Squaw Dance. Please do not attend unless invited by a Navajo family.

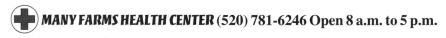 **MM 37 Tsaile Butte and Chuska Mountain** East, in the distance

MANY FARMS

Dá'ák'ehaláni, the Navajo name for Many Farms, means large cultivated fields. A good name for the more than 700 small farms run by Navajo families since 1937. There is a very large lake two miles east of Many Farms that has largemouth bass, channel catfish and black bullhead.

✚ **MANY FARMS HEALTH CENTER** (520) 781-6246 Open 8 a.m. to 5 p.m.

LODGING: **Many Farms Inn** *(from the intersection of Navajo Route 59 and U.S. Hwy 191 head north one mile on Hwy 191. Turn left at the Many Farms High School sign. Follow the signs for another mile to the entrance of the Inn.)* This Inn was made possible through a School-to-Work federal grant project to give high-school students a chance to learn the hospitality industry. The school converted a vacant dormitory and be-cause it was a dormitory, bathrooms are shared. Each room has two single beds. Rates are $30 per room, single or double occupancy. There is a tele-vision lounge, pay phone, coffee and vending machines only. Because lodg-ing is hard to find in the summer, this will probably be happy news for some travelers.

REGIONAL RUG DESIGN- *Yé'ii bicheii*

From the area around Many Farms are many weavers who make the *Yé'ii bicheii* design. The *Yé'ii bicheii* is an important night ceremonial when hu-

mans dress like *yé'iis,* or Navajo gods, for the pur-pose of healing. The dancer's pro-portions are life-like and the weaver places them in her rug according to the requirements of the ceremony. (Lamb, 1992)

Yé'ii bicheii, ca. 1910-1930
Photograph by Gene Balzer, Museum of Northern Arizona

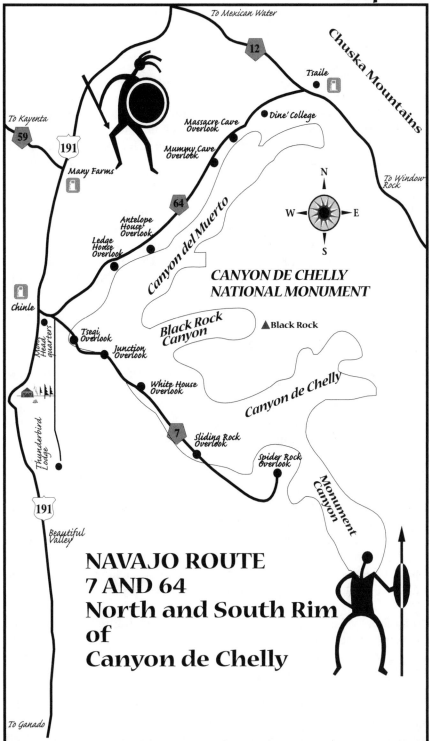

Chapter 15

To Mexican Water

12

Chuska Mountains

Tsaile

To Kayenta

59

191

Many Farms

Massacre Cave Overlook

Mummy Cave Overlook

Dine' College

To Window Rock

64

Canyon del Muerto

N
W — E
S

CANYON DE CHELLY
NATIONAL MONUMENT

Antelope House Overlook

Ledge House Overlook

Chinle

Park Head quarters

Tsegi Overlook

Junction Overlook

Black Rock Canyon

▲ Black Rock

White House Overlook

Thunderbird Lodge

Canyon de Chelly

191

7

Sliding Rock Overlook

Spider Rock Overlook

Monument Canyon

Beautiful Valley

**NAVAJO ROUTE
7 AND 64
North and South Rim
of
Canyon de Chelly**

To Ganado

NATIVE ROADS

⚡ CHINLE

The Navajo name for this community is *ch'inlih,* which means "water flow-ing." Prior to 1941, many magazine writers referred to the town as Chin Lee. Father Leopold Osterman established the first Franciscan mission here in 1904. You can see the original Catholic church, dedicated in 1912, as you drive to Canyon de Chelly on Navajo Route 7. It is about one mile (1.6 km) on the south side of the road, behind the new hogan-style Catholic church.

In 1906, *Doyalthi'ih,* "the silent one," kidnapped Indian agent Reuben Perry for forcing Navajo children to go to boarding school in Fort Defiance about 90 miles (145 km) away. Convicted of kidnapping, Doyalthi'ih served one year in Alcatraz in San Francisco and then Fort Huachuca in southern Arizona. A BIA boarding school was built here in 1910. (Van Valkenburgh, 1941)

⚡ GARCIA'S TRADING POST (North)

Now the Holiday Inn, located about three miles heading east from the junction of Hwy 191 and N.R. 7. The first trader in this area was *Naakaii Yazzi,* a Mexican who ran his store from a tent in 1882. In 1886, a small one-room building with a floor made of Arbuckle coffee boxes was built on this site and is now under the kitchen area of the new Holiday Inn. (Navajo Nation)

Lorenzo Hubbell and his partner C.N. Cotton traded in Chinle in 1886 out of an old rock hogan on the grounds of what would become Garcia's Trading Post. But due to a nationwide depression that caused a downturn in livestock and wool prices, Hubbell and Cotton let their trading license in Chinle expire. After the depression ended, Hubbell returned in 1900 and built a two-story trading post down the road, that included rooms for the many visitors to Canyon de Chelly that he believed would soon be coming.

With the arrival of the Atchison, Topeka & Santa Fe Railroad in Gallup, his prophesy was to come true. To help tourists see the canyon, Hubbell started a stage coach line in 1915 that picked passengers up in Gallup, took them by his post in Ganado, and then brought them to Canyon de Chelly.

Camillo Garcia, known to the Navajos he traded with as the "Mexican who blinked all of the time," took over the post in the 1920s and enlarged the compound to include eight buildings. Garcia ran the post successfully until the 1960s when he and his son were killed in a plane crash at the Chinle airport. The Holiday Inn took over the site in 1992 and built this 100–room motel with a restaurant and swimming pool. (Reid, 1992)

CANYON DE CHELLY NATIONAL MONUMENT HEADQUARTERS

Perhaps the most obvious question about this canyon is why is it named de Chelly (pronounced de-shay)? The generally accepted answer is that de Chelly is the Spanish mispronunciation of the Navajo word *Tséyi'*, meaning "rock canyon."

People have lived in Canyon de Chelly since 2,000 years before Christ. First inhabited by the Anasazi and later by the Navajo who many believe migrated to the canyon in the 17th Century. They developed large peach orchards and farms which continue today. According to Richard Van Valkenburgh, an Indian Service anthropologist in the 1930s, it was the Hopi and Jemez Indians who gave the Navajo the peach tree. Forced to Canyon de Chelly because of the Pueblo uprising against the Spanish in 1680, these refugees slowly became part of the Navajo Tribe through intermarriage and are known as the *Ma'ideshgezhnih* clan. (Van Valkenburgh, 1941)

At the height of Kit Carson's slash-and-burn campaign, Canyon de Chelly and the Chinle area were his primary targets because of the many farms on the canyon floor. Carson signed the peace treaty with the Navajos in 1864 on the knoll where the Canyon de Chelly Monument Headquarters sits today.

Canyon de Chelly became a National Monument in 1931. But the Navajo Tribe holds claim to the land, unlike all other U.S. national monuments. The park is administered by the National Park Service and this headquarters provides valuable information about the ethnohistory and geology of the Canyon.

The Southwest Parks and Monuments Association operates a nonprofit book store in the visitors center specializing in books and maps about the local area and the Navajo and Hopi nations.

Cowboys in Canyon de Chelly, ca. 1930s
Fred Harvey Collection, Museum of Northern Arizona Photo Archives 301-3-114.

CANYON DE CHELLY TOUR GUIDES

You will probably want to hire a Navajo guide to take you on a tour of various parts of the Canyon. You may not enter the canyon without an authorized guide. White House Ruin trail is the only access to the canyon without a guide.

Tsegi Guide Association: They offer four-hour interpretative hikes or customized tours as requested. The fee is $10 per hour; three-hour minimum. You can also hire someone to take you for a vehicle tour through the canyon, using your own four-wheel-drive. Make arrangements at the visitors center.

De Chelly Tours: Offers daily morning hikes, including White House Ruin and overnight pack trips. (520) 674-3772 or 674-5433

Canyon Hiking Services: Offers scheduled and custom hikes. P.O. Box 362, Chinle, AZ 86503

Justin Tso Horse Rental: Offers two to three hour to overnight guided trail rides into the canyon. (520) 674-5678.

Twin Trail Tours: Offers two to three hour rides to Antelope House and Mummy Cave and overnight rides. (520) 674-8425.

COTTONWOOD CAMPGROUND

Free, year-round camping on a first–come, first–served basis. Five day limit per visit or 14 days per year. From April through October facilities include restrooms, picnic tables, water. From November through March, portable toilets and picnic tables only. There are no shower facilities. RVs are allowed but are restricted to 35 feet (11 m). A dump station is available.

Sam E. Day's Trading Post, Chinle, Arizona , 1902
Photograph by Ben Wittick
Courtesy School of American Research Collections in the Museum of New Mexico 15988

THUNDERBIRD LODGE

In 1902, Sam Day built a trading post that would eventually grow into the beautiful Thunderbird Lodge of today. Sam Day, originally from Canton, Ohio, came to Arizona in 1883 as a homesteader at Cienega Amarilla (St. Michaels) and worked with the survey party to determine the boundaries of the Navajo Reservation. He sold his land at St. Michaels and built a log trading post, facing east, that became the social center of the Chinle area.

Because of competition from Lorenzo Hubbell, Sam Day sold his trading post in 1905 to Charles Wiedemeyer from Fort Defiance. Day continued to own trading posts in Cienega Amarilla and Navajo, Ariz., and served as a member of the Arizona legislature. His favorite causes were the prohibition of alcohol on the Navajo Reservation and ending gambling.

His son Charles married the daughter of Chief Manuelito, Kate Roanhorse, in 1912 and continued his work on the preservation and documentation of Navajo life ways.

In 1919, "Cozy" McSparron, a legend in trading circles because of his good humor and creative storytelling, bought the trading post and turned it into a dude ranch called the Thunderbird Ranch. He developed the Thunderbird logo for promotional brochures, and the Fred Harvey Co. included the Thunderbird Ranch in its itinerary for the Harveycar Motor Cruises. Wanting more of a wild west atmosphere at his ranch, Cozy offered gambling and boxing matches on Saturday nights.

In 1931, Herbert Hoover declared Canyon de Chelly a national monument and Cozy became its temporary custodian for two years until a permanent custodian was named. Cozy and his wife Inja were host to many movie stars filming in the area from 1930 to 1950. Stars included Claudette Colbert, Guy Madison and Rory Calhoun.

When Cozy's health failed, he sold the Thunderbird Ranch to the Nelsons who were former employees of the Babbitt Brothers in Flagstaff. One of the Nelsons suffered a heart attack and the ranch was again up for sale.

The LaFonts took over operation in 1960 and built the first motel units to accommodate the increasing number of visitors to the monument. Odessa LaFont further developed the image of the Thunderbird Ranch as an oasis in the desert by expanding many of the plants, lawns and trees that Cozy had started. Not long after they purchased the trading post and ranch, the LaFonts asked for permission from the Navajo Tribe to close the trading post. They did this because most of the local people came to eat in the new cafeteria rather than trade. The Navajo Tribe approved the closure and you can dine in this popular cafeteria located in the original 1902 trading post built by Sam Day .

In 1984, the LaFonts sold the ranch to Mary Jones who proceeded to develop the lodge, and, in 1986, added the new pueblo style motel rooms in the back of the original trading post and motel. (Harrison, 1989)

The Thunderbird Lodge offers half or full-day **Jeep Tours** of Canyon de Chelly. Half-day tours will take you to Antelope House and White House. The jeeps are open so bring a hat and sunscreen.
Half-day Tours: Departure 9 a.m. or 2 p.m. $31/person plus tax.
Full-Day Tour: Departs at 9 a.m. returns at 5:30 p.m. $50/per person plus tax, includes lunch. For reservations call: (800) 679-2473 or (520) 674-5841.

 **REGIONAL RUG DESIGN- CHINLE**

One of the more common rug designs woven throughout the Navajo Nation because of its relatively easy pattern is the Chinle design. It is simply a banded rug without borders. Developed during the Revival Period of weaving, from 1920 to 1940, the Chinle Rug has solid lines of color alternating with more complex bands that contain geometric designs. (Lamb, 1992)

Chinle, ca . 1947
Gene Balzer Museum of Northern Arizona

In 1923, Cozy McSparron, in collaboration with Mary Wheelwright of the Wheelwright Museum, encouraged the re-use of natural vegetal dyes used before the introduction of commercial dyes in 1870.

Some weavers felt limited by the colors available in natural dyes so a dye expert from the DuPont Chemical Co. came to Chinle to research the kind of natural coloring and variety the weavers were seeking. That same year, DuPont introduced the new dyes to the reservation but the weavers had to mix the dangerous acid components themselves. In 1932, the Diamond Dye Co. came out with a dye called "Old Navajo" that did not require mixing but still offered the variety and subtle color shading so admired by the weavers. Because of this influence, the Chinle Rug style may have either vegetal or commercial dyes or both in its coloring. (James)

SOUTH RIM OF CANYON DE CHELLY

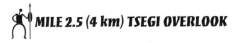 **MILE 0**

No mile markers on the South Rim so set your odometer to zero at the visitors center.

 **MILE 2.5 (4 km) TSEGI OVERLOOK**

Blade Face from Tsegi Overlook, no date.
Courtesy Museum of New Mexico, #68800

Tséyí means canyon in Navajo. From this overlook you can see the traditional homes and farms where Navajos live in the summer. They move to their winter camps on the rim when the weather turns colder.

Across the highway from this overlook are sand dunes just like the ones that formed the de Chelly sandstone more than 200 million years ago. The de Chelly sandstone makes up the majority of the vertical cliffs that line the Rio de Chelly. If you look closely you can see lines in the rock indicating that the wind that formed the sandstone came from the north.

NATIVE ROADS

ᐤ MILE 3.9 (6.2 km) JUNCTION OVERLOOK

Named for a ruin that sits at the junction of Canyon del Muerto and Canyon de Chelly. James Stevenson of the Smithsonian Institute gave Canyon del Muerto its name, meaning the "canyon of the dead," because his expedition found prehistoric Indian burials in this canyon. **First Ruin** is across the canyon on your left. It was given this name because it was the first ruin to be explored and chronicled by archeologist Cosmos Mindeleff in 1882.

ᐤ MILE 5.7 (9.2 km) TURN-OFF TO WHITE HOUSE OVERLOOK

This is the only ruin in the park that you may hike to without a Navajo guide. It is about 1 1/4 miles (2 km) one way to the ruin with an elevation change of about 500 feet (152 m). You can find the trail to your right, close to the rim. Because of the high temperatures in summer, it is always a good idea to carry at least a quart (1 L) of water with you on this hike. This trail is not wheelchair accessible. You can buy a White House trail guide at the visitor center for 50 cents which explains the history of the ruin, as well as the geology and plant life found along the trail.

WHAT IS DESERT VARNISH? On the canyon wall above White House ruins is a good example of desert varnish. It is a blue-black color caused by the leaching over centuries of iron and manganese oxide from the sandstone. If there happens to be a crack where water collects, lichen forms, turning the rock orange and green. (Chronic, 1988)

ᐤ MILE 12.9 (21 km) SLIDING ROCK OVERLOOK

On your walk to the overlook you will walk across sandstone that has eroded into shallow basins. These basins are an important source of fresh water for humans and animals after a rain storm. The larger ones can hold water for several weeks.

Across the canyon on a narrow ledge is **Sliding Rock Ruin,** named appropriately because the ancient people who lived here had to build retaining walls to keep their homes from sliding into the canyon.

ᐤ MILE 21.8 (35 km) SPIDER ROCK OVERLOOK

The trail is 200 yards (183 m) from the parking lot to your right down a paved trail. Spider Rock, or *Tse' Na'ashjé'ii*, is the center point of the junction of Canyon de Chelly and Monument Canyon and stands 800 feet (244 m) from the base of the canyon floor.

Spider Rock
The Kansas State Historical Society,4/D-16.12

SPIDER ROCK RV & CAMPGROUND: *Just before the turn-off to Spider Rock.* Owned by Navajo business man Howard Smith, this 44 site primitive area is a spectacular place to camp. The family is working on upgrading the grounds but right now there is only a chemical toilet and tank water, no hook-ups. $10/night, RV's up to 44 ft. are welcome. Reservations are a good idea (520) 674-8261.

SERVICES IN CHINLE
LODGING
Best Western Canyon de Chelly Inn: *South just as you turn onto Indian Route 7 from U.S. Route 191.* Open year-round and has an indoor pool and restaurant. Summer rates: two people, two double beds, $96 plus 8 percent Navajo tax. AAA and AARP $86 plus tax. (800) 327-0354 or (520) 674-5875.

Holiday Inn: Room Rates: June through August, two double beds $99 double or single plus tax. (800)-HOLIDAY or (520) 674-5000.

Thunderbird Lodge: Summer: two people/two double beds, $83 plus tax. AARP 10 percent discount. The older rooms have been recently remodeled in a Southwestern motif and are very comfortable. Cable TV. (520) 674-5841; (800) 679-2473.

RESTAURANTS
Bashas' Deli: Open 8 a.m.-10 p.m., Monday through Saturday and 8 a.m.-8 p.m. on Sunday. (520) 674-3464

Burger King Open 6:30 a.m-11 p.m. (520) 674-3700

Holiday Inn Restaurant: Open 6:30 a.m.-10 p.m. (520) 674-5000.

Junction Restaurant: *Next to the Canyon de Chelly Inn.* Mexican, Navajo, American. Open: 6:30 a.m.-10 p.m. (520) 674-8443

Taco Bell: 7 a.m.-10 p.m. (520) 674-5376

Thunderbird Lodge: Cafeteria style, specials are good, try their blue corn pancakes for breakfast. Open 6:30 a.m.-9 p.m.

AUTOMOBILE SERVICES
Auto Service Center	(520) 674-3241
Garcia's Towing Service	(520) 674-3318

BANKING SERVICES
Norwest Bank: Hours 9 a.m.-2 p.m. and 3 p.m.-5 p.m. Monday-Friday. ATM in lobby 24 hours.

Chapter 16

NORTH RIM OF CANYON DE CHELLY

No mile markers -- use the visitors center as mile zero on your trip odometer.

MILE 5.4 (8.7 km) LEDGE RUIN

It's .8 mile (1.3 km) to the viewpoint. As you stand at the viewpoint, Ledge Ruin is directly in front of you in an alcove about 100 feet (30 m) above the canyon floor. The pottery found in the ruin dates from between 1050 to 1275 A.D.

MILE 8.2 (13.2 km) ANTELOPE HOUSE

Travel down this road for two miles to the viewpoint. Antelope House Ruin gets its name for the antelope painted on the wall to the left of the ruin. Navajo artist *Dibé Yázhí* (Little Sheep) painted the antelope around 1830. Hands and figures painted in white next to the antelope are probably the work of the Anasazi who lived here around 693 A.D.

The **Tomb of the Weaver,** about 50 feet (15 m) above the canyon floor across from Antelope House, is a carefully constructed crypt so finely made

that even in this windblown country, no dust or sand had worked its way into the burial house. Inside was the well-preserved body of an old man, believed to be a weaver because of a spindle whorl found sitting atop skeins of cotton yarn. A blanket of golden eagle feathers wrapped the body and a bow and arrow, cornmeal, corn, pinyon nuts, beans and salt were laying on top of the blanket. Under the feather shroud was a cotton blanket so white that when archeologists unearthed the crypt in 1920, the blanket looked like it had just been woven.

Antelope House, ca. 1890s
Photo by Ben Wittick
Courtesy School of American Research Collections, Museum of New Mexico, 149225

NAVAJO FORTRESS VIEWPOINT

The fortress is the sandstone butte directly across the canyon from Antelope House Viewpoint. Fortress rock was one of the many hiding places for Navajos hunted by the Spanish and later by Kit Carson's troops. On the east side of the butte, that you can't see from the overlook, is a trail leading to the top of the fortress. Log poles were used to climb to the nearly inaccessible top and are still visible on a jeep tour through the canyon. Once the Navajos climbed on top of the butte, they pulled the poles up after them. Rock walls were used as shields to hide behind while throwing rocks on their tormentors below. At night, Navajo men would sneak down to get water and food for the people but vigilant Kit Carson waited at the bottom until the starving Navajos surrendered to him in 1864.

Mummy Cave Ruins, ca. 1890s
Photo by Ben Wittick
Courtesy School of American Research Collections in the Museum of New Mexico, 149217

MILE 17.5 (28 km) MUMMY CAVE TURN-OFF

Travel 1.6 miles (2.6 km) to the overlook. Col. James Stevenson, who named Canyon del Muerto, found two mummies at this site in 1880 and called the ruins Mummy Cave. This is one of the longest continuously-inhabited ruins in Canyon de Chelly, believed to have been occupied from 300 to 1300 A.D. Set in two caves, the architecture is like that found at Mesa Verde in southwestern Colorado. Both ruins have similar masonry and both have a three-room tower. The ceiling timbers in the tower were cut in 1284 A.D. In 1938, this 711-year-old tower was in danger of collapsing but was saved with financial assistance from the Bureau of American Ethnology and the Southwestern Monuments Association. Earl Morris, well-known for his renovation of the Temple of Warriors at Chichen Itza, was able to stabilize the ancient structure. (Morris, 1938)

MILE 21 (33.8 km) MASSACRE CAVE OVERLOOK

The Spanish were not welcome in the Navajo homeland and raids against them by Navajo warriors were common. To put an end to their attacks, Lt. Antonio de Narbona was sent to Canyon de Chelly in 1805. A bloody battle ensued according to his reports sent back to the Spanish governor in Santa Fe. Narbona reported killing 90 men, 25 women and children and capturing another 36 women and children. The Navajo version of what happened was quite different. Hosteen Tsosi, a life-long resident of Canyon de Chelly, told anthropologist Richard Van Valkenburgh in an interview in 1940, that the 90 men allegedly killed by Narbona were away in the Lukachukai Mountains hunting deer. Defenseless and fearing for their lives, all of the women, children and elders hid in a nearly–inaccessible cave across from the north rim when they saw the Spanish coming.

Narbona didn't know where the group was hiding as he rode above them on the canyon rim. But a woman in the cave, a former Spanish slave, could not resist taunting the Spanish solders. Once sharp shooters identified the location of the woman's voice, musket balls were ricocheted off the cave's ceiling, killing most of the helpless people huddled there. There was no escape to the canyon floor because the Spanish had worked their way below the only exit from the cave.

Hosteen Tsosi's grandmother survived the attack by hiding under a big rock. When the Spanish made their way up to the cave to finish off survivors with their bayonets, they did not find the little girl. Two days later, the Navajo men returned from their hunting trip. Realizing what had happened, the hunting party took off after the Spanish to revenge their loved ones' deaths. They caught up with the Spaniards around Wide Ruins but were no match against the Spanish muskets and inflicted little damage on the troops. (Van Valkenburgh, 1940)

MILE 25 (40.2 km) DINE' COLLEGE

This was the first tribally controlled community college in the United States, founded in 1968 by an act of Congress. Today there are 29 tribal colleges.

The name was changed by tribal resolution in 1997 from Navajo Community College to Diné College. This was done so the college could begin to develop four-year degrees. The first degree will be the result of a partnership with Arizona State University creating the Diné Teacher Education Program.

The college philosophy is *Sá ah Naasgháí Bik'eh Hózhóón*. It summarizes the Navajo philosophy of life that places all human beings in harmony with the earth and the universe. The entire campus is laid out like a giant hogan, designed to promote the philosophy of *hozhóó* (harmony). As in a hogan, the buildings used for sleeping, eating, living and spiritual well-being are in traditionally–prescribed locations on the campus. Medicinemen blessed the campus with white corn meal and yellow corn pollen during the groundbreaking ceremony which represent the four footprints of the Navajo people. The logo of the college is an arrowhead within a *yé'ii* rainbow. The arrowhead stands for protection from danger and the rainbow represents harmony with all creation. Diné College has campuses in Shiprock, Tuba City, Chinle, Crownpoint and Ganado. It offers two-year associate degrees as well as transfer programs to a university setting. A major focus of the college is Diné Studies and teaching and preserving the Navajo language.

Ned Hatathli Museum and Gallery: *Open 8 a.m.-12 noon and 1 p.m.-4 p.m. Monday through Friday; Closed weekends and holidays.* On the third and fourth floors of the six-story glass hogan is a wonderful museum that explains the history of the Navajo people with displays of cultural artifacts and local artists' work.

HOGAN: On the second floor is a beautiful sanctuary in the shape of a hogan. Its dirt floor is actually connected to the earth by a chimney that extends through all six floors to the sky. The walls of the anteroom leading to the hogan depict the history of the Navajo people. They were handpainted by Paul Willeto, now dean of instruction at the college.

SERVICES AT DINE' COLLEGE

Dormitory: Rooms with two single beds and a shared bathroom are available to tourists for $20 single; $30 double. It's a good idea to bring your own towels and soap. You can make reservations by calling the NCC Housing Office at (520) 724-6782 from 8 a.m. to 5 p.m., Monday through Friday. It may be difficult to get a room during the academic semesters which run from around Aug. 29 to Dec. 15 and from Jan. 10 to May 4 every year.

Summer school begins in early June and lasts through August. Dormitory vacancies are most likely during the summer.

Cafeteria: Meals are available only when school is in session. Breakfast, $3; lunch or dinner, $4.00. The cafeteria is open only from the hours of 7 a.m.-8 a.m., 11:30 a.m.- 1 p.m. and 5 p.m.- 6 p.m., Mon.-Fri; Sat. and Sun.10 a.m. to 11 a.m. (Brunch); 4 p.m. to 5 p.m. (Dinner). A snack bar is open all day, Monday through Friday, during the school year.

Bookstore: Excellent collection of Native American books and T-shirts. Open from 8 a.m.-12 noon and 1 p.m.-5 p.m. Monday through Friday.

TSAILE LAKE

Driving halfway around the college's circular drive, you will come to three very large gas tanks. Head south on the dirt road to the lake. Fishing is allowed here with a tribal fishing license, available at the gas station on the corner of Navajo Routes 12 and 64. If you continue to the end of the dirt road, stop where a wash obviously crosses the road. To the west of the wash, at the edge of the canyon, is a seasonal waterfall that runs after heavy rains or during the spring snow melt. This is the start of Canyon del Muerto. Walter Jensen, Student Services Director at the college can arrange private tours of the Tsaile area, (520) 724-6743.

Towering over Tsaile Lake is beautiful **Tsaile Butte** or *Tsézhin Dits'in*.

COYOTE PASS HOSPITALITY

One of the first and best-known Navajo Bed and Breakfast is owned and operated by Will Tsosie, Jr. who lives in Tsaile. He will serve as your guide, explaining the complexities of the Navajo traditional way of life including oral tradition, ethnographic interpretation, ceremonies, herbology and philosophy. Guests are invited to stay in a traditional hogan at *Beauty Under the Tree* located in a pine forest in Tsaile or *Green Canyon Meadow* in the Tsosie desert wintering camp in Lukachukai or *Horse Line Cliffs* in the Chuska Mountains. A traditional Navajo breakfast is included. The Bed and Breakfast fee is seperate from the cultural instruction or tours. Call Will Tsosie at (520) 724-3383 or write Coyote Pass Hospitality, P.O. Box 91, Tsaile, AZ 86556.

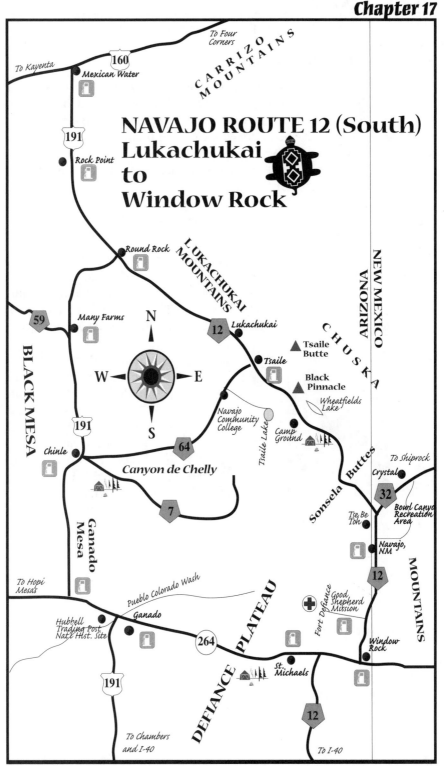

**NAVAJO ROUTE 12 (South)
Lukachukai
to
Window Rock**

To Four Corners

To Kayenta

160

Mexican Water

CARRIZO MOUNTAINS

191

Rock Point

Round Rock

LUKACHUKAI MOUNTAINS

59

Many Farms

N

W E

S

12 Lukachukai

Tsaile

Tsaile Butte

Black Pinnacle

CHUSKA

ARIZONA

NEW MEXICO

Wheatfields Lake

191

Navajo Community College

Tsaile Lake

Camp Ground

Chinle

BLACK MESA

Canyon de Chelly

64

Sonsela Buttes

Crystal

To Shiprock

32

Bowl Canyon Recreation Area

Tse, Be Toh

Navajo, NM

7

Ganado Mesa

To Hopi Mesas

Pueblo Colorado Wash

Hubbell Trading Post Nat'l Hist. Site

Ganado

264

Fort Defiance

Good Shepherd Mission

12

MOUNTAINS

Window Rock

191

DEFIANCE PLATEAU

St. Michaels

12

To Chambers and I-40

To I-40

56 miles (90.1 km) from Lukachukai to Window Rock

NIZHONI FIVE FINGERS, INC.

Located in this area is a small business owned by Annie Tsosie Kahn, a member of the Water Clan. Annie has offered workshops for many years for Navajos and non-Navajos interested in learning more about the lifestyles and beliefs of the Diné. She offers women a traditional sweatlodge and the chance for both men and women to experience the beauty of the Lukachukai region and Navajo life. For more information, write to Annie Kahn, P.O. Box 1347, Lukachukai, AZ 86507.

LUKACHUKAI (East)

Lók'a'ch'égai is the Navajo word for "slender reeds." It is descriptive of the cove at the base of the pass over the Lukachukai Mountains, located at the end of town. Many people use this dirt road to cross the mountains but it is not recommended, especially in winter. The Lukachukai Creek runs through town and divides the Lukachukais from the Chuska Mountains.

George Barker started the first trading post here in 1892. The friars from St. Michaels built a church in 1912 and added a dispensary in the 1950s. This offered the only health care in the area for many years.

Lukachukai Catholic Church, not dated.
St. Michaels Photo Collection of the Franciscan Friars at St. Michaels, Ariz.
Museum of Northern Arizona Photo Archives, MS 119-181-3511

COMMUNITY OF TSAILE (West)

Tsééh yílí (pronounced say-lee) means "flows into the rocks" and refers to Tsaile Creek which flows into Canyon Del Muerto.

 MM 69 TSAILE BUTTE (East)

This sacred place, known as *Tsezhin Dits'in*, is frequently visited by medicinemen to collect herbs needed for ceremonies. It is an igneous volcanic formation.

CHUSKA MOUNTAINS (East)

You will follow this mountain range from Lukachukai all the way to Window Rock. In Navajo, *ch'ooshgaii* means "white spruce or fir." In Navajo tradition, the spruce is a sacred tree that attracts rain.

The Chuska Mountains are one part of a system of mountain ranges, or cordillera, that form a sacred male figure called *Yoo tzill,* or "Goods of Value Range." The head of the male figure is the Chuska Mountains. The Lukachukais form the body and the Carrizo Mountains make up the legs. (Van Valkenburgh, 1941)

In some historic accounts of the area there are frequent references to the Tunecha Mountains. This is because in 1851 the U.S. military cartographers separated the Chuska mountain range into two sections. They called the northern section the Sierra de Tunecha and the southern section Sierra de Chusca. The U.S. Geological Survey added the Lukachukai Mountains as the third section in 1892. Today the entire range is known as the Chuska Mountains. (Granger, 1960)

MM 65 BLACK PINNACLE (East)

The Navajos know this volcanic ridge as "where the bear lives." The Indian Service built a fire lookout station here in 1937 to protect the pine forests surrounding the volcano. (Van Valkenburgh, 1941)

MM 60 WHEATFIELDS LAKE (East)

Col. John Washington traveled through here in 1849 and reported numerous Navajo wheat fields, thus its name. Wheatfields Creek feeds the lake with runoff from the Chuska Mountains. It has the best fishing for rainbow and brook trout on the Navajo Nation. You can purchase a tribal fishing license at the Wheatfields store, or in Tsaile or Navajo. Camping is free for two weeks. There is no running water; outhouses only.

MM 60 WHITECONE (East)

An important place for gathering healing herbs, this mountain is called *Sei' heets'ozii,* or "slender female sand." It's a good name for a mountain made of friable Chuska Sandstone.

MM 51 SONSELA BUTTES (East and west side of road)

These buttes have rather unusual vertical basaltic lava at their top with the rest of the butte consisting of Chuska and Entrada Sandstone.

MM 44 Junction Indian Route 12 and Route 32 to Shiprock

MM 44 to MM 45 GREEN KNOBS (East)

A most amazing but subtle color change occurs around this volcanic plug. You're traveling along at 55 mph (89km/hr) enjoying the beautiful red rock sandstone when suddenly the area turns green, then back to red again. The reason is that peridotite, a volcanic rock made up of green ferromagnesium minerals and olivine, covers this area. This material forms the semi-precious stone, peridot. (Trauger, 1967)

Green Knobs is a highly-sacred place to the Navajo people. Please do not walk on or take any of these fragile rocks.

MM 43 NAVAJO LAKE: This wetland is home to many aquatic birds.

MM 41.5 BOWL CANYON RECREATIONAL AREA TURN-OFF

Head east for about nine miles (14.5 km) on a dirt road to get to this campground. At the entrance to the area is **Cleopatra's Needle**. As you travel into the bowl made from a dry lake bed, you'll see **Venus Needle**. Camp Assayi for children is located in the recreation area. There are cabins and running water but they are not open to visitors. You may camp anywhere in this 645,000-acre (2,600 sq km) designated area but RVs are not recommended because of the rough road.

MM 45 NAVAJO, NEW MEXICO

Highway 12 dips into New Mexico for a short distance then returns to Arizona before entering Fort Defiance. Located 15 miles (24 km) from here is Tanner Springs, known as "sitting willows" to Navajos. Part of Chee Dodge's expansive ranch was here and included a two-story house where he held many parties and entertained guests from throughout the country. (See page 204 for more on Chee Dodge.)

Dodge's most famous offspring, **Annie Wauneka**, grew up here. Today she's a living legend and role model to the Navajo people. She had a major impact on the tribe's public health policies in her effort to eradicate tuberculosis.

In 1929, Annie became the first woman elected to the Navajo Tribal Council. In her role as chairperson of the council's health committee, she took the lead in learning about the horrendous health conditions of the Navajo people and deadly diseases like tuberculosis.

TB was especially tricky to educate the people about because of its transmission through the air. Navajos were long-accustomed to sharing the same dwelling, eating from the same bowl, drinking from the same cup, even spitting on the hogan's dirt floor, all very easy ways to spread TB from one person to another. In addition, Dr. Wauneka had to persuade medicinemen that she was not out to discredit their methods of spiritual curing. She participated in innumerable ceremonies with families during her years of traveling the reservation, going from hogan to hogan. Many times she had to hide the fact that she was not eating or drinking from the same vessel used by others in ceremonies or meals so as to not offend her hosts or the medicineman. She persevered and taught families about the cause of TB and why it was important to follow the "white man's" treatment for the disease.

Annie had the difficult task of convincing many Navajos to leave the reservation to spend months at a time in a sanitarium. She explained that TB affects people all over the world and that the power of the medicineman alone was not going to be able to cure this disease. She taught the concept of germs, and that TB was spread by tiny unseen creatures that lived in saliva and spread from one person to another through coughing.

Wauneka's efforts at health education alone did much to slow the epidemic spread of the disease. For this, President Lyndon Johnson honored her with the Presidential Medal of Freedom in 1964. (Nelson, 1972)

Navajo is also the site of the tribal sawmill which generated jobs and revenue from the processing of the tribe's 600,000 acres (2,437 sq km) of ponderosa pine on the Defiance Plateau. Managed by the Navajo Forest Products Industry, the mill closed in 1994 because of a $7 million debt.

 **THE BEAST** **East, behind the Pine Forest building.**

This is a volcanic plug that's also called Frog Rock on the U.S. Geological Survey's topographic map.

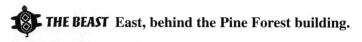 **FORT DEFIANCE**

Take a right at the stoplight if you are traveling south from Tsaile. If you are traveling from Window Rock, continue straight ahead through the stop light. Go all the way to the end of the road to the Indian Health Service hospital. The fort was located at the end of the canyon but no ruins remain.

Col. Edwin Sumner, known as Bull Head Sumner after a musket ball bounced off his head without causing any damage, was in charge of building Fort Defiance in 1851. He chose this site, at the junction of Bonito and Black Creeks, for its defensive position in a box canyon. Bonito Canyon surrounds the fort with sheer red cliffs on the east, north and west. The top of the cliffs are the boundaries of the Defiance Plateau. Actually, this site was not a very secure position because the Navajos could spy on the soldiers' activities from the top of the plateau.

The First Dragoons, the fighting regiment assigned here, named it Fort Defiance because they had come to defy the Navajos. The word dragoon means to harass, or to force into submission by violent measures. (Woolf, 1973)

The original fort is no longer standing because it deteriorated so badly during the Civil War when troops went back east to fight. Because of the absence of the Army, Navajo raids on white settlers and miners increased and became an obstruction to settlement of the West. To protect the settlers, the military reopened the fort in Bonito Canyon and renamed it Fort Canby for the commander of the New Mexico forces in 1860. Fort Canby was the first stop on the 300-mile (484 km) journey to Fort Sumner for 2,500 Navajos Kit Carson had managed to starve out of hiding in Canyon de Chelly. The Long Walk ended on the Pecos River in New Mexico in a place called "the round grove," or Bosque Redondo. President Lincoln set this land aside for the Navajos and any other "unruly Indians." The other unruly

Indians at the time were Apaches and Mescaleros. All of these people tried to survive on the same small desolate reservation. After four long miserable years, and the complete failure to turn Navajos into farmers, the survivors were allowed to return to their own homeland. See page 18-19 for more on Bosque Redondo.

Officers Quarters, Fort Defiance, Arizona, not dated.
Museum of Northern Arizona Photo Archives

Fort Defiance was one of the boundaries of the new reservation created for the Navajos and would become the first Indian Agency for the Bureau of Indian Affairs. See page 19 for a map of the original reservation boundaries. (Sleight, 1953)

The first licensed reservation trading post opened in Fort Defiance in 1868 to accommodate the needs of the Navajos returning from Bosque Redondo. Licensing of all traders on the reservation was a requirement of the Indian Service and is now required by the Navajo Tribe.

✚ FORT DEFIANCE INDIAN HEALTH SERVICE HOSPITAL

The area in front of the hospital, planted in cottonwoods, was the parade ground used by the military at Fort Defiance. The Episcopalians at the Good Shepherd Mission down the road were actually the first to provide health care to the people in this area. The Indian Service built a 110-bed hospital and tuberculosis sanitarium here in 1938. (Sleight, 1953) **Emergency room number: (520) 729-3209.**

THE LADY OF THE BLESSED SACRAMENT CATHOLIC CHURCH

On the left just past the post office. This church was built in 1915 with native sandstone by the Franciscan friars at St. Michaels.

*Anna Curley weaving a pictorial rug of the
Fort Defiance Catholic Church, not dated.*
Museum of Northern Arizona Photo Archives
Photo Collection of the Franciscan Friars at St. Michaels, Az.
MS 119-181-3497

 BIA BOARDING SCHOOL

*Located across from the Indian Health Service hospital. The buildings
now house BIA administrative offices.* These buildings housed the very
first government boarding school built on the Navajo reservation. It was
established in 1881, 13 years after the signing of the peace treaty that promised an education for every child from age six to 16. (Frink, 1968)

Even though the signers of the treaty saw the benefit of educating their
children they did not know it would mean sending their children to boarding school. As one mother said, "It is like giving up our hearts." In 1887,
Congress passed a law to force Navajo parents to send their children to
school. This led to even more problems and hard feelings between parents
and Bureau of Indian Affairs officials. Mission schools became popular at
this time because parents were able to choose where their children would
go to school rather than being forced by government authorities.

GOOD SHEPHERD MISSION

*As you head back out onto the four-lane road, the mission is on the left
about half-way to the stop light before you get to the high school.* The
Episcopalians came to Fort Defiance in 1892, five years after the U.S.
government required all children to attend school. They had actually
"drawn" the Sioux Reservation under the Grant Peace Policy of 1869. It
was the Presbyterians who were responsible for educating the Navajos but
all of their attempts to establish a school and mission at Fort Defiance had
failed.

Women played an important role in the development of the Good Shepherd Mission. The "woman who laughs," Eliza Thackara, superintendent
of the mission, opened the first hospital in Fort Defiance in 1897 on a 48-
acre (0.19 sq km) plot deeded to the Episcopalians. As you drive through
the mission gates, the old hospital is the first building on the right. It is now
the administrative building.

Trachoma in the early 1900s was one of the most debilitating diseases treated at the new hospital. Caused by a highly-contagious rickettsia microorganism that frequently resulted in blindness at an early age. The only treatment at the time was the painful scrubbing of the everted eyelid with "blue stone" three times a day. Because the treatment forced patients to stay at the hospital for a long time, some children lost contact with their parents and the mission eventually became an orphanage. (Anderson, 1992)

To generate more donations for her growing hospital, Miss Thackara wrote a frantic letter to her benefactors in New York, telling them that "(the Roman Catholic Church) ...is about to establish a large school at a mission nine miles (14 km) from us at St. Michael's... they always have money." Rev. Mother Katharine Drexel opened the St. Michael's Boarding School in 1902. (See pages 153-155 for more about St. Michaels Mission.)

The **Chapel of the Good Shepherd**, the first building to the left as you drive through the entrance, honors the charitable work of one of the mission's more generous contributors, Cornelia Jay of New York. It was built in 1954 by architect John Gaw Meem who was renowned for his Southwestern style of architecture. Some of his most famous buildings are the La Fonda Hotel in Santa Fe, and Scholes Hall and Zimmerman Library on the campus of the University of New Mexico in Albuquerque. (Bunting, 1983)

 **MM 27 BLACK ROCK (West)**

This is a volcanic intrusive rock formed from molten lava. It's a natural landmark along the old military road that ran more than 200 miles (323 km) to Albuquerque. The road was heavily used from 1851 to 1864 and the military grazed their horses here because of its abundant water supply. The Navajos call Black Rock "Big Snake House." It plays an important role in the Wind Way Ceremony. (McFarland, 1960)

WIND WAY CEREMONY

Navajos attribute much power to the wind. Because it is everywhere, taking different forms and colors, it may be a source of illness for some people. To overcome its effects, a Wind Way Ceremony may be prescribed as the necessary curing treatment. Through this ceremony the patient regains harmony with the supernatural power of the wind and is protected in his future travels. (Wyman, 1962)

 BEALE WAGON ROAD

In 1857, Lt. Edward Fitzgerald Beale surveyed the trail that would eventually become part of Route 66, the famous highway connecting the east and west coasts. His assignment was to find a direct route from Fort Defiance to the Colorado River on the California border. To expedite his mission, Beale used camels to carry his heavy load of supplies.

It was Jefferson Davis, then secretary of war, who first suggested the use of camels. Beale, who had traveled over the American Southwestern deserts with Kit Carson, agreed with Davis because of the need to carry water and feed for their riding and pack animals. With the help of Davis, Beale persuaded Congress to appropriate $30,000 for the purchase of 23 Arabian camels from Egypt and Arabia. He purchased 44 more in Asia Minor and shipped them all to a valley outside of San Antonio, Texas. Here they rested before making the long trip to Fort Defiance.

The trip from San Antonio to Fort Defiance took 66 days. The camels did extremely well. Able to carry almost 1,000 pounds (2,200 kg), the camels handled the rocky terrain with ease because they pick up their spongy feet for each step rather than shuffling them like a mule. They could eat anything and especially liked creosote bushes.

Given all of these wonderful characteristics, why didn't the camel catch on as a pack animal in the desert Southwest? Primarily because mule drivers felt threatened by their abilities and cowboys didn't want to treat them gently. In their traditional homeland, attendants pamper their camels and treat them like members of their family.

Because of their unpopularity with the wranglers, some camels "escaped" during Beale's expedition. Encountered in the wild many years later, they were surviving quite well. In 1901, a crew surveying the International Boundary Line between the U.S. and Mexico reported seeing very healthy camels in southern Arizona. None survive today.

Take a left at the light and follow the signs to Window Rock Tribal Park.

NAVAJO NATION TRIBAL COUNCIL CHAMBERS

This beautiful 1923 building is constructed in the shape of a traditional Navajo hogan with the door facing east to allow the Holy People to enter. Handpainted murals by Navajo artist Gerald Nailor depict Navajo history and cover the interior walls of the council chamber. A bell given to the Navajo Tribe by the Santa Fe Railroad sits next to the entrance. It commemorates all of the Navajos who helped build the railroad.

The Bureau of Indian Affairs created the Navajo Tribal Council — now the Navajo Nation Council — to facilitate the signing of oil leases with American oil companies wanting to tap the large oil reserves discovered near Farmington.

This is the largest Indian legislature in the country, composed of 88 delegates from the 110 chapters, or communities, of the reservation. Chapters operate like town councils, except meetings are conducted in the Navajo style. Anyone who wants to may speak on a subject, generally uninterrupted, until finished. Because of this, meetings can last long into the night.

A complete reform of the tribal government occurred in 1991 to create a three-branch tribal government with executive, legislative and judicial branches. This action was due primarily to former tribal chairman Peter MacDonald's conviction in tribal and federal courts on corruption and conspiracy charges. A four-term chairman of the Navajo Tribe, he is now serving a 14-year prison term. See pages 198-199 for more on Peter MacDonald.

The council holds regular sessions four times a year but calls many special sessions as well. Much of its deliberations are in Navajo. You are welcome to visit the council chambers during the day. All of the tribal council meetings are open to the public. For more information call the Office of the Speaker at (520) 871-7160.

WINDOW ROCK

The "window" in the Cow Springs Sandstone formed from water and wind erosion. Called *Tse'gha'hoodzáni'*, or "perforated rock," this is one of the four places medicinemen collect water for use in the Waterway Ceremony. (Van Valkenburg,1941)

In 1936, John Collier, then-commissioner of Indian Affairs, centralized in Window Rock all federal agencies governing the Navajo. Instead of Window Rock, some wanted to call the new capital, *Ni' 'ałníí'gi*, meaning

"earth's center." But medicinemen objected because it is inappropriate to use a ceremonial name in everyday conversation. It was also a difficult word for the many non-Navajos working for the Indian Service to pronounce. So the name Window Rock was adopted.

Window Rock, ca. 1890
Photo by Ben Wittick, Courtesy School of American Research Collectionsin the Museum of New Mexico,

For services in Window Rock see pages 158-159.

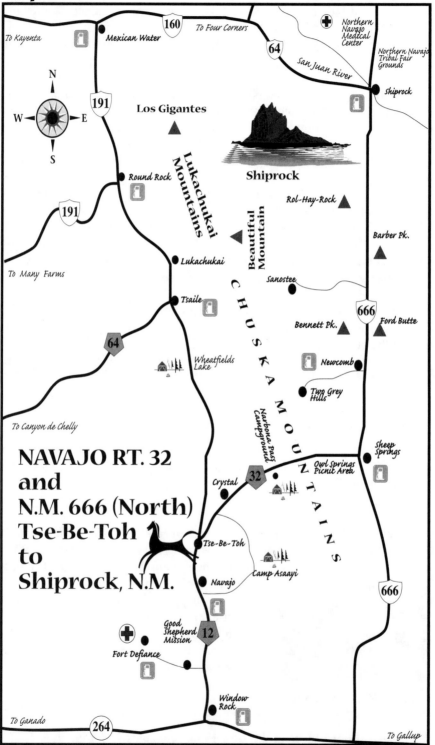

Chapter 18

To Kayenta

Mexican Water

160 To Four Corners

Northern Navajo Medical Center

64

San Juan River

Northern Navajo Tribal Fair Grounds

Shiprock

191

Los Gigantes

N
W E
S

Shiprock

Round Rock

Rol-Hay-Rock

Lukachukai Mountains

Barber Pk.

191

Beautiful Mountain

To Many Farms

Lukachukai

Sanostee

666

Tsaile

C H U S K A

Ford Butte

64

Bennett Pk.

Wheatfields Lake

Newcomb

Two Grey Hills

To Canyon de Chelly

M O U N T A I N S

Narbona Pass Campground

Sheep Springs

NAVAJO RT. 32 and N.M. 666 (North) Tse-Be-Toh to Shiprock, N.M.

Crystal

32

Owl Springs Picnic Area

Tse-Be-Toh

Camp Asaayi

666

Navajo

Good Shepherd Mission

12

Fort Defiance

Window Rock

To Ganado

264

To Gallup

60 miles (97 km) from Tse-Be-Toh to Shiprock, N.M.

TSE BE TOH Navajo Housing Authority Project

MM 18 CAMP ASSAYI AND BOWL CANYON (South)

A few miles down a rough dirt road, not recommended for RVs. Camping is allowed but there are no services. The elevation here is 7,800 feet (2,377 m) with frequent monsoons in summer. The average temperature is 75 degrees (23.8° C) during the day. You must have a Navajo tribal fishing permit to fish in Lake Assayi.

MM 18 CRYSTAL TRADING POST (North)

J.B. Moore was the trader at the Crystal Trading Post from 1890 to 1912. Like Lorenzo Hubbell, he wanted to improve the quality of the Navajo rug. One of the unusual features of rugs woven for Moore was that he had weavers bring in raw wool for him to send back east for machine processing. Clean wool was easier to weave and made exceptional rugs.

Crystal Trading Post, not dated.
Photo by Milton Snow, Courtesy Museum of New Mexico, # 46046

 **REGIONAL RUG DESIGN-CRYSTAL**

The Crystal design has two or three complex bands with arrows, stars, crosses or triangles. Traditionally woven using natural colors like brown, grey and rust but modern weavers may use pink, light green and yellow pastels. (Lamb, 1992)

Crystal, ca. 1910-1925
Photograph by Gene Balzer, Museum of Northern Arizona

MM 14 Blue Spruce, Aspen, Ponderosa Pine Forest

MM 12.5 NARBONA PASS (Elevation 8,150 feet or 2,484 m)
Referred to as Washington Pass on most maps until a group of Navajo Community College students fought to rename the pass in honor of Navajo leader Narbona.

Following the signing of the Treaty with Mexico in 1840 and the addition of land to the U.S. (which would later become New Mexico and Arizona), the U.S. military turned its attention to controlling Navajos. Lt. Col. John Macrae Washington rode into the Chuska Mountains to meet with Narbona and his son-in-law, Manuelito. He hoped to sign a treaty with the Navajos to end raids against the Mexicans as promised in the Treaty of Guadelupe de Hidalgo. To make his point, Washington noticed that one of the horses in Narbona's party belonged to the Mexicans and ordered the horse and rider seized. When the rider took off running, Washington's troops fired, killing Narbona. Witnessing his father-in-law's death, Manuelito vowed never to negotiate with the military again.

The headwaters of the Rio de Chelly start in Washington Pass at Coyote Wash. Known as "sparkling water" to the Navajo.

MM 12.5 NARBONA CAMPGROUND (South)

MM 10 OWL SPRINGS PICNIC AREA

Junction Navajo Route 32 with New Mexico Highway 666 to Shiprock, turn north.

At this junction is the community of **Sheep Springs**. This was a popular camping site for the military in 1847 because of the spring that flows here. Charles Newcomb established a trading post here in 1912. (Van Valkenburgh, 1941)

MM 59 NEWCOMB (West)
Originally named *Pesh-do-clish* but renamed Newcomb after the family who purchased the trading post in 1914.

Newcomb's Trading Post, not dated.
St. Michaels Photo Collection of the Franciscan Friars at St. Michaels, AZ. MS 119-186-4010

Franc Newcomb and her husband Arthur developed a close relationship with the famous Navajo medicineman, sandpainter and weaver, Hosteen Klah. Over the years, Franc attended many healing ceremonies conducted by Klah. She had a photographic memory capable of memorizing the intricacies and colors of each sandpainting Klah and other medicinemen made for their patients. Once home she drew more than 450 designs on paper. (Newcomb, 1964)

As Klah got older, the apprentice he had trained to take over his ceremonies died. This left Klah with no one to learn his complex ceremonies. Because of his fear that all of his knowledge would be lost, Klah consented to the recording and interpretation of his ceremonies by Franc Newcomb

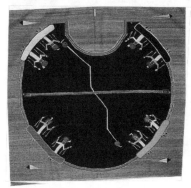

and Mary Wheelwright, a wealthy anthropologist from Boston. In an unprecedented move, Klah also wove many of his sandpainting designs into rugs. To preserve these valuable cultural artifacts, Mary Wheelwright built the Museum of Navajo Ceremonial Arts in Santa Fe specifically to house Klah's sandpaintings and weavings.This sandpainting rug pictured is from the Nightway Ceremony.

Klah Sandpainting Rug, ca. 1930-1936
Photographer Gene Balzer, Museum of Northern Arizona

In 1926, the Crown Prince of Sweden and his wife Princess Louise stopped at the Newcomb Trading Post for lunch on their way to Mesa Verde. The Prince wanted to see the ruins where his father, the King of Sweden, had purchased prehistoric artifacts for the Royal Museum of Stockholm. With only two hours prior notice, Mrs. Newcomb was expected to feed the entire royal entourage. The party was so large that Henry Ford sent six Lincolns from Detroit to Gallup, N.M., by rail to accommodate the prince's ground trip to Mesa Verde.

Traders were accustomed to feeding travelers who stopped by their trading post without notice, so the luncheon came off without a hitch. Upon meeting Klah, the Prince asked Arthur Newcomb if Klah was the Navajo king because of his dignified manner. (Newcomb, 1964)

 REGIONAL RUG DESIGN-TWO GREY HILLS

Down the road from Newcomb is the Two Grey Hills Trading Post, established in 1897, famous for the rug pattern of the same name. Originally based on J.B. Moore's Crystal design, weavers soon discarded his use of red and other bright colors in favor of subtle, natural, undyed colors of white, gray, brown and black. By 1925, Moore's design was completely abandoned. A design that focused on a center piece with surrounding smaller designs in each corner emerged to take its place. The Two Grey Hills is a finely woven rug with as many as 120 wefts to the inch compared to 30-to-50 wefts found in other high-quality rugs. All of the wool is hand spun. To get different shades of color, weavers card different colors of wool together. (Lamb, 1992; James, 1976)

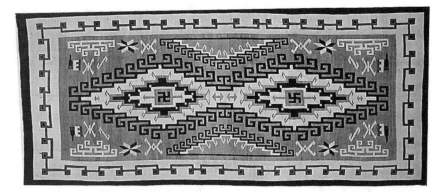

Two Grey Hills, ca. 1920-1940
Photographer Gene Balzer, Museum of Northern Arizona

In the center of the two diamonds of this particular rug are "whirling logs" designs,ancient symbols used by many Indian tribes. They have no connection with the European swastika. To the Hopi, it symbolizes the direction the clans traveled on their migrations. To the Navajo it represents the four sacred directions.

The primary setting for Tony Hillerman's fictitious novel *The Ghostway* is the Two Grey Hills Trading Post. The surrounding Chuska Mountains are also featured as well as Shiprock, Jim Chee's first assignment as a police officer.

MM 64 BENNETT PEAK (West)

This peak is known as Black Rock in Navajo. Narbona placed warriors on this peak to send smoke signals when Washington's troops were approaching in order to give him enough time to defend his people. He also used this pinnacle to warn of the arrival of Ute and Apache raiders.

MM 64 FORD BUTTE (East)

Both Bennett Peak and Ford Butte are igneous formations with dikes similar to Shiprock. (Trauger, 1967)

MM 67 SANOSTEE

Six miles (9.7 km) off Route 666 to the west is the small community of Sanostee. This is the birthplace and traditional home of Narbona. Renowned for his strong leadership and strategic skills, he is said to have led more than 1,000 men into battle. (Newcomb, 1964)

MM 70 BEAUTIFUL MOUNTAIN (West)

Standing at an elevation of 8,340 feet, this mountain was the site of the Beautiful Mountain Uprising of 1913. About 35 Navajos went into hiding here in protest of the government's stand against plural marriages, a traditional practice not commonly seen today. (McIlhaney, 1983)

MM 78 BARBER PEAK (East) Volcanic intrusive rock associated with Shiprock.

MM 78 TABLE MESA (West)

MM 85.5 SHIPROCK SCENIC PULL-OUT (West)

*Tsé Bit'á*í, or the Winged Rock, rises 1,700 feet (518 m) above the earth and has many volcanic dikes radiating from the center of the plug. The southern dike is 10 feet (3 m) wide and two miles (3.2 km) in length. The geologic cause of this spectacular rock formation was an explosion of built-up gases below the surface of the earth. When Shiprock exploded more than five million years ago, swamps and vegetation of all types covered this area. At the time, the top of the volcano was level with the surrounding plateau. Gradually, as the seas receded and the region turned to desert, the plateau was worn away from wind and water erosion, leaving the impregnable volcanic core standing alone on the landscape. There are hundreds of volcanic plugs throughout the Colorado Plateau, including Agathla Peak and Church Rock in Kayenta.

To the Navajo people, Shiprock represents one of the battles to cleanse the world of the evil monsters that tried to kill the Earth Surface People. Changing Woman's twin sons, Monster Slayer and Child-Born-of-Water, fought the man-eating eagle here and won. At the top of the monolith are the sharp feathers pointing up to the sky. At the base are the wings of the bird that trail into the ground. (Underhill, 1953)

In the first edition of *NATIVE ROADS* I said that "the Sierra Club of California attempted to climb Shiprock in 1939 but Navajo medicinemen objected. No further attempts to climb the volcanic plug have been made since." But I have received numerous letters from readers telling me that this is not true. According to Eric Bjornstad, author of *Desert Rock,* four members of the California Sierra Club, did successfully climb "America's toughest climbing problem" in 1939. After 12 failures by Colorado climber, Robert Ormes, the California team was successful because of the development and use of new technology–the expansion bolt. According to Bjornstad, in 1952 there were three more ascents on Shiprock and by 1963, 86 ascents had taken place with the last group removing 27 expansion bolts and 15 pitons.

✦ SHIPROCK COMMUNITY

Bureau of Indian Affairs Superintendent William Shelton was in charge of this area in 1903. Shelton, called "Tall Boss" by the Navajo, initiated an agricultural program here using irrigation water from the San Juan River. The original buildings and homes in Shiprock were made of logs and adobe. Most were swept away in the flood of 1912. In the reconstruction that followed, the new bridge across the San Juan replaced the ferry that "Jimmy the Boatman" ran for many years.

In 1921, oil, gas and helium were found close to Shiprock. This led to a period of increased oil exploration and discovery on Navajoland, making the tribe one of the richest in the country. In the 1950s and 1960s, uranium was found in the Carrizo Mountains, turning Shiprock into a boom town for about 20 years. The community had a hotel and a few more restaurants at that time.

✚ NORTHERN NAVAJO MEDICAL CENTER

This is a U.S. Indian Health Service facility. Non-Navajos are seen on an emergency basis only. **(505) 368-4971**

NORTHERN NAVAJO TRIBAL FAIR: Held in October, this fair features the *Yé'ii bicheii* ceremony, or Nightway Chant. This is a lengthy and expensive ceremony used to treat patients with a chronic illness or someone experiencing visual, hearing or mental disturbances.

A "hand trembler," someone gifted with the ability to diagnose illness through touch, determines the need for the ceremony. If the diagnostician prescribes this ceremony, it is conducted only "after the thunder sleeps" in the winter.

This ceremony is a complex and laborious commitment from the family that agrees to hold it for their ill relative. The host must feed everyone who attends the nine-night ceremony, and the medicineman and his many helpers must be paid. The most popular part of the ceremony is when the *yé'iis*, or Holy People, dance in public on the seventh and ninth nights. The dancing lasts all night and is open to anyone. However the healing ceremony and sandpainting in the hogan are for the patient's family and invited guests only.

The Northern Navajo Fair in Shiprock is usually held the first weekend in October. The "Two Yé'iis Coming" dance starts on Saturday afternoon with the yé'ii bicheii dancing in the evening. The sacred masked dancers begin late on Saturday night and continue in the morning on Sunday. No photography is allowed at the Yé'ii bicheii ceremony. For more information contact Shiprock Navajo Fair, Inc., P.O. Box 1893, Shiprock, NM (505) 368-5108.

SERVICES IN SHIPROCK

MOTELS There are no motels in Shiprock, the closest motel is in Farmington, N.M., 30 miles (48 km) to the east.

Anasazi Inn	903 West Main St., Farmington	(505) 325-4564
Basin Lodge	701 Airport Drive, Farmington	(505) 325-5061
Comfort Inn	555 Scott Avenue, Farmington	(800) 221-2222
Encore Motel	1900 E. Main, Farmington	(505) 325-5008
Days Inn	2530 Bloomfield Hwy., Farmington	(505) 327-4433
Farmington Lodge	1510 W. Main, Farmington	(800) 833-4792
Holiday Inn	600 E. Broadway, Farmington	(800) Holiday

The Inn Best Western	700 Scott Avenue, Farmington	(800) 528-1234
Journey Inn	317 Airport Dr., Farmington	(505) 325-3548
La Quinta	675 Scott Ave., Farmington	800) 531-5900
Motel 6	1600 Bloomfield Hwy, Farm.	(505) 326-4501
Motel 6	510 Scott Ave., Farmington	(505) 327-0242
Redwood Lodge	625 E. Main, Farmington	(505) 326-5521
Sage Motel	301 Airport Dr., Farmington	(505) 325-7501

Silver River Adobe Inn (Bed and Breakfast)

| | 3151 W. Main, Farmington | (800) 382-9251 |
| Super 8 | 1601 Bloomfield Hwy, Farm. | (800) 800-8000 |

RESTAURANTS IN SHIPROCK

Kentucky Fried Chicken	Breakfast, lunch and dinner.	
	7 a.m.-10 p.m.	(505) 368-4805
Little Ceasars Pizza	11 a.m.-10 p.m.	(505) 368-5682
That's-a-Burger	7 a.m.-10 p.m.	(505) 368-4019
Taco Bell	7 a.m.- 10 p.m.	(505) 368-5957
City Market Bakery	6:30 a.m.-10 p.m.	(505) 368-4248
& Deli		

AUTOMOBILE SERVICES IN SHIPROCK

Buck's Tire and Towing Service	(505) 368-5774
Dineh Express Lube	(505) 368-4846
El Navajo Garage	(505) 368-4998
Montano's Towing	(505) 368-5261
and Wrecking Service	

SHIPROCK NAVAJO POLICE: (505) 368-4383

Located on the north corner of the junction of New Mexico 666 and 64.
This was the first assignment for Tony Hillerman's fictional character, Jim
Chee, before he was transferred to Tuba City.

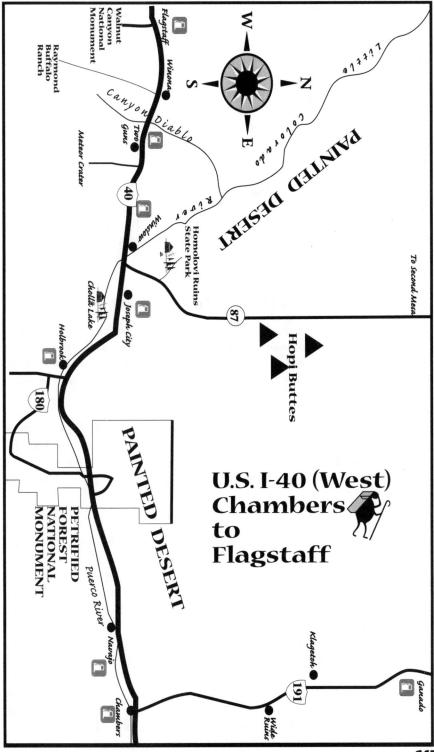

CHAPTER 19

U.S. I-40 (West)
Chambers
to
Flagstaff

140 miles (225 km) from Chambers to Flagstaff

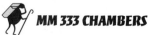 **MM 333 CHAMBERS**

Chambers prospered through the sale of bentonite clay deposits used in the manufacture of fine porcelain china.

 **MM 325 NAVAJO, ARIZ.**

Not to be confused with Navajo, N.M., Navajo, Ariz., also known as Navajo Springs, was a popular watering stop for settlers and western explorers. It was here on Dec. 29, 1863, that John Goodwin of Maine took the oath of office as the first governor of the newly-formed territory of Arizona.

MM 311 PETRIFIED FOREST AND PAINTED DESERT NATIONAL PARK

There are two entrances to the forest. If you're pressed for time and want to see only the petrified wood, enter the park at the south entrance. At Holbrook, take U.S. Highway 180 south and follow the signs to the Painted Desert. The road from the south to the north entrance is 26 miles (40 km) one way. Entrance fees at either the north or south end are $10 per car or $5 per person on bicycle or foot. Golden Eagle, Golden Age and Golden Access passes are accepted. There are no camping facilities or motels. There is a restaurant at the north end of the park next to the Painted Desert Visitors Center. Open 7 a.m. - 7 p.m. in summer and 8 a.m. - 5 p.m. (MST) the rest of the year. Closed Dec. 25 and Jan. 1. (520) 524-6228

The Chinle Formation is responsible for much of the beauty of northern Arizona. It is in this layer of geologic time that we see the beautiful red, brown, purple, gray and green shales of the Painted Desert plus the phenomenon known as petrified wood. More than 220 million years ago, this area was the site of a large Triassic lake and floodplain heavily covered with vegetation. Most of the logs found in the park are *Araucarioxylon arizonicum*, distant relatives of trees found today only in wet areas of New Zealand, Australia and South America. (Ash, 1990)

Over time the Chinle Formation, rich with minerals, encased the fallen vegetation and trees. Eventually, where the conditions were just right, the organic matter in the wood was replaced with minerals, or "petrified."

The Painted Desert Visitors Center shows a 17-minute movie every half-hour that explains how wood is petrified. (Baars, 1972, Ash 1990.)

The Petrified National Forest contains the largest collection of entire petrified logs but smaller pieces of wood decorate much of northern Arizona.

Petrified Logs, ca. 1889
Detroit Publishing Company Collection
Cline Library, Special Collections and Archives, NAU PH 516.30

As more settlers moved into this area, petrified wood was used to make everything from coffee tables to lamps. Eastern towns ordered truck loads of the stones for various commercial uses and the new Atlantic & Pacific Railroad cut right through the Petrified Forest helping to speed up the export of these rare stones. An enterprising entrepreneur even built a mill in Jasper Forest to grind petrified wood into abrasives. This venture failed, however, because cheaper abrasives were on the market. Alarmed at the rapid destruction of this natural treasure, local citizens petitioned Congress for protection. In 1906, President Theodore Roosevelt set the area aside as a national monument with the Painted Desert section added in 1932. (Ash, 1990)

SCENIC DETOUR

Starting from the north entrance in the Painted Desert section of the park.

PAINTED DESERT INN MUSEUM

Originally built in the 1920s, the Civilian Conservation Corps rebuilt the Painted Desert Inn for the National Park Service in 1938. The Fred Harvey Co. became the concessionaire at the park and asked Mary Colter to design the interior of the Inn. She combined the Spanish theme of the building with native Indian designs. Fred Kabotie, the artist who painted murals in Colter's Grand Canyon Desert View Watchtower, painted the Buffalo Dance in the dining room of this hotel. (Grattan, 1992) No longer a hotel, the Painted Desert Inn has been preserved as a museum and is a National Historic Landmark. Behind the Inn is the sweeping vista of the Painted Desert.

PUERCO INDIAN RUINS (East)

After leaving the Painted Desert Inn, continue south six miles (9.5 km) to these ruins, dated to 1100 A.D. This was a desirable location for farming because of the nearby Puerco River. But in 1200 A.D., the site was abandoned because of a great drought. In 1300 A.D., it was reinhabited but abandoned for the last time in 1400 A.D., possibly because of the damaging erosion of the Puerco River on the farming area which made it too difficult to grow a sustaining crop.

NEWSPAPER ROCK (West)

Down the road about one mile (1.6 km) is an overlook where you can view a rock art location covered with hundreds of petroglyphs.

WHAT ARE PETROGLYPHS? These pictures and symbols, pecked into the surface of rocks many centuries ago, are extremely common in the Southwest, particularly on the Colorado Plateau. Some think they were used by prehistoric people as a way to communicate with the supernatural powers which they believed controlled the universe and the tribe's success or failure. Many of the images, pecked into the soft sandstone, have to do with fertility, rain or abundant hunting animals. Some of the supernatural beings depicted include *Ye'iis*, (Navajo), Kachinas (spirit beings), migration and clan symbols and myriad other images that probably played a part in the band's ceremonial life. **Pictographs** are rock paintings which often depict the same images as petroglyphs. Naturally-occurring colors like hematite,

---

a iron-laden mineral, for red, charcoal for black and clay for white are used as paint. You will find most rock art is near springs, places where people lived or along commonly traveled routes. (Weaver, 1984)

Newspaper Rock, Petrified Forest, not dated.
Mary Jane Colter Rock Art Collection, Museum of Northern Arizona, MS 301-5-415

Leaving Newspaper Rock, turn south to travel though the **Tepees**, part of the Painted Desert badlands and on to the Petrified Forest section of the park. Interesting stops are the **Jasper Forest** where you can see petrified logs with root systems indicating that some of the trees grew in this area. **Crystal Forest** was given its name because of the many amethyst and quartz crystals found here by gem collectors before the area became a national park. The **Agate House** is an interesting stop because this 1050 A.D. pueblo is made entirely of petrified wood. The **Rainbow Forest Museum** at the south entrance to the park has interesting displays about the petrified wood and ethnohistory of the area.

MM 285 HOLBROOK

Holbrook was born a classic Western town. It developed around Horse-head Crossing where the skull of a horse hung on a post to mark the safest crossing across the treacherous quicksand of the Little Colorado River.

Holbrook, named for the chief engineer of the Atlantic & Pacific Railroad, Henry R. Holbrook, was little more than a sleepy little town before the railroad arrived in 1866. It soon turned into one of the wildest burgs in the Southwest, boasting the only churchless county seat in the U.S. (Johnston, 1981)

To help subsidize the expense of building a transcontinental railroad, the government gave the railroad company land grants extending 20 miles (32 km) on either side of the tracks that could be sold to generate capital.

The Boston financiers who were charged by President Chester A. Arthur to build the railroad from Albuquerque to California liked the rich grazing land the railroad passed through in northern Arizona. They saw an opportunity for a new business venture. Under the laws of the state of New York, the owners of the railroad created the Aztec Land & Cattle Co. They then bought one million acres of grazing land around Holbrook at 50 cents an acre (.004 sq km). The Hash Knife outfit in Texas sold 33,000 head of cattle to the new cattle company and sent them by railroad to Holbrook.

Holbrook turned into a bustling, dangerous city overnight. Hundreds of

cowboys, many with criminal records, headed for the town looking for work with the Aztec Cattle Co. When off the range, the cowboys spent most of their free time and their $25 monthly wages at the **Bucket of Blood Saloon**. The original but now-abandoned saloon still stands at 119 E. South Central in Holbrook. It is one of Holbrook's first stone buildings constructed after the fire of 1888 which destroyed the entire town. (Johnson, 1956)

Horsehead Crossing of the Little Colorado, Arizona. Ca. 1882-83.
Photo by Ben Wittick
Courtesy School of American Research Collections in the Museum of New Mexico, 15813.

To give you an idea of what it was like to be thrown into jail during this time in history, stop by the **Navajo County Courthouse**. This 1898 jail came completely assembled by railroad from St. Louis to be placed in the courthouse. The courthouse is located on the northeast corner of Navajo Blvd.

One of the first **Harvey Houses** opened in Holbrook in 1884 and was staffed by Harvey Girls who gave prompt and efficient service during the 30-minute stop for meals. To speed up the service, rail passengers ordered their dinner selection from the conductor who signaled ahead how many of each menu items to prepare. The meals were hot and waiting for the passengers as soon as they arrived. The most popular item on the menu was steak imported from Kansas City. But passengers also had the choice of oysters, turtle, quail or antelope. (Grattan, 1992)

The restaurant sat right next to the train depot in five converted railroad cars, painted bright red and decorated in an Indian motif. Unfortunately, with the drop in rail travel over the years, the Harvey Houses, in railroad towns like Holbrook and Winslow, are long gone.

SERVICES IN HOLBROOK

LODGING

Best Western Adobe Inn	615 West Dr.	(520) 524-3948
Best Western Arizonian Inn	2508 E. Navajo Blvd.	(520) 524-2611
Brad's Motel	301 West Dr.	(520) 524-6929
Budget Inn	602 Navajo Blvd.	(520) 524-6263
Comfort Inn	2602 E. Navajo Blvd.	(520) 524-2611
Econo Lodge	2596 Navajo Blvd.	(520) 524-1448
Day's Inn	2601 E. Navajo Blvd.	(520) 524-6949
El Rancho Motel	867 E. Navajo Blvd.	(520) 524-3332
The Inn	235 West Dr.	(520) 524-3809
Holiday Inn Express	1308 E. Navajo Blvd.	(520) 524-1466
Moenkopi Motel	464 Navajo Blvd.	(520) 524-6848
Rainbow Inn	2211 E. Navajo Blvd.	(520) 524-2654
Super 8 Motel	1989 Navajo Blvd.	(520) 524-2871
Western Holiday Motel	720 Navajo Blvd.	(520) 524-6216

CAMPGROUNDS

KOA	102 Hermosa Dr.	(520) 524-6689
Full hook-ups $20.95		
OK RV	1526 Navajo Blvd.	(520) 524-3226
Full-hook ups $16.50		

RESTAURANTS

Arizona Country Cafe	Jct. N. Hwy 77 & I-40	(520) 524-2686
Denny's Restaurant	2510 E. Navajo Blvd.	(520) 524-2893
El Rancho Restaurant	867 Navajo Blvd.	(520) 524-3332
Jerry's Restaurant	2602 E. Navajo Blvd.	(520) 524-2364
Joe & Aggies Cafe	120 West Dr.	(520) 524-6540
Pizza Hut	538 West Dr.	(520) 524-2216
Plainsman Restaurant	1001 West Dr.	(520) 524-3345
Roadrunner Cafe	1501 E. Navajo Blvd.	(520) 524-2787

Sundown Café	915 West Dr.	(520) 524-3785
Wayside Drive-In	1150 West Dr.	(520) 524-3167

AUTOMOBILE SERVICE

Arizona Towing	(520) 524-2222
Chuck's Performance Towing	(520) 524-2444
Scotty & Son Towing	(520) 524-6442

 MM 277 CHOLLA LAKE COUNTY PARK

This man-made lake has a campground patrolled by three rangers. Basic camping is $7 per night. Camp sites with electricity and water are $10 per night. There are community bathrooms and showers but no dump site for RVs. Sites given out on a first-come, first-served basis. The rangers lock the gates to the park at 9 p.m. (MST) and if you want to get out earlier than 8 a.m. they will give you the combination. For more information call (520) 288-3717.

MM 274 JOSEPH CITY

This is the only one of four Mormon settlements to survive along the Little Colorado River during the late 1800s. First called Allen's Camp for the mission's leader, the community members decided to change the name to St. Joseph in honor of their prophet Joseph Smith.

The original group, sent here by Brigham Young, was to establish Mormon communities based on the social concept of a United Order. Successful in Brigham City, Utah, the United Order idea was based on the principle of cooperation rather than competition. Article 1 of the incorporation of Allen's Branch of the United Order of 1877 read: "Resolve that we the under-signed of our own free will and choice form ourselves into a Company and combine all of our means and labor that we may more fully carry out our agricultural, manufacturing and all other industrial pursuits necessary for our mutual benefit."

This would prove to be a beneficial way for the people of Allen's Camp to survive in this harsh country. If they were to be successful farmers, irrigation from the Little Colorado was a necessity. Over a period of 18 years, the settlers built 12 dams on the Little Colorado. It was a river like nothing they had ever seen before. It had a mind of its own, one year a raging torrent and the next year completely dry.

Their first attempt at dam building came in March 1876. It was a simple design relying on tons of rock brought to the river from a nearby quarry and dumped on the sandy river bottom. But in July, when the seasonal monsoons hit, the river rose in flood to erase any sign of their hard work. They tried other types of dams. One suggested by engineers from the nearby Atlantic & Pacific Railroad consisted of wooden piles driven deep into the river bed. Although this was a successful design for the railroad, it failed for the Mormons. But they persevered and finally, in 1894, they built a dam that held for 29 years.

Life along the Little Colorado was hard. Just to have a cool, clean drink of water was a luxury reserved for trips to the mountains or Tuba City. St. Joseph's drinking water came from the Little Colorado River and was laden with salt, gypsum and tons of sediment. They called it the river that was too thick to drink and too thin to plow. Yet for almost 40 years this was the only source of potable water. Even when wells were dug, the resulting water was not much better than the river because of its high concentration of salt.

In 1923, the town's name of St. Joseph changed to Joseph City because the mail kept being confused with St. Joseph, Missouri. A half-mile (0.8 km) east of Joseph City is a marker placed by the Daughters of the Utah Pioneers commemorating the spot where the St. Joseph Fort stood. (Tanner, 1977)

MM 257 HOMOLOVI RUINS STATE PARK (North)

The visitors center is open 8 a.m. - 5 p.m. everyday except Christmas. The ruins are open from 8 a.m. to sunset. Entrance fees are $3 per car, per six people. All park facilities have been designed for access by physically-impaired visitors. If you have difficulty walking any distance, check at the visitors center for alternate access to Homolovi II. The center is also developing information in braille and has sign language interpreters available for their public workshops if you call in advance. This is an Arizona state park so Golden Eagle passes are not accepted. (520) 289-4106

In the Hopi language, Homol'ovi means "the place of little hills." This settlement is an ancestral home to some clans currently living in Hopi villages to the north. It's a different kind of interpretative site to visit because most of the 300 ruins have not been excavated. This gives you an idea of the effort required to restore many of the ancient sites you may have already visited. At Homol'ovi II, thought to have more than 1,000 rooms, you'll have the opportunity to look inside an ancient kiva.

NATIVE ROADS

Homolovi is one of the pueblos built by ancestors of the present-day Hopi along the ancient **Palatkwapi Trail**. In Hopi legend, it is believed that when the Hopis emerged from the underworld, some went to live at Palatkwapi, or "the place of the red rocks" in the Verde Valley. Here they became lazy and failed to continue their migrations, as *Maa'sau* instructed, before permanently settling down in one place.

As their lifestyle deteriorated, a great flood came to punish the people. They had no choice but to abandon their paradise. The clans at Palatkwapi began to gradually move northward, building pueblos at various springs along the trading route, one of which was Homol'ovi. The Palatkwapi Trail begins at the village of Walpi, passes by springs located about every 15 to 30 miles (24-48 km), crosses the Little Colorado at Sunset Crossing by Winslow where there is solid rock and less danger of quicksand, skirts around the impassable Canyon Diablo and drops down into Verde Valley to the mineral-rich, modern-day towns of Jerome and Prescott. (Byrkit, 1988)

At the Homolovi visitors center take the short walk to the **Sunset Cemetery** that overlooks the Little Colorado River. Mormon leader Lot Smith founded a community named Sunset near here in 1876. Because of floods and drought, the group could not survive and abandoned the town in 1887. Smith then moved to Tuba City where he prospered raising dairy cattle but died in a shootout with a Navajo. His body was brought back to Sunset to be buried in this cemetery. (See page 162 for more about Lot Smith.)

The Homolovi visitors center has exhibits, video programs and a great book store specializing in the local native cultures, natural history and Southwest archaeology. Throughout June and July you can watch archaeologists working Monday through Friday in the field. The last weekend in July is the park's annual archeology day with tours of the summer's excavations. All of the ruins are reburied to protect them during the rainy season, which usually starts by early August.

Homolovi Campground

Fifty-three sites with electricity, dump stations, and restrooms year round. Water hook-ups and showers available from mid-April through mid-October. Pull-through sites available for large RV's and some pads for tents are available. $8 without hook-up, $13 with hook-up.

MM 257 LITTLE COLORADO RIVER

Its name in Hopi is *Paayu* and it is a constant source of water throughout the year. Even when it looks dry, there is water just inches below the surface. During prehistoric times, the river flowed year round. But since upstream damming, there is no surface flow during the dry season.

MM 257 WINSLOW

Before the coming of the railroad, Winslow was called Sunset Crossing and was the only safe way across the treacherous Little Colorado River. In 1866, the Navajos called Winslow "iron lying down" because of the iron rails stored here during construction of the railroad heading west.

The town is named for Gen. Edward Winslow, president of the St. Louis & San Francisco Railroad which also owned most of the Atlantic & Pacific Railroad. (Yost, 1958)

Famous Grand Canyon architect and designer Mary Colter built the **La Posada Hotel and train depot** in Winslow in 1929. Believing that a building should be an extension of its surroundings and blend with the history of the area, Colter designed La Posada in the grand hacienda style of the Southwest.

La Posada, The Last Great Railroad Hotel,
A National Historic Landmark
Photograph courtesy Alan Affeldt

La Posada was Colter's favorite project, and in its day it was the finest small hotel in the Southwest. There were 75 guest rooms, six dining rooms, grand public spaces and acres of beautiful gardens full of the smell of orchards and flowers.

Colter filled the Hacienda with furniture from around the world–century old Spanish engravings, Mexican chandeliers, Navajo rugs, Italian benches and beds made by her own craftsmen working on site.

It cost the Santa Fe Railroad $1 million to build La Posada and another million to landscape and furnish, but the beautiful retreat survived only 27 years. Doomed from the start, the hotel's grand opening came one year after the worst stock market crash in the history of Wall Street. Luckily, the Santa Fe Railroad did see the value in keeping the building and turned it into their division headquarters. But they sold all of the expensive, hand-made La Posada furniture and fixtures at auction. Finally in 1993, the Santa Fe announced plans to move out of La Posada and it looked like Mary Colter's love was doomed.

But local historians began a fight to save this treasure and got protection for the building through its designation as a National Historic Landmark. Alan Affeldt, with city and state support, bought the old hotel in 1997 and today it is considered one of the top five historic hotels in Arizona. There are 20 guest rooms now available and La Posada is open for tours every day. AMTRAK stops daily at the depot and PBS, the History Channel and Garden TV have all produced specials on the restoration of La Posada. *For more information and a brochure call (520) 289-3873.*

Hubbell's Trading Post, Winslow, Arizona, not dated.
Arizona Historical Society-Pioneer Museum

Lorenzo Hubbell owned a large wholesale trading post and warehouse here on Hicks and First streets. This location provided access to the railroad to ship Hubbell merchandise throughout the Four Corners area and the country. A spur line came up beside the building. The building is now owned by the Arizona Historical Society and the Affiliation of Native American Groups is working to renovate the building for office space to provide needed programs to Natives living in Winslow.

Winslow is also famous for a stretch of old **Route 66** found at Second and Third streets. Called the "Mother Road" by novelist John Steinbeck, Route 66 was, at one time, a destination in itself. Chartered in 1926 but not completed until 1938, it connected Chicago with Los Angeles and popularized the great American tradition of driving across country for summer vacation.

The ruins of **Brigham City**, one of the four Mormon United Order settlements of the Little Colorado River, is located just north of the interstate at N. Park Drive. (See page 254 for more on the United Order.) A local community group hopes to restore the fort and other historic buildings for visitors to enjoy.

SERVICES IN WINSLOW

LODGING

American Inn	701 W. 3rd St.	(520) 289-4605
Bel Air Motel	1003 E. 2nd St.	(520) 289-2459
Best Western Adobe Inn	2301 North Park Dr.	(520) 289-4638
Best Western Townhouse	W. Highway 66	(520) 289-4611
Comfort Inn	520 W. Desmond	(520) 289-9581
Delta Motel	W. Highway 66	(520) 289-3897
Earl's Motel	512 E. 2nd St.	(520) 289-9987
Easy 8 Motel	1000 E. 3rd St.	(520) 289-5130
Econolodge	I-40, Exit 253	(520) 289-4687
Entre's Motel	W. Highway 66	(520) 289-2476
Mayfair Motel	1925 W. Highway 66	(520) 289-5445
Motel 10 Inn	725 W. 3rd St.	(520) 289-3903
Price Right Motel	1216 E. 3rd St.	(520) 289-2491
Royal Motel	1221 E. 3rd St.	(520) 289-4631
Sand & Sage Motel	912 W. 2nd St.	(520) 289-3328
Super 8 Motel	2140 W. Highway 66	(520) 289-4606
Westerner Motel	500 E. 2nd St.	(520) 289-2825
Winslow 6 Motel	1901 W. 2nd St.	(520) 289-2458

RESTAURANTS

Arby Roast Beef	2121 North Park Dr.	(520) 289-5565
Brown Mug Café (Mexican)	308 E. 2nd St.	(520) 289-9973
Burger King	W. Highway 66	(520) 289-4449
Casa Blanca Cafe	1201 E. 2nd St.	(520) 289-4191
Church's Fried Chicken	300 E. 2nd St.	(520) 289-2515

Crosswinds Restaurant	1701 North Park Dr.	(520) 289-4638
Dairy Queen	1304 E. 2nd St.	(520) 289-3282
Darrel's Root Beer Stand	1001 Williamson Ave.	(520)289-2891
Denny's	410 Mike's Pike	(520) 289-5117
El Papagayo	1942 W. 3rd St.	(520) 289-3379
El Torito	908 Central	(520) 289-2714
Entre' Restaurant	W. Highway 66	(520) 289-2141
Falcon Restaurant	1113 E. 3rd St.	(520) 289-2342
Gabrielle's Restaurant	918 E. 2nd St.	(520) 289-2508
Graffiti's Diner	2201 North Park Dr.	(520) 289-9531
Highway Diner	320 E. 2nd St.	(520) 289-3629
Joe's Café (Chinese)	W. Highway 66	(520) 289-4155
McDonald's	1501 North Park Dr.	(520) 289-5710
Sonic Drive-In	1520 E. 3rd St.	(520) 289-3278
Sue's Place	725 W. 3rd St.	(520) 289-5589
Taco Bell	1605 North Park Dr.	(520) 289-4212
Town House Restaurant	W. Highway 66	(520) 289-4611
Two Stars Café 101	E. 2nd St.	(520) 289-5103

 **MM 233 METEOR CRATER (South)**

This is a privately-owned commercial venture. It's a five-mile (8 km) drive one-way to the visitors center where there is a snack shop, curio shop and entrance to view the crater. Entrance fees are $7 for adults, $6 for adults over 60, $2 for 13-17 years, $1 for 6-12 years. Not affiliated with the National Park Service so Golden Eagle passes are not accepted.

Dr. D.M. Barringer was the first person in the late 1880s to think that the huge bowl, more than a mile (1.6 km) wide and 800 feet (243 m) deep was a meteorite crater. Most experts in geology at the time believed the crater was the result of a steam explosion. Dr. Barringer, a mining engineer, disagreed with this explanation because the usual cause of steam explosions, volcanic activity, is completely absent in this area.

For 20 years, Dr. Barringer scoured the crater and surrounding area for evidence to support his theory. His problem was that he could not find any recognizable meteorite big enough to have caused this kind of depression. He theorized that the meteorite hit the earth at an angle and broke into small pieces from the force of the impact. To prove his theory, Barringer hired a driller and finally found extraterrestrial material at a depth of 1,346 feet (410 m).

Evidence of other small meteor craters in the world began to surface. One was discovered in Odessa, Texas, in 1923. Eight years later, 13 craters were found in Australia, all with only small chunks of meteorite in the vicinity. This was the proof Dr. Barringer needed for his theory to gain world-wide support. Unfortunately, he died before his theory became universally accepted. To honor the man who spent more than 30 years of his life and a substantial portion of his own money to prove that this is a meteorite crater, the Meteoritical Society officially named it Barringer Meteorite Crater. A crater on the far side of the moon also honors Barringer.

No one knows exactly when the meteorite hit the earth but scientists think it occurred around 20,000 to 50,000 years ago. The meteor hit the earth so hard that it displaced 300 million tons of rock in the center and pushed the edge of the crater 150 feet (45 m) high. Scattered over an area of 100,000 acres (405 sq km) are meteorite chunks of nickel and iron, some as heavy as 200 pounds (30.7 kg). One of these large pieces can be seen at Verkamps, a curio shop next to the Hopi House, on the south rim of the Grand Canyon.

RV PARK: *There are 71 pull-through spaces, full hook-ups, private restrooms with showers. Two adults, $18 plus 6 percent tax. Each additional adult, add $2. Each child 5 and under, add $1. (520) 289-4002.*

First Trading Post, Canyon Diablo, ca. 1870
Kansas State Historical Society, Topeka, Kansas ATSF.1/0074

 **MM 230 CANYON DIABLO (North)**

In 1540, when Coronado failed to find the Seven Golden Cities of Cibola in the Zuni villages of New Mexico, he dispatched Lt. Garcia Lopez de

Cardenas to the west to look for the possibility of gold in the Hopi villages. The Hopis told Cardenas about a magnificent river even farther west where he might find gold. The expedition pushed on, crossing the Little Colorado at Winslow. Encountering Canyon Diablo, Cardenas named the canyon after the devil because it was so difficult to cross.

In 1857, Lt. Edward Beale reported Canyon Diablo to be a major obstacle in his attempt to survey a road from Fort Defiance to the Colorado River. His party had to travel 40 miles (64 km) out of its way to find a way across. Herman Wolff built the first trading post in the area, about 10 miles (16 km) from here, in 1870. Because of the nearly impassable canyon, Wolff had to bring freight from Albuquerque, more than 300 miles (482 km) away. In 1882, the Atlantic & Pacific Railroad built an iron bridge with a span of 520 feet (158 m) across Diablo Canyon. Standing 254 feet (77 m) above the canyon floor, the bridge ended the problem of hauling supplies by wagon over such a long distance.

After Wolff's death, S.I. Richardson and his uncle, George McAdams of Red Lake, bought the post. S.I managed it alone for a couple of years. The Babbitt brothers later bought the post but sold it a short time later to an inexperienced eastern archaeologist named Leander Smith.

One day, thinking Navajos would enjoy his joke, Smith displayed a human skull in the front window of his store. Smith had found the skull while excavating around his post and was obviously unaware of Navajo beliefs regarding death and human remains. To his surprise, customers shunned the post and he was soon out of business. Because of this serious *faux pax*, the Wolff post never reopened and lies in ruin today.

Charles Algert set up his first trading post along the canyon in an abandoned box car to serve the needs of the railroad crews. Following the completion of the railroad, he shifted his attention to trading with Navajos and built a limestone trading post north of the tracks. He sold his post to Frederick Volz in 1897 and moved to Tuba City to open the Tuba Trading Post. Aware of tourists' interest in the Hopi snake dance, Volz began to haul people by the hundreds from the train station at Canyon Diablo to the Hopi mesas. To accommodate the travelers on this dry, hot journey of more than 62 miles (100 km), Volz built another post called "the fields" along Oraibi Wash, half-way between Canyon Diablo and Oraibi. (Babbitt,1986)

In 1898, Volz bought some interesting iron pieces from two sheepherders and sent them to a metallurgist. The specimens turned out to be meteorites. The iron sold for 75 cents a pound (.45 kg), so Volz hired local laborers to collect meteorites around Meteor Crater and sold two railroad cars-full.

Canyon Diablo, Arizona, ca. 1883
Photograph by Ben Wittick
Courtesy School of American Research Collections, Museum of New Mexico, 51054

MM 230 TWO GUNS (South)

The ruins of the town of Two Guns are on private property and the owner does not want visitors because of liability issues. You can see the ruins from the highway.

It is hard to believe that anything of interest ever happened here. But because of major trails heading east to Albuquerque and west to Flagstaff, this was an important stopping off place. Navajos used a trail through Two Guns that ran north and south to the Mogollon Rim where they traded and fought with Apaches.

Various accounts tell of a massacre that occurred near here in 1878. Fifty Navajo men, women and children were killed by Apache warriors. Seeking revenge, a party of Navajo men headed south over the well-used trail in pursuit of the murderers. For some time they were unable to find any trace of the war party but then by chance, overheard the sound of voices and smelled smoke coming from beneath the earth. Looking through a limestone fissure, they saw the Apaches and their horses hiding inside a large cave. The Navajos shot arrows at their enemies through the earth cracks and built a fire at the cave's only opening. Desperate to survive, the Apaches butchered their horses in a vain attempt to extinguish the fire with the animal's blood. Finally, overcome with smoke, all 42 Apache warriors died. This later became known as the "Apache Death Cave."

In 1923, Harry "Indian" Miller leased the land surrounding the "death cave" from then owner Earl Cundiff and renamed it "Mystery Cave." Hoping to entice tourists interested in the macabre, he built a fake pueblo at its entrance and decorated the cave with the skeletal remains of the Apache warriors. More than once he was told by local Navajos that the cave was cursed and should be avoided, but Miller was determined to turn Two Guns into a popular tourist destination.

Harry's trouble started not long after opening his business venture. In 1926, Earl Cundiff was mysteriously murdered and Harry was the primary suspect but was never taken to trial. Later, he was seriously mauled by wild cats he kept caged in his zoo. The zoo was part of the now ruined, pueblo style tourist town he built over the opening to the cave. But it was after the death of his 17 year-old daughter in a car accident on the newly opened Route 66 that Miller believed there really was a curse on the "death cave." He left Two Guns in 1934 and opened a new tourist attraction called the "Cave of the Seven Devils" across the border in New Mexico. (Kildare,1967;Thomas, 1993)

Famous Navajo trader S.I. Richardson bought Two Guns as an investment when he retired from the trading business at the age of 80. When he died in 1959 he left the property to his children. His son, Gladwell, also known as Toney Richardson, was a prolific southwestern novelist and travel writer. In 1968 he wrote a book about Two Guns filled with history and interesting anecdotes he heard from local Navajos and his famous trading father and uncles over the years. One interesting story is about the popular Arizona theme of finding and losing a fortune in gold.

As elsewhere in northern Arizona, the first non-Indian explorers were with Coronodo's gold-seeking expedition of 1540. It is believed that in 1769, Franciscan fathers actually found silver somewhere in central Arizona. Traveling from their mines and loaded down with silver, the padres came through Two Guns on their way back to Santa Fe. Indians attacked the expedition, but the friars were too encumbered by the silver packed on their mules and horses to escape. To lighten their load, they hid their silver bars in what they thought was an abandoned Indian village. Splitting up, half the party took off toward California and the other half tried to get through to Santa Fe.

In 1902, a treasure hunter found a map of the location of the alleged cache of silver in the archives of San Miguel Mission in Santa Fe. Hordes descended on the Two Guns area to find the lost treasure, but it was a local sheepherder who found one bar of silver weighing a hefty 64 pounds (29 kg). The rest of the silver from the Lost Mines of the Padres was never recovered. (Richardson, 1968)

MM 225 RAYMOND BUFFALO AND ANTELOPE RANGE (South)

This range, purchased from Dr. R.O. Raymond by the Arizona Game and Fish, covers 15,000 acres (961 sq km) compared to the 60,000 acres (243 sq km) at the buffalo ranch in House Rock Valley. (See pages 92-94 for information about House Rock Valley.) The smaller area makes it a little easier to find the 85 bison living here. Wildlife Manager Earl Breese and his wife Ann have lived at the ranch for 18 years and are willing to help visitors find the herd. Call ahead to make an appointment at (520) 774-5045.

MM 211 WINONA (North)

Once a tourist camp in 1920, Winona is now a picturesque little community next to the railroad and one of the stops on Route 66 memorialized in song. (Richardson, 1968)

SCENIC DETOUR

MM 204.5 WALNUT CANYON NATIONAL MONUMENT (South)

Open 8 a.m. - 5 p.m. (MST) every day except Thanksgiving and Christmas. Entrance fee is $4 per car. Golden Eagle, Golden Access and Golden Age passes are accepted. No campground or services available in the park. Water and bathrooms are available at the visitors center. Unfortunately, most of the park is not wheelchair accessible.

This beautiful Kaibab Limestone canyon was formed more than 60 million years ago. The canyon housed the prehistoric Sinagua Indians named by Harold S. Colton, founder of the Museum of Northern Arizona. Colton conducted an extensive archeological survey of the more than 300 ruins found under ledges in the canyon. He took the name Sinagua from the Spanish name for the area, *Sierra Sin Agua*, or "mountains without water."

Like all native peoples of the Southwest, the Sinagua understood how to survive on very little water. Using the dry farming techniques still practiced by modern-day Navajos and Hopis, the Sinagua built dams to catch run-off and farmed in washes to capture every available drop of moisture. They supplemented their diet with wild plants and nuts like the plentiful pinyon and the Arizona black walnuts, from which this canyon is named.

Flute Player Petroglyph ca. 1930s
Walnut Canyon National Monument
Fred Harvey Collection
Museum of Northern Arizona Photo Archives

The Sinagua moved into the Walnut Canyon area around 1120 A.D. and were part of a large community of Sinaguan people that extended from Wupatki National Monument to the Verde Valley where Montezuma Castle and Tuzigoot are located.

It is amazing that there is anything left to see at Walnut Canyon. When the railroad reached Flagstaff at the end of the 1800s, pothunting was one of the recreational pursuits of many tourists and local settlers. It was not uncommon for people to brag about the artifacts they found in many of the cliff dwellings in Walnut Canyon. This grew to such an extreme that one group dynamited the ruin's walls to make their job less difficult. Prompted by concerned local citizens, Woodrow Wilson declared Walnut Canyon a national monument in 1915.

One of the truly important discoveries at Walnut Canyon was the burial site of a Sinaguan man. Archaeologist John McGregor found the tomb in the 1930s. Inside were hundreds of offerings such as hand-painted pots, arrowheads and 12 hand-carved wands resembling hooves of animals and human hands.

Not sure of what he had found, McGregor asked the nearby Hopi if they had any clues to his puzzle. Some present-day Hopi clans claim Walnut Canyon as their ancestral home and it is known that the people of Old Oraibi were building their village at the same time the Sinaguans lived comfortably in Walnut Canyon. It is because of their sophisticated oral history carried down through generations that the present day Hopi were able to describe the purpose and name of each item found in the ancient grave. (Thybony,1988)

Island Trail: Behind the visitors center is a paved trail that descends into the canyon to allow you to visit more than 25 ruins. The trail drops 185 feet (56 meters) and can be strenuous for someone not accustomed to the 7,000-foot (2,134 m) elevation. There is also a rim walk.

SERVICES IN FLAGSTAFF Contact the Flagstaff Chamber of Commerce at (520) 774-9541.

Flagstaff, Arizona, July 1883
Photo by Ben Wittick
Courtesy School of American Research, Collections in the Museum of New Mexico, 15796

Native Roads

Ahmann, Steve, et al. "Native Uses of Plants of Canyon de Chelly," Chinle High School Science Department, Chinle Unified School District No. 24, N.D.

Anderson, Owanah. *The Good Shepherd Mission in the Navajo Nation 1892-1992*, Good Shepherd Mission, Fort Defiance, Arizona, 1992.

Anderson, Roger, et al. *Guidebook of the Black Mesa Basin: Northeastern Arizona*, New Mexico Geological Society, Ninth Field Conference, 1958.

Anonymous, "Tuba City and the Charlie Day Spring," *Museum Notes*, Vol. 3, No. 11, May, 1931, pp. 1-4.

Anonymous, "The Tsegi Country," *Museum Notes*, Museum of Northern Arizona, Flagstaff, Arizona, 1934.

Ash, Sidney. *Petrified Forest: The Story Behind the Scenery*, Petrified Forest Museum Association, 1985.

Baars, Donald L., *Red Rock Country: The Geologic History of the Colorado Plateau*, Doubleday/Natural History Press, 1972.

Babbitt, James. *Rainbow Trails: Early-Day Adventures in Rainbow Bridge Country*, Glen Canyon Natural History Association, Page, Arizona, 1990.

Babbitt, James. "Trading Posts Along the Little Colorado," *Historic Trading Posts*, Museum of Northern Arizona 1986.

Babbitt, John. G., "The Babbitt Brothers Trading Company: An Address Before the Newcomen Society," April 15, 1967, Privately Printed, 1967.

Bailey, Lynn. "Thomas Varker Keam: Tusayan Trader," *Arizoniana*, Volume II, 1961, pp. 15-19.

Barnes, Will C., Rev. by Ryrd H. Granger, *Arizona Place Names*, The University of Arizona Press, Tucson, 1960.

Barrs, Don. *San Juan Canyons: A River Runner's Guide*, Canon Publishers Ltd, Lawrence, Kansas, 1986.

Berggren, Karen. Park Manager, Homolovi Ruins State Park, Winslow, Arizona, Personal Communication, April, 1995.

Bingham, Sam and Janet. *Navajo Farming*, Rock Point Community School, Chinle, Arizona, 1979.

Brechner, Kevin Cloud. Time River Productions, Personal Communication, April, 1995.

Breed, William, J. *The Age of Dinosaurs in Northern Arizona*, Museum of Northern Arizona, Flagstaff, Arizona, 1968.

Boars, Donald L. *Red Rock Country*, Doubleday/Natural History Press, 1972.

Broderick, Johnson H., *Navajo Education at Rough Rock*, Rough Rock Demonstration School, D.I.N.E., 1968.

Brooks, Juanita. *The Mountain Meadows Massacre*, University of Oklahoma Press, Norman, Oklahoma, 1974.

Brown, Bonnie et al. *The Complete Family Guide to Navajo-Hopi Land*, Navajo Tribe, Office of Tourism, 1986.

Brugge, David. *Hubbell Trading Post: National Historic Site*, Southwest Parks and Monuments Association, Tucson, Arizona 1993.

Butler, Kristie Lee. *Along the Padres' Trail: St. Michaels Mission to the Navajo 1898-1939*, St. Michaels Museum, St. Michaels, Arizona, 1991.

Byrkit, James W. *The Palatkwapi Trail*, Museum of Northern Arizona, 1988.

Cerquone, Joseph. *In Behalf of the Light: The Domínquez and Escalante Expedition of 1776,* Domínquez-Escalante Bicentennial Expedition, Inc., 1976.

Chronic, Halka. *Roadside Geology of Arizona,* Mountain Press Publishing Company, Missoula, Montana, 1986.

Chronic, Halka. *Pages of Stone: Geology of Western National Parks and Monuments,* The Mountaineers, 1988.

Clark, H. Jackson. *The Owl in the Monument: And Other Stories from Indian Country,* University of Utah Press, Salt Lake City, Utah, 1993.

Cleeland, Teri A. *The Cross Canyon Corridor Historic District in Grand Canyon National Park: A Model for Historic Preservation,* A Thesis Submitted in Partial Fulfillment of the Requirement for the Master of Arts in Anthropology, Northern Arizona University, August 1986.

Correll, J. Lee. "Events in Navajo History," *The Navajo Times,* March 3, 1966, p. 8.

Crampton, C. Gregory. *Sharlot Hall on the Arizona Strip: A Diary of a Journey Through Northern Arizona in 1911,* Northland Press, 1975.

Deedra, Don. *Navajo Rugs: How to Find, Evaluate, Buy and Care for Them,* Northland Publishing, Flagstaff, Arizona, 1990.

Dennison, Johnson. Presentation at the *Advance Navajo Cultural Orientation for Health Professionals,* Farmington, New Mexico, 1994.

Donovan, Bill. "Where is Peter McDonald?" *Window Rock Scene,* February, 1993, p. 17.

Erisman, Fred. "Tony Hillerman," *Western Writers Series No. 87,* Boise State University, Boise, Idaho, 1989.

Evans, Edna. *Tales From the Grand Canyon: Some True, Some Tall,* Northland Press, Flagstaff, Arizona, 1985.

Fireman, Bert. *Historical Markers in Arizona Vol. I,* Arizona Development Board, 1957.

Frink, Maurice. *Fort Defiance and the Navajos,* Pruett Publishing Company, Boulder, Colorado, 1968.

Gillmor, Frances and Wetherill, Louisa Wade. *Traders to the Navajo: The Story of the Wetherills of Kayenta,* The University of New Mexico Press, 1934.

Good, John. *Grandview Grand Canyon Trail Guide,* Grand Canyon National History Association, 1985.

Guernsey, Samuel James. "Basket-maker caves of northeastern Arizona; report on the explorations, 1916-1917," *The Museum,* 1921.

Granger, Byrd Howell. *Arizona's Names: X Marks the Place,* The Falconer Publishing Company, 1983.

Grattan, Virginia. *Mary Colter: Builder Upon the Red Earth,* Grand Canyon Natural History Association, Grand Canyon, Arizona 1992.

Grey, Zane. *The Rainbow Trail,* Harper & Row, 1915.

Hardeen, George. Interview with Ben Muneta, M.D., Epidemiologist, 1992.

Hardeen, George. "Hogans in Hospitals: Navajo Patients Want the Best of Both Worlds," *Tribal College,* Winter, 1994, pp. 20-21.

Hardeen, George. "Jacob Hamblin's Vision Resulted in Settlement," *Navajo-Hopi Observer,* Wednesday, July 20, 1985.

Hargrave, Lyndon. "The Tsegi Country," *Museum Notes, Vol. 6, No. 11*, May, 1934, pp. 51-54.

Hamm, R. *The Navajo Detective Novels of Tony Hillerman: A Bridge Between Cultures,"* Submitted to the College of Graduate Studies Texas A & I University in partial fulfillment of the requirements for the degree of Master of Arts, August 1989.

Harrison, Laura Soulliere, et al. "Historic Structure Report Chinle Trading Post, Thunderbird Ranch, and Custodian's Residence Canyon de Chelly National Monument, Arizona," National Park Service, Southwest Regional Office, Santa Fe, New Mexico, October 1989.

Hegemann, Elizabeth Compton. *Navajo Trading Days,* University of New Mexico Press, Albuquerque, 1963.

Hewett, Edgar L., "Origin of the Navajo Name," *American Anthropologist*, Kraus Reprint Corporation, New York, New York, Vol. 8,1906, p. 193.

Holt, Ronald. *Beneath These Red Cliffs: An Ethnohistory of the Utah Paiutes,* The University of New Mexico Press, Albuquerque, New Mexico, 1992

Hooper, C.R., "Guest Register at Willow Springs," *Outdoor Arizona*, July 1977, pp. 20-22.

Hooper, Mildre et al., "Blue Canyon: Wonderland in Stone," *Outdoor Arizona*, September, 1978, pp. 17,31,36.

Houk, Rose. *The Painted Desert: Land of Light and Shadow*, Petrified Forest Museum Association, 1990.

Indermill, Roc H. "Roadside Fever: The Social Organization of Roadside Frontage Tenure in the Context of the Navajo Beadwork Trade, 1928 to 1988," A Thesis Submitted in Partial Fulfillment of the Requirements for the Degree of Master of Arts in Anthropology, Northern Arizona University, December, 1990.

James, Harry C. *Pages From Hopi History*, The University of Arizona Press, 1994.

James, H.L. "Navajo Rugs: The Regional Style," New Mexico State Highway Department, Albuquerque, New Mexico, 1973.

Jett, Stephen. "Red Rock Country," *Plateau*, Vol. 37:3, 1965, pp. 80-84.

Johnson, . "The Hash Knife Outfit," *Arizona Highways*, June, 1956, pp. 2-7.

Jones, Anne Trinkle, et al. *A Sketch of Grand Canyon Prehistory*, Grand Canyon Natural History Association, 1979.

Johnston, Lyle. *Centennial Memories: Holbrook, Arizona 1881-1981*, Friends of the Holbrook Public Library, Holbrook, Arizona 1981.

Kelly, Charles. "Chief Hoskinnini," *Utah Historical Quarterly*, July 1953, pp. 219-226.

Kelly, Charles. "John D. Lee's Lost Gold Mine," *The Desert Magazine*, August 1946, pp. 9-11.

Kildare, Maurice. "Cave of Death," *Desert Magazine*, Sept. 1967, pp.30-31.

Kinnear, Willis. "House of Three Turkeys," *Desert Magazine*, May, 1965, pp. 32-33.

Kinsey, Joni Louise. *Thomas Moran And the Surveying of the American West*, Smithsonian Institution Press, 1992.

Klinck, Richard. "Movie Making In Monument Valley," *Guidebook to Monument Valley and Vicinity,* Arizona and Utah, New Mexico Geological Society, Twenty-Fourth Field Conference, October 4-6, 1973.

Lanner, Ronald. *The Piñon Pine: A Natural and Cultural History*, University of Nevada Press, 1981

Lamb, Susan. *A Guide to Navajo Rugs*, Southwest Parks and Monuments Association, Tucson, Arizona, 1992.

Loving, Nancy J. *Along the Rim: A Road Guide to the South Rim of Grand Canyon*, Grand Canyon Natural History Association, 1981.

Luckert, Karl W. *Navajo Mountain and Rainbow Bridge Religion*, Museum of Northern Arizona, Flagstaff, Arizona, 1977.

MacDonald, Peter. *The Last Warrior*, Orion Books, New York, 1993.

Malotki, Ekkehart. *Hopi Ruin Legends*, University of Nebraska Press, 1993.

Mann, Timothy. *A Guide to Grand Canyon Village Historic District*, Grand Canyon Natural History Association.

Markward, Anne. *Monument Valley Navajo Tribal Park*, Companion Press, Santa Barbara, California, 1992.

Matthiessen, Peter. *Indian Country*, Penquin Books, New York, New York, 1984.

Mayes, Vernon. *Nanisé A Navajo Herbal*, Navajo Community College Press, Tsaile, Arizona, 1989.

McGibbeny, Joseph Howard. "The Niman Ceremony," *Arizona Highways*, July 1959, pp. 16-28.

McFarlane, Mary. *Motorist Guide to the Navajo Reservation Publications*, Gallup, New Mexico, 1960

McIlhaney, Sam. "The Blue-Eyed Navajo," *Albuquerque Journal Magazine*, Jan. 25, 1983, pp. 12-15.

McPherson, Robert S. *Sacred Land Sacred View*, Brigham Young University, Salt Lake City, Utah, 1992, pp. 21-22.

McNitt, Frank. *The Indian Traders*, University of Oklahoma Press, 1962.

Miller, William C., "Records in Rock of A 1054 A.D. Star Explosion," *The Desert Magazine*, January, 1963, p. 30.

Moon, Samuel. *Tall Sheep*, University of Oklahoma Press, 1992.

Morris, Earl H. "Mummy Cave," *Natural History*, September, 1938, pp. 127-138.

Muench, Joseph. *Arizona Highways*, March 1963, pp. 14-33.

Nations, Dale, et al. *Geology of Arizona*, Kendall/Hunt Publishing Company, 1981.

Navajo Nation Archaeology Department, "National Register of Historic Places Registration Form," Window Rock, Arizona, N.D.

Nelson, Mary Carroll. *Annie Wauneka*, Dillion Press, Minneapolis, Minnesota, 1972.

Nequatewa, Edmund. *Truth of a Hopi: Stories Relating to the Origin, Myths and Clan History of the Hopi*, Northland Printing, 1967.

Newcomb, Franc Johnson. *Hosteen Klah: Navajo Medicine Man and Sand Painter*, University of Oklahoma Press, Norman, 1964.

Nininger, H.H., "Visitor From a Distant Planet," *Desert Magazine*, July, 1942, pp. 9-11.

Noble, David Grant. *Wupatki and Walnut Canyon*, Ancient City Press, Santa Fe, New Mexico, 1993.

Parker, Charles Franklin. "The Kaibab and the North Rim," *Arizona Highways*, May, 1957, pp. 4-9.

Peterson, Willis. "Sixty Miles an Hour on the Hoof," *Arizona Highways*, June 1956, pp.32-37.

Price, Theresa, et al. *A Picture Tour of Old Ganado Mission*, The College of Ganado, Ganado, Arizona, 1991.

Reid, Betty. "Making room for a new hotel: trading post to be cleared," *The Gallup Independent*, Jan. 31, 1992, p. 2.

Richardson, Gladwell. "My Wonderful Country by Joe Lee," *Frontier Times*, Feb.-March, 1974, pp. 6-56.

Richardson, Gladwell. *Navajo Traders*, The University of Arizona Press, Tucson, Arizona 1986.

Richardson, Gladwell. *Two Guns, Arizona*. Blue Feather Press, Santa Fe, New Mexico, 1968.

Richardson, Toney. "Traders at Tonalea," *The Desert Magazine*, January, 1948, pp. 17-20.

Richardson, Toney. "Trail to Inscription House," *The Desert Magazine*, May, 1948, pp. 14-16.

Rigby Keith J., *Field Guide Northern Colorado Plateau*, Brigham Young University, Provo, Utah, Kendall/Hunt Publishing Company, Dubuque, Iowa, 1976.

Rusho, W.L., *Lee's Ferry:Desert River Crossing*, Cricket Productions, Salt Lake City, 1992.

Seaman, David. *Hopi Dictionary*, Northern Arizona University Anthropological Paper No.2, 1985.

Scott, Kenneth. *Zane Grey Born to the West*, G.K. Hall & Co., 1979.

Shinkle, James D., *Fort Sumner and the Bosque Redondo Indian Reservation*, Hall-Poorbaugh Press, Inc., 1965.

Sleight, Eleanor Friend. "Fort Defiance," *El Palacio*, January, 1953, pp. 3-11.

Smith, Ida. "The Mystery of the Little Trees," *Arizona Highways*, September, 1962, pp. 32-35.

Stegner, Wallace. *Beyond the Hundredth Meridian*, Penguin Books, 1992.

Stein, Pat. *The Basques in Arizona From Spanish Colonial Times to the Present*, Arizona State Historic Preservation Office, Phoenix, Arizona, 1991.

Suran, William. *The Kolb Brothers of Grand Canyon*, Grand Canyon Natural History Association, Grand Canyon, Arizona, 1991.

Tanner, George et al. *Colonization on the Little Colorado*, Northland Press, Flagstaff, Arizona, 1977.

Thomas, Bob. "Two Guns: A Big Tourist Draw?," *The Arizona Republic*, April 18, 1993, p. T6.

Thybony, Scott. *Walnut Canyon National Monument*, Southwest Parks and Monuments Association, 1988.

Trueger, Frederick D. Editor, *Guidebook of Defiance-Zuni-Mt. Taylor Region*, Arizona and New Mexico, Eighteenth Field Conference, 1967, New Mexico Geological Society, 1967.

Underhill, Ruth. *Here Come The Navajo*, United States Department of the Interior, Branch of Education, 1953.

Van Valkenburgh, Richard. *Dine' Bikeyah*, United States Department of the Interior, Office of Indian Affairs, Navajo Service, Window Rock, Arizona,1941.

Van Valkenburgh, Richard. "Inscription at Hwoye Spring," *Desert Magazine*, January 1941, pp. 9-11.

Van Valkenburgh, Richard. "Sacred Places and Shrines of the Navajo Part 1: The Sacred Mountains," *Museum Notes*, Vol. 11, No. 3, September 1938, pp. 29-34.

Van Valkenburgh, Richard. "Tsosi Tells the Story of Massacre Cave," *The Desert Magazine*, February, 1940, pp. 22-25.

Vokes, H.E., "The Goosenecks of the San Juan," *Natural History*, May, 1942, pp. 272-273.

Vokes, H.E., "Rainbow of Rock," *Natural History*, October, 1942, pp. 148-152.

Vokes, H.E., "The Story of Shiprock," *Natural History*, April, 1942, pp. 212-215.

Walters, Harry. Presentation at the *Advanced Cultural Orientation for Health and Social Service Providers*, Farmington, New Mexico, 1994.

Weatherburn, Stephen. "Bashas' in Chinle Using Navajo Labels," *Navajo-Hopi Observer*, April, 12, 1995.

Weaver, Donald E., Jr., *Images on Stone: The Prehistoric Rock Art of the Colorado Plateau*, The Museum of Northern Arizona, 1984.

Wheat, Joe Ben. *The Gift of the Spider Woman: Southwestern Textiles The Navajo Tradition*, The University Museum, University of Pennsylvania, 1984.

Whiteley, Peter. *Bacavi: Journey to Reed Spring,* Northland Publishing, Flagstaff, Arizona, 1988.

Wicoff, Mary. "Visiting Baby Rocks, peaceful, eerie, awesome," *Gallup Independent*, August 27, 1993, p.11.

Wicoff, Mary. "Old Hopi Writings Marred," *Gallup Independent*, June, 1990.

Willson, Roscoe G., "How the Buffalo Came to Arizona," *Arizona Days and Ways Magazine*, October, 16, 1960, pp. 24-25.

Woolf, Henry Bosley Editor, *Websters New Collegiate Dictionary*, G & C Merriam Co., 1973

Wyman, Leland C., *The Windways of the Navaho*. The Taylor Museum of the Colorado Springs Fine Art Center, 1962.

Yazzie, Ethelou. *Navajo History, Volume 1*, Navajo Community College, Tsaile, Arizona 1971.

Yost, Billie Williams, *Bread Upon the Sands*, The Caxton Printers Ltd., Caldwell, Idaho, 1958.